Overview

Contents

CHECK AT BACK FOR CD ROM

JavaServer Pages Application Development

Development

Ben Forta, et al.

SAMS

201 West 103rd St., Indianapolis, Indiana, 46290 USA

JavaServer Pages Application Development

International Standard Book Number: 0-672-31939-x

Library of Congress Catalog Card Number: 00-102818

Printed in the United States of America

First Printing: November 2000

03   02   01   00   4   3   2   1

Trademarks

Warning and Disclaimer

ASSOCIATE PUBLISHER
Michael Stephens

ACQUISITIONS EDITOR
Angela Kozlowski

DEVELOPMENT EDITOR
Jeff Riley

MANAGING EDITOR
Matt Purcell

PROJECT EDITOR
Andy Beaster

COPY EDITORS
Gene Redding
Pat Kinyon

INDEXER
Tim Tate

PROOFREADERS
Matt Wynalda
Tony Reitz

TECHNICAL EDITOR
Brian Powell

TEAM COORDINATOR
Pamalee Nelson

MEDIA DEVELOPER
Matt Bates

INTERIOR DESIGNER
Anne Jones

COVER DESIGNER
Anne Jones

PRODUCTION
Steve Geiselman
Liz Patterson

About the Authors

Ben Forta is Product Evangelist at Allaire Corporation, the company responsible for the JRun and ColdFusion application servers. He has over fifteen years of experience in the computer industry in product development, support, training, and marketing. Ben is the author of the best-selling *ColdFusion Web Application Construction Kit* (now in its third edition) and its sequel, *Advanced ColdFusion 4 Development* (both published by Que), as well as books on WAP, SQL, Windows 2000 development, Allaire HomeSite, and Allaire Spectra. He is a frequent lecturer and columnist on Internet-related technologies and is a much sought after speaker. Born in London, England and educated in London, New York, and Los Angeles, Ben now lives in Oak Park, Michigan with his wife Marcy and their six children. Ben welcomes your email at ben@forta.com and invites you to visit his Web site at http://www.forta.com.

Scott Stirling is proud of having graduated *summa cum laude* with a degree in Classical Greek and Latin languages in 1997 from Saint Anselm College in NH. He's now married and living with his wife and three cats in Massachusetts. Scott is a QA engineer for JRun at Allaire and has worked with JRun since Allaire acquired the product. His main interests are server-side Java APIs and architectures and Java Virtual Machines. In his free time, he enjoys reading English and classical literature. He is Webmaster and co-founder of the Propylaean Academy at http://www.propylaean.org.

Edwin Smith is a software architect at Allaire Corporation and works closely with all aspects of JRun engineering, particularly Java/native integration, system architecture, and performance optimization. Ed is also an avid motorcycle enthusiast and road racer, winning the amateur lightweight superbike national title at Daytona in 1996.

Larry Kim has an undergraduate degree in electrical engineering from the University of Waterloo in Canada. He is the Product Manager for the JRun Server and is taking graduate studies in the field of distributed computing at Harvard.

Roger Kerr is a consultant who specializes in server-side Java technologies. He has implemented JSP- and servlet-based solutions for several top-tier companies of the financial service industry. Roger is now providing J2EE solutions for small to medium-size enterprises as well as training courses for JavaScript and DHTML.

As his mother is fond of recounting, **David Aden** started his computer experience (this lifetime anyway) with a small plastic and metal toy given to him for Christmas too many decades ago to admit. By placing thin plastic sheaths over strategically placed metal knobs and sliding an armature back and forth, the toy could be "programmed" to mimic basic binary calculations or the "logic" of an elevator. Many years later, after a long, fun, rewarding stint in public affairs and community activism, David went on to run a UNIX-Windows network for a small non-technical business in

Massachusetts. As he was wrapping up work there, he discovered some newfangled "language" called HTML and wrote an interactive job description that provided detailed instructions to his successor as well as links that kicked off automatic administrative processes. From there, he went to HP's Distributed Computing Environment (DCE), followed by work at an MCI local development lab in Virginia. In 1997, he arrived at Careerbuilder, Inc., where he hooked up with current web-world studios, inc., partner John Stanard to work on his first real Web project using ColdFusion. Since then, he's worked on a variety of ColdFusion projects for Microsoft, CNET, Cable & Wireless USA, and others. David became an early adopter of Allaire's Spectra and co-authored Ben Forta's *Allaire Spectra e-Business Construction Kit*. He has continued working with Spectra and has now plunged into the large, growing world of Java and JSP.

Andre Lei has been involved with JSP since the 0.92 specification and has seen the support for JSP grow tremendously to what it is today, an integral part of Sun's J2EE. He has been with Allaire's JRun product group since early April 1999 as a JSP Application Engineer for LiveSoftware's internal and external sites. After rolling out JRun's Management Console, a DHTML-based administration console with a JSP backend, he is now working on Allaire's packaged systems product, Spectra. Prior to his gig at Allaire, Andre was busy consulting for places such as McAfee.com, SoftwareBuyLine.com, and Autoweb.com. In his free time (yeah, right) he enjoys watching movies (big screen and DVD), playing games like UT/Diablo2/AoK Conquerors, playing badminton, and trying to think up the next killer Web app. He vows some-day to put up good stuff on RunHere.com and LocalLang.com.

Dedications

To my wife, Catherine Stirling, for her love, and to Dan Smith, for getting me started with JRun.
—Scott Stirling

To Jessica Nguyen—for staying up with me late at night when she could have been sleeping and for making me something to eat whenever I'm hungry. Gosh, I'm gonna marry this girl someday... depending on market conditions. =)
—Andre Lei

To L. Ron Hubbard, whose insights and writings on the subject of study remain a marvel of simplicity and practicality. In this age of constantly changing technology, it is no small comfort for me to know about, understand, and have the tools to handle the three primary barriers to effective study. Thank you.
—David Aden

To my mom.
—Edwin Smith

To Dilip, Gerard, and my profs at Waterloo.
—Larry Kim

This book is dedicated to my friends and family who provide me with countless opportunities for a more abundant life.
—Roger Kerr

Acknowledgments

First, I'd like to thank my coauthors, Edwin Smith, Larry Kim, Scott Stirling, Andre Lei, David Aden, and Roger Kerr, for providing the bulk of the content of this book. David and Larry deserve special acknowledgment for going above and beyond the call of duty when those pesky deadlines were looming.

Thanks to the Allaire JRun team for all their help and support—and for a killer product.

Thanks once again to everyone at Macmillan, especially Andrew Beaster and Jeff Riley, for their hard work and dedication to this project. A very special thank you to my acquisitions editor, Angela Kozlowski, for putting up with me once again (the next one will be easier on you, I promise).

And finally, a special thank you to the most dedicated, selfless, and hard-working person I know—my wife Marcy. It is she who makes all I do possible.

—Ben Forta

I thank the JRun Team at Allaire, especially Paul Colton, Andre Lei, Paul and Tom Reilly, Dan Smith, Edwin Smith, Spike Washburn, and Clement Wong, for being so open and helpful to a new guy in 1999. Thanks to Karl Moss, who fully understands the labor of writing books. Thanks to Jim Squarey for helping me reach my goals and stick it out. The JRun Team's collective intelligence, ingenuity, and hard work is awesome and inspiring. I would like to thank Ben Forta for conceiving this book, finding all the authors, and overseeing its development. And thanks to everyone on `jrun-talk@houseoffusion.com` for keeping the interest in servlet and JSP programming alive, and for challenging me and JRun to keep up with you.

—Scott Stirling

I'd like to acknowledge Paul Reilly and Karl Moss for the sample code and authentication handlers used for the security chapter.

—Edwin Smith

I have the usual people to thank for their help while working on this book. Because that help came, by and large, in non-technical form, they bear no responsibility whatsoever for mistakes or problems with what I wrote while at the same time getting credit for anything good about it. It takes a remarkable amount of time to write a book of any length or complexity and my respect for those people that do it often and well has definitely grown over the last six months. My webworld studios, inc., partner, John Stanard deserves thanks for accommodating my absences from usual duties while working on this. The rest of the webworld studios developers and staff—Steve, Erin, John, Andrew, Debbie, Dmitry, Mike, and Teo—have also been great. Thank you for all the good work you do. And, of course, I want to thank my sons, Jason (himself a fine Spectra developer) and Jesse, who've managed to grow into a couple of young men with whom I enjoy spending time and of whom I am very proud. Last, but not least, to my wife who continues to motivate and amuse.

—David Aden

Paul Colton, for creating JRun and giving me the opportunity to work with him, which eventually led to his dragging me to Allaire. Spike Washburn, Clement Wong, Scott Stirling, Tom Reilly, Dan Smith, Edwin Smith, and Karl Moss, for their outstanding knowledge and their willingness to share it. Ben Forta, for having written *Cold Fusion Web Database Construction Kit* (ISBN 0-7897-0970-8), which helped me land one of my first "Web Applications Engineer" positions in this whole crazy World Wide Web. And of course, giving me the chance to be part of a wild ride on this book.

—Andre Lei

Tell Us What You Think!

As the reader of this book, *you* are our most important critic and commentator. We value your opinion and want to know what we're doing right, what we could do better, what areas you'd like to see us publish in, and any other words of wisdom you're willing to pass our way.

As an Associate Publisher for Sams, I welcome your comments. You can fax, email, or write me directly to let me know what you did or didn't like about this book—as well as what we can do to make our books stronger.

Please note that I cannot help you with technical problems related to the topic of this book, and that due to the high volume of mail I receive, I might not be able to reply to every message.

When you write, please be sure to include this book's title and authors, as well as your name and phone or fax number. I will carefully review your comments and share them with the authors and editors who worked on the book.

Fax:	317-581-4770
Email:	Samsfeedback@macmillanusa.com
Mail:	Michael Stephens
	Sams
	201 West 103rd Street
	Indianapolis, IN 46290 USA

Introduction

JSP, or JavaServer Pages, is a unique language, one that is fast changing the face of Web application development. There is good reason for this.

By now almost everyone has heard of Java, the highly portable object-oriented development language created by Sun Microsystems. In a short time, Java has matured into a robust and reliable language, one that continues to gain acceptance within the development community. It is worth noting that Java was never intended to be used purely on the Internet or the Web. Java is a development language (as well as a complete development platform) and can be used to create complete applications, from desktop to server—and it can also be used to power Web applications.

But as powerful and popular as Java is, one thing it is not is simple—at least not as simple as scripting languages like Microsoft's ASP, Allaire's ColdFusion, or even Perl. This is why scripting languages remain dominant for Web development. After all, it is the simplicity of HTML that helped make the Web the success it is, and it makes sense to keep building the Web on that same simplicity. When faced with a choice between the power of Java and the simplicity of scripting, developers more often opted for the latter.

But JSP changes all that. JSP represents a new interface to Java, an interface so important that it is part of the Java 2 Enterprise Edition (J2EE) specification. JSP combines the best of both worlds—the raw power of Java and the simplicity of scripting—giving developers a new choice for Web application development. JSP uses an XML-based, tag-based syntax (much like HTML itself) and uses a page-oriented metaphor for coding. JSP also provides access to the full spectrum of Java classes and functions, and JSP code is compiled into binary servlets for faster processing.

JSP truly is the best of both worlds, and this is why it is starting to capture the attention of Web developers everywhere.

Who Should Use This Book

This book is designed to teach you JSP, even if you have no Java experience whatsoever. In fact, as long as you know HTML and the basics of Web page creation, you have the knowledge you need to get started.

If you are an HTML developer looking for ways to extend your Web sites, then this book is for you. If you have Web application development experience with a scripting language (such as ASP, Perl, PHP, or ColdFusion) and want to harness the power of Java, then this book is for you. And if you are an experienced Java developer looking for a way to apply your hard-earned knowledge in Web development, then this book is for you.

From Internet basics to Java acronyms and lingo, from Java fundamentals to JSP syntax, from interaction with beans to writing your own tag libraries, from database integration via JDBC to email interaction via JavaMail, from security to session state management, from EJB use to LDAP integration, you'll find it all in this book, and all in a format that is highly readable and very code-centric.

How to Use This Book

This book is designed to be used in two ways. Beginners should work through the book systematically, beginning with the very first chapter and continuing from there. More experienced developers will find that the extensive index and cross-references make this book an invaluable reference tool.

What You'll Learn

Chapter 1, "Understanding JSP," explains what JSP is, how it relates to Java, what all those acronyms mean, and what servlets are.

Chapter 2, "Creating a JSP Page," walks you through the creation of your first JSP page, explaining how to use Java objects and methods in your code.

Chapter 3, "Using Scripting Elements," covers JSP scripting in detail, including working with variables, expressions, and scriptlets.

Chapter 4, "Using Available Objects," explains objects, packages, scope, and how they are used.

Chapter 5, "Using Beans," explains JavaBeans and how to use them from within your JSP code.

Chapter 6, "Connecting Pages," covers URLs and page linking, as well as how to pass data from one page to another.

Chapter 7, "Working with Forms," continues this discussion with an explanation of HTML forms and their use in JSP (including coverage of dynamically generated forms and elements).

Chapter 8, "Interacting with Databases," teaches the use of the JDBC interface, which is used to facilitate database integration within your code.

Security is an important part of any Web application, and Chapter 9, "Securing Your Applications," covers security implementations and user authentication issues.

Chapter 10, "Managing Session States," explains how session state management works and how to use it properly.

Chapter 11, "Integrating with Email," covers the JavaMail libraries and explains how to provide POP, IMAP, and SMTP support within your applications.

Chapter 12, "Developing Custom Tags," explains the new tag library support in JSP and covers in detail the creation and use of tag libraries.

Chapter 13, "Interacting with Enterprise JavaBeans," teaches the basics of EJB (Enterprise JavaBeans) and how to use this technology in your code.

Chapter 14, "Handling Errors," covers error trapping and handling so that you can provide a consistent and professional user experience.

Chapter 15, "Debugging and Troubleshooting," explains what can go wrong and what you can do about it.

Appendix A, "JSP Syntax," provides a quick reference of the JSP tags and their use, complete with syntax and examples for each.

Appendix B, "Using Popular JSP Servers," lists the major JSP servers, with brief usage notes for each.

Appendix C, "Using Java Methods to Retrieve CGI Environment Variables," lists the methods you can use to retrieve CGI information.

And with that, turn the page and start coding. You'll be a JSP expert in no time at all.

NOTE

Of course, you'll need a JSP server installed and running before you go much further. Refer to Appendix B for a list of popular JSP servers, and also see the CD-ROM that accompanies this book.

Understanding JSP

IN THIS CHAPTER

This book is intended for a combined audience. It aims to engage and address skilled Web developers and programmers interested in learning the latest and greatest in Web development and server-side Java technology. It is also for people interested in getting involved with serious Web development for the first time. JavaServer Pages (JSP) provide a nice entrée to the field of Web development. Basic Web development skills such as JavaScript, HTML, and CSS can be applied nicely in learning and using JSP. JSP can be barebones simple like HTML, or it can be very deeply technical and challenging. Of course, it can also be rewarding at all the shades in between.

In this chapter we will go through some Internet and World Wide Web basics, recapping some of the Web's past to bring us up to date quickly. Then we will discuss Java, the basis for everything in JSP. If you are interested in the Java programming language, then JSP is a great way to start learning it. If you aren't, then you don't have to learn it. There is a lot you can do with JSP without knowing Java, although this will be truer in the near future than it is as we are writing this book.

Internet and World Wide Web Basics

One crucial distinction to make in understanding the World Wide Web's history is between the Internet and the Web. They aren't exactly the same thing, nor are they the same age, though a common perception is that they are. Learning this distinction is a good basis for any budding Web developer. If you are already wise to this distinction and the history of the Web, please bear with us for a moment.

The Internet

The Internet began in the late 1960s as a small network of computer systems run by the United States Department of Defense. The original name for the network was ARPANET, which stood for Advanced Research Projects Agency Network. Over the years, the network extended to American universities and colleges, then international ones. Email, `telnet`, Usenet newsgroups, Ethernet, FTP, and a host of other Internet fixtures were invented and developed in the 1970s. Corporations built their own private networks while the government and communications companies expanded and interconnected the original ARPANET and other networks. By 1990, TCP/IP, NNTP, DNS, and IRC had all been invented. But the *Internet*, as it had been known since the early 1980s, was home primarily to the military, scientists, students/researchers, and serious computer geeks.

The World Wide Web

In the early 1990s, Tim Berners-Lee, a scientist at the CERN physics research center in Switzerland, began developing a software application for visually rendering documents transferred over the Internet. He worked on this graphical tool while also contributing to the development of two related technologies. One was Hypertext Transfer Protocol (HTTP), a simple protocol layered over the existing TCP/IP protocols that had been the basis for Internet communication since the early 1980s. The other was a simple derivation of SGML (Standard Generalized Markup Language) called Hypertext Markup Language (HTML), which allowed documents and other information to be formatted, linked and cross-referenced in a very user-friendly way across the Internet. Thus was born the *World Wide Web*, which was the original name for this software application. The World Wide Web browser/editor originally ran only on NeXT computers, and the first full alpha version wasn't released until 1993.

You can see that the World Wide Web as we know it has only existed since 1993 at the earliest. The Internet far precedes the Web. But the interesting thing is that, as soon as HTML, HTTP, and a Web browser became available, the World Wide Web took off like a rocket, and the Internet provided the foundation.

Web Browsers and Web Servers

The National Center for Supercomputing Applications (NCSA), University of Illinois, Urbana-Champaign, was a hotbed of activity for World Wide Web development. The NCSA developed a Web browser called *Mosaic* that quickly became widely used. It seemed that putting a user interface on the Internet suddenly made it much more accessible. Eventually, Marc Andreessen, who led NCSA's Mosaic team, started up a company called Netscape and developed a Web browser we all know as Navigator.

Also at the NCSA was one of the first and most popular pieces of Web server software, called *httpd*, for Hypertext Transfer Protocol Daemon. A Web server was originally a simple but necessary piece of client/server software used to send responses to client requests for HTML documents. However, soon an interested party of Webmasters and budding Web server developers got together and coordinated their efforts to patch and extend the original httpd, developed by Rob McCool at NCSA. This little group, founded by Brian Behlendorf and Cliff Skolnick, wound up calling its server Apache, because it was a cool-sounding pun that described their "patchy" server. Now Apache is the most widely used Web server on the Internet. Apache and other popular servers such as Microsoft's Internet Information Server (IIS) and Netscape's iPlanet do far more than just manage the transfer of text documents over the Internet.

Web servers typically perform user authentication, datastream encryption (using Secure Sockets Layer (SSL)), and dynamic content generation. This last capability is where servlets, JavaServer Pages, and a host of other technologies come into play. Some technologies, such as Perl and ASP, extend the server via pluggable components that can be tied tightly to the Web server by integrating with its native application programming interface (API). Others are tied more loosely to the Web server but handle special processing for the server and hand back results via the common gateway interface protocol (CGI).

To the user, all this processing is transparent. The only inkling most users have of how a Web server is doing its work is by watching the URLs in the browser. For example, if you see files being served with a `.cfm` extension, then the server is using Allaire's ColdFusion application server. If you see `.php`, they are PHP pages. If you see `.asp`, those are Microsoft's Active Server Pages. If you see `https://` instead of `http://` in the URL, then you know the connection you are currently making to the server is SSL encrypted, and so on. Static content is still prevalent, but dynamic content is here to stay. Most Web sites are a combination of the two.

Application Servers

Client/server computing has been a great success. It's a distributed approach to computing, allowing for easier distribution of computing resources across a network. The "old" way of enterprise-level computing was that of connecting lots of "dumb terminal" clients directly to the mainframe. Mainframes are massive and powerful computers capable of handling thousands of simultaneous users at a time. The earliest business computers were mostly mainframes, often filling an entire room. Now mainframes are about the size of refrigerators, but they are still incredibly powerful. Mainframes probably aren't going anywhere. There are too many computers with major investments in them and thousands upon thousands of custom programs written for them. Most major companies use mainframes or somewhat smaller computers called midrange computers for their critical business data and systems.

Nevertheless, there is a need to "Webify" nearly everything in business these days. Whether it's business-to-business (for example, Ford ordering engine parts from one of its automotive parts suppliers) or business-to-consumer (for example, you buying books online from www.books.com), every business needs to integrate its data and business systems with other people and businesses across the country and the world.

There is a huge area between the client's PC and the enterprise's mainframes or databases, referred to as the "middle tier." The middle tier can pretty much consist of anything that helps get data from one place to another. Some sort of processing needs to happen, especially when that data needs to go from a large warehouse-like repository to an end user. Data in its raw form is usually pretty ugly. A user likes to see his online shopping cart represented as a little icon he can click on; he likes to click on buttons and see data organized visually into colorful tables on the Web. The middle tier is where intermediate systems process raw data (whether it's stored in hexadecimal, ASCII, or binary form) from databases into nice-looking Web pages.

Likewise, when you are shopping on www.amazon.com, browsing a public library's holdings online, or retrieving your bank statement via an online banking system, the user interface that makes navigation and interaction (hopefully) intuitive to you is all bells and whistles. Behind the scenes, it's all bits and bytes, abstracting the raw data away from the user interface again and storing it in a database, usually after some sort of business logic has been applied to it.

When Web servers were first being extended to do more than just serve HTML pages, there was no connection to enterprise systems—no middle tier. But that soon changed. Web servers became the front line of larger back-end systems that handled business processing for Web-based clients. It made sense to use the popular World Wide Web for retail business as well as business-to-business transactions. Web servers couldn't handle all the work, so extensions were written. The extensions evolved into the middle tier. The whole application on the server side, from handling the business process from the Web server to the database and back, started being called an *application server*.

Application server is a rather vague term. For some people it refers to the whole back end of their Web site, including all the various components and containers, from the server software to the middleware to the database. Microsoft ships products that it calls "servers," which has probably helped confuse the issue. When you buy Microsoft's Back Office Server, you get a Web server (IIS), database (SQL Server), messaging server (Exchange), and more. It's all one huge package. The main disadvantage to this scenario is that everything resides on one system, provided by one vendor, written to proprietary APIs. And in the case of Windows, you have both vendor lock-in and platform lock-in.

Others take the term *application server* to refer to any piece of middleware that's sophisticated enough to provide everything you need for connecting your Web server to your database and other back-end components. These application servers tend to be more modest than Microsoft Back Office. They shoot for a different market, aiming to fill in the gap between server and enterprise rather than to be a complete drop-in solution. Examples of these sorts of application servers include ColdFusion Application Server, PHP, and any server that's branded as J2EE, the Java 2 Enterprise Edition.

Sometimes these application servers plug directly into your Web server as if they were Web server extensions. ColdFusion and PHP are like that. Others, like Orion and JRun, can plug into your Web server or run standalone and receive requests directly from clients. The key advantages of these kinds of application servers are that they do not lock you into a single vendor for your total server-side business solution, and they typically run on multiple platforms. ColdFusion, for example, runs on Linux, Solaris, HP-UX, and Windows. A pure Java J2EE implementation will run on any platform that has a Java 2 JVM.

Components, Containers, and Connectors

The Java 2 Enterprise Edition (J2EE) is a pure Java framework and set of APIs for building application servers in both senses given above. There are enough APIs and specifications to support the construction of the largest business back ends in pure Java. On the other hand, the J2EE technologies are as separable as they are complementary. That is, you can use aspects of the J2EE platform to extend your Web site without having to implement more than you need.

There are two main categories of JSP and servlet users:

- One set is made up of users who want to build dynamic Web sites, probably connecting to a database somewhere along the line.
- The second set is comprised of users who are building complex, secure, transactable middleware for in-house or commercial distribution.

In the former case, users can treat JSP as a standalone technology, an alternative to PHP, ASP, CFML, PERL, or what have you. In the latter case, users must understand the role of JSP technology in the larger scheme of J2EE; JSP has a specific functional role in the enterprise application server.

Whichever category you fall into, the following J2EE terminology will help you categorize the pieces of your application as you go about developing it.

Components

Components are the main building blocks of your application. Components include things like servlets, JavaBeans, JSPs, HTML pages, Enterprise JavaBeans (EJBs), and the like.

Containers

Containers are the applications that run components. If your app is built of JSP and servlet components, you need a servlet container (formerly known as a servlet *engine*) that incorporates JSP support. If your application is built of EJBs, you need an EJB container. (There is a technical distinction between an EJB container and an EJB server, but it's only recently been clarified in the EJB 2.0 specification, so it's academic as far as we are concerned.)

Connectors

Typically, connectors are drivers—that is, software that allows your application to communicate directly with other pieces of software (as opposed to using a public protocol like HTTP). Connectors bridge the gap between the middle tier and the enterprise. They also bridge the gap between the pure Java APIs that Java programmers deal with and the native APIs that most database and messaging servers use. Web server connectors could also fall under this category. Connectors enable you to write code that will run on any platform without worrying about how your code actually connects to Oracle or Sybase or MQ Series. The connectors do a lot of under-the-covers magic to make this possible. JDBC drivers are the most common example.

Components, containers, and connectors are used with these specific meanings in the J2EE literature. You may find them useful in categorizing things in the non-J2EE domain. Virtually everything in J2EE is based on a non-Java version of something else, so you should find that these terms have a broader application than just J2EE.

The Java Advantage

As was hinted above, Java can give some unique advantages when developing and deploying applications. In this section we will talk a little about Java as a programming language and as a platform for server-side development. We will also go over some of the key acronyms everyone using Java ought to know.

Understanding Java

Java was written from the ground up by Sun Microsystems to be a portable, object-oriented programming language for the Internet. Originally it was designed for communication between consumer devices (a use which is seeing a renaissance with JINI technology), but that idea got scrapped as interest in the World Wide Web picked up. Sun released a pure Java Web browser for the Internet called HotJava that could download Java extensions called *applets* and run them in the browser. Netscape released a version of its browser that could run Java applets in process. Dynamic content on the Internet was born. Applets were secure (meaning they ran in a software "sand box" that prevented them from deleting or changing anything on your hard drive, among other things), platform neutral, and network aware—three of the main features designed into the language when it was primarily intended for consumer devices.

One of the key advantages of client-side Java applets was that they could do a lot of cool multimedia stuff because, unlike HTML, they were little applications that ran inside the browser. A major disadvantage to client-side Java was that it was slow and buggy, and the applets themselves, unless they were extremely simple (and hence uninteresting), took considerable time to download. Also, because of their security restrictions, applets were severely limited in what they could do.

Many of the failures of client-side Java have been pretty much overcome. Applets can be signed now, so they can do anything on your computer if you let them. The advent of faster download speeds has made downloading an applet almost unnoticeable. Java is much faster and more stable on the client now. But there are other challenges. The advent of JavaScript (which has no relation to Java other than a marketing deal between Sun and Netscape embedded in the name), style sheets, and DHTML pretty much killed the need for applets unless they were very complex. There are still some very cool applets being written and used, but they are few and far between. All the old Java applets tricks can now be done in JavaScript and DHTML, which access the Web browser APIs directly.

For mainstream client applications with a graphical interface, Java has never been fast enough to beat natively compiled languages like C++. C++ is another object-oriented language and is several years older than Java, but Java's syntax is intentionally based on it (to make it easier for C++ programmers to learn Java). C++ is used to write applications end users are most familiar with, such as Microsoft Word and Excel, Netscape Communicator, and so on. So even though Java is much faster than it used to be on the client, it's often not fast enough to warrant abandonment of older, faster compiled languages like C++. If you write a client application in Java now, it is more for considerations of portability than speed.

A few years ago, people began writing server-side Java, where speed is less important, but also where Java's CPU-intensive graphics libraries aren't used. Java on the server began to take off while it seemed that Java on the client was reaching an all-time low. Once again, the destiny of Java changed course based on a natural course of development, rather than on any plans laid by Sun.

Java on the server has been an unprecedented success. While improvements continue to be made on the client side, where Java may someday be a strong contender, Java has already taken the server by storm. Many APIs have sprung up in the server domain, strides in performance and scalability increases have been made, and whole corporations now base their business systems on a combination of Java and legacy technology.

The Java Virtual Machine

The Java Virtual Machine (JVM) is the key to Java's portability. It is a software program typically written in C. Java source code is compiled to an intermediate binary language called *byte code*. When you execute the byte code (when you want to run the application), the byte code is loaded and interpreted in a JVM. Most JVMs these days use some degree of Just in Time (JIT) compilation to compile byte code into platform-specific machine code on-the-fly. JIT allows Java to perform at speeds approaching native code.

The source code and byte code levels are where Java is completely platform neutral. That is, once you have compiled your Java program, you can run it on any computer that has a JVM. Here's the secret: The JVM is not written in Java, and it is completely tied to the platform on which it runs; you can download a pure Java application and run it on any JVM, but you can't download a JVM and run it on any platform. The JVM has to be customized and compiled to native code for each platform that it runs on.

There are many different versions of the JVM out there. There is some competition among vendors in the JVM market, but not that much. IBM and Sun (and the Sun technology branch known as JavaSoft) are the two biggest contenders in the JVM market, and they both give away their JVMs free. Appeal (www.jrockit.com) is a small company making an excellent and easy to use JVM that competes extremely well with Sun's and IBM's most cutting-edge JVMs.

It seems odd to many who are new to Java to hear that all Java programs run inside another program called a JVM. It is a little odd (more because Java has been so successful even though it's inherently slower than native code), but it's not unique to Java. Perl is an interpreted language, as are Smalltalk, Python, and Tcl/Tk. Other languages can be compiled to byte code and run on a JVM as well, which is kind of neat but rarely done in practice.

Java Terminology

Here is where we encounter some of the most common TLAs (three letter acronyms) in the Java world.

JDK, JRE, and JVM

We take these three together because they are related, and people often confuse them.

The JDK is also called the SDK because, ever since Java 2, Sun has referred to it inconsistently as the Java Software Development Kit *and* the Java Development Kit. It includes tools used for software development. It also includes a JRE.

The JRE is the Java Runtime Environment. The JRE includes all the runtime libraries needed to run any basic Java program. It also includes a JVM.

As discussed above, the Java Virtual Machine (JVM) is the software that runs all Java applications. The JVM is usually just a couple of files buried in the JDK or JRE directories, one of which is usually a shell that instantiates the JVM and gets it running on the native operating system. You can't run a JVM without running a Java program on it. The name of the JVM from the user's perspective is "java." If you are on Solaris, for example, the java command is a standard command. When you execute it, you are executing the JVM. If you execute a JVM without giving it the name of a Java program to run, it will do nothing or just print out a usage listing.

The term *JVM* has a couple of different connotations in ordinary speech. In one sense, it refers to the actual binary file on your file system that you installed when you installed your JDK or JRE. That is the sense people mean when they say, "What version of JVM are you using?"

The second sense is used to refer to a particular instance of the JVM wile it's running. When you execute a Java program, an instance of the JVM (think of it as a copy) is loaded into the computer's memory, and it runs as a process on your operating system. But the binary file on your hard drive doesn't change or get loaded. It stays where it is. Thus, you can run multiple instances of the JVM on your computer simultaneously. They can be running different copies of the same Java program or completely different programs. This is the sense people mean when they say "The JVM crashed" or "That program is running inside a JVM." Sometimes people drop the *J* and refer to it as just a *VM*.

Java Files

Java files are Java source code files that end in a .java extension. Java programmers write Java programs and save them in Java files. Then they run these files through the compiler when they want to convert them into runnable byte code. JSP coders write Java code, but they save their files with a `.jsp` extension. That's actually configurable on most servlet containers, but that's beside the point. Java compilers recognize the `.java` file extension as a signal that this is a Java source code file.

Class Files, Byte Code

These two terms are related. When you compile a Java source code file, the Java compiler outputs a series of byte codes in a file and names the file with a `.class` extension. Class files are the executable form of Java programs.

Byte codes are byte-sized machine codes for the Java Virtual Machine.

JavaBeans

JavaBeans are discussed in depth in Chapter 5, "Using Beans." It's enough to say here that *JavaBeans* is just a cute name for reusable Java code components. They used to be more specifically tied to GUI development and Java developer IDEs, but they are now more general purpose. Virtually any Java program or any piece of a Java program can be written as a JavaBean, which offers no special significance other than that JavaBeans adhere to a few basic conventions that make them a little more amenable to reuse.

JAR Files

JAR files are Java archive files. Java archives are simply compressed files that have been created using the JDK's jar utility. The compression technique used is the same as that used by popular zip utilities. In fact, WinZip and pkunzip can be used on Windows for opening JAR files. Emacs on UNIX/Linux can browse JAR files' contents just as it can ZIP and TAR files. If you are familiar with the standard TAR (Tape ARchive) utility on UNIX/Linux, then you can see where the name came from.

It is convenient for programmers and Java application vendors to deploy and distribute their applications as JAR files. That way, everything can be zipped up into a single file, which may or may not need to be expanded when the application is run. The `java` command allows you start a Java program that is stored in a JAR file as long as you use the `-jar` option.

J2EE

The Java 2 Enterprise Edition has been mentioned before and will come up again later in this book. There are three main editions of the Java Software Development Kit. Each edition comes with a JVM and all the standard tools needed for development. Where each differs most is in the JVM version and Java development libraries it ships with. They are all prefixed with "Java 2" because they are all part of the Java language, version 1.2, also known (confusingly) as Java 2. The funny thing is that version 1.3 of Java is also called Java 2.

The *Java 2 Micro Edition* (J2ME) comes with a slimmed-down set of runtime libraries and a JVM optimized for handheld and embedded devices.

The *Java 2 Standard Edition* (J2SE) comes with the standard set of runtime and development libraries for general Java development and deployment. It comes with a JVM optimized for client-side use.

The *Java 2 Enterprise Edition* (J2EE) includes everything in the J2SE, plus a host of APIs and libraries for developing and deploying enterprise-level applications, such as transaction processing systems, Web servers, servlet engines, messaging services, and so on. It comes with the same JVM as the J2SE, but there is an optimized server-side version of the JVM called HotSpot Server VM that can be downloaded separately.

JSP and Servlets

As people realized that server-side Java was a good idea, a proposal was made for developing an API specifically designed to make server-side Java programming easier and more standardized. The Java Servlet API was soon released and adopted by many Java programmers who were working on extending the server-side functionality of Web servers. The Servlet API cleanly handled many of the problems faced by server-side Java programmers and gave a standard base on which vendors could build engines for servlets. Servlet engines started to come on the scene, providing programmers with a server on which to run their servlets. Some servlet engines ran in process with Web servers, and some ran out of process but could plug into Web servers. All of them provided runtime features and sandbox security, which made programming servlets much easier for the Java developer.

Servlets had their shortcomings. For one thing, it was very tedious to have to write `out.print()` statements for every piece of HTML code you wanted to output to the client. For another, servlets required quite a bit of Java knowledge to write. There were competing technologies out there, such as ASP and CFML, that allowed HTML programmers to develop dynamic content for the Web. ASP and CFML were scripting languages, which hid most of their implementation from the programmer. This made programming in ASP and CFML much easier than coding raw Java in servlets. It would have been nice to bring the full power of Java servlets to the large and ever-expanding Web scripting and coding community, without requiring everyone to learn Java.

The first public JavaServer Pages specification draft was released by Sun in early 1998. It was JSP version 0.91, and it looked more like Microsoft's ASP than any of the later revisions (for instance, the ASP-like `<SCRIPT runat= . . .>` tag was replaced with `<%! . . . %>` by the time the first 1.0 public draft came out). The next public draft was JSP 0.92, which came out in October 1998.

> **NOTE**
>
> Sun Microsystems has the *Java Community Process* (JCP), a formalized process by which independent companies, organizations, and individuals can participate with Sun in planning the future of Java. Briefly, interested companies, organizations, and individuals pay dues and select representatives to participate in the development of Java APIs and technology specifications. The whole JCP is documented at Sun's Javasoft site at `http://java.sun.com/aboutJava/communityprocess/`.
>
> The JCP is where public drafts of specifications, such as the JavaServer Page spec, originate. After the specification group representatives involved in the planning of an accepted *Java Specification Request* (JSR) have developed a somewhat polished draft, it is made public for comments and input from the general Java community.

JSP 0.91 and 0.92 were pretty raw when compared to the refined and quite different 1.0 specification that followed almost one year later. Between the first two drafts, a few tags and directives were changed or dropped, and the specification grew in number of words as more features and concepts were introduced. But many changes, including formalization of JSP semantics, removal of an SSI (Server Side Include) tag, and many other refinements, were made between the second draft and the first full specification. JSP 1.0 became final on September 27, 1999. By then there were plenty of implementations of the specification, including those that supported the earlier revisions of the spec as it was in the process of being developed. Even though the 0.92 draft was never a full specification from Sun, there are entire Web sites out there written to the 0.92 draft.

JSP 1.1 followed quickly, on December 17, 1999. The most significant changes between 1.0 and 1.1 were the full fleshing out of the custom tag library concept and the repositioning of the specification to be based firmly on the Servlet 2.2 API. As of JSP 1.1, the Java Servlet API is the official foundation for JavaServer Page technology. JSP 1.2 is in the works now. In JSP 1.2 there may be cool things such as the capability to write custom JSP tags in JSP itself. Another closely related specification under a separate release cycle is the JSP Standard Tag Library. When that specification is released, there will be a full-featured library of standard tags, which all JSP containers will be required to support.

Putting Java to Work

Hopefully, you are now ready to embark on the journey of learning some JSP and Java. We try to balance them in this book, empowering you with enough Java as you go that you can take full advantage of what JSP technology offers. As JSP matures, users will need to know less and less Java to efficiently apply the full power of J2EE. Until that happens, you will need to know some Java to be *really* dangerous, and this book will teach you what you need to know.

The first part of this book focuses on the standardized core of JSP, its syntax, and its uses in Web application development. The second part of the book deals with more complex application development and covers the extensible custom tag features of JSP 1.1.

Creating a JSP Page

IN THIS CHAPTER

Now let's see what a JavaServer Page looks like. First we will look at the simplest possible JSP. I'll show you a JSP source file, and then we'll look at the translated Java source files that several servlet engines produced from it. The page developed by the JSP programmer (you or me) and the end result seen by our Web clients are consistent, but the servlet that generates the response is implementation dependent, as you'll see.

Getting Under the Hood

I want you to notice a couple of things in these examples. One is the similarities between the outputs of the different servlet engines. Many of the similarities are based on constraints of the Java programming language or of the JSP specification. For example, every translated JSP has to import certain packages and implement certain methods. The second thing to notice is the differences. For example, JRun outputs a lot more Java source code than Resin does. This is partly due to the fact that JRun outputs extra debugging information so that if an error occurs in processing, the exact line number of the JSP source can be correlated with the Java source.

I don't expect you to understand these Java files unless you already know Java. But by the end of this book you should be able to refer back to these listings and at least partially understand them. Plus, I think it's good just to see what goes on when a JSP gets translated, so that you better understand the process, from the initial client request to your page to the server's response via the JSP container.

Hello World

Listing 2.1 is an example of the simplest JSP one could write. It contains no Java and no JSP syntax. It's just some HTML code in a page saved with a .jsp file extension.

LISTING 2.1   Hello.jsp—A Hello World JavaServer Page

```
<html>
<title>Hello World</title>
<body>
<h1>Hello World</h1>
</body>
</html>
```

Getting the Request

When a client first requests a new or updated JSP page, the JSP container has to locate the source file of the JSP and begin the process of translating it into a Java file. The .jsp file extension tells the Web server (or a Java extension to the Web server, depending on how your JSP container is implemented) that this file should be handled by the JSP container if it is requested, just as naming a file with .cfm or .asp signifies that a file needs special processing by a server extension.

JSP containers that run out-of-process from the Web server and link to the Web server via a socket usually have a native (that is, non-Java) connector that runs in-process with the Web server. An in-process connector is written in conformance with the Web server's API, such as the NSAPI for Netscape Enterprise Server or the module API for Apache. These connectors usually operate by scanning all requests, which come to the Web server in the form of URLs, and filtering requests with special prefixes and suffixes to the JSP or servlet container. JRun, Resin, and Tomcat (introduced more fully below) can operate in this mode.

Another way to do it is to have the Web server as part of the JSP container by implementing a Java-based HTTP server. Most Web-enabled application servers, including JRun, Tomcat, Resin, and Orion Application Server, can operate in this mode. In the latter case, no socket is involved and no request filtering is necessary. Rather, requests for JSPs come directly to the JSP container from clients.

Translating the Page

Normally, JSP source files are kept in the document root of your Web server, in a subdirectory of the document root, or in any directory you configure the JSP container to search. The JSP container first searches for, finds, and reads in the JSP source file. Then the JSP engine parses and translates the JSP source into a Java file (there may or may not be an intermediate temporary or permanent file, such as an XML file, produced in this phase). This process is implementation dependent, but one way of doing it is to transform the JSP source into an XML file on-the-fly and then use an internal XSL (eXtensible Stylesheet Language) sheet to transform the intermediate XML file into Java code. The JSP engine then calls a compiler to convert the Java source file into a Java servlet class file. The resulting Java class is then loaded as a servlet into the JSP container's servlet engine, and the servlet outputs the response to the client. After the initial request, the JSP is not retranslated, recompiled, or reloaded into memory unless the JSP source file changes or the servlet container is stopped and restarted.

Viewing the Source

The listings that follow are taken from some of the leading JSP container implementations on the market. Each of them offers an implementation of the latest servlet and JavaServer Page specifications.

JRun

First we will look at JRun, a Web-enabled application server from Allaire Corporation (http://www.allaire.com/products/jrun/).

Listing 2.2 is the Java source that the JRun 3.0 JSP container translated our Hello.jsp file into.

LISTING 2.2 JRun Java Source Example

```java
// Generated by JRun, do not edit

import javax.servlet.*;
import javax.servlet.http.*;
import javax.servlet.jsp.*;
import javax.servlet.jsp.tagext.*;
import allaire.jrun.jsp.JRunJSPStaticHelpers;

public class jrun__Hello2ejspa extends allaire.jrun.jsp.HttpJSPServlet
➥ implements allaire.jrun.jsp.JrunJspPage
{
    ServletConfig config;
    ServletContext application;
    Object page;
    JspFactory __jspFactory;

    public void _jspService(HttpServletRequest request,
                          HttpServletResponse response)
        throws ServletException, java.io.IOException
    {
        response.setContentType("text/html; charset=ISO-8859-1");
        PageContext pageContext = __jspFactory.getPageContext(this, request,
                              response,  null, true, 8192, true);
        JspWriter out = pageContext.getOut();
        HttpSession session = pageContext.getSession();

        try {

    out.print("<html>\r\n<title>Hello World</title>\r\n<body>\r\n<h1>Hello
➥       World</h1>\r\n</body>\r\n</html>\r\n");

        } catch(Throwable t) {
            if(t instanceof ServletException)
                throw (ServletException) t;
            if(t instanceof java.io.IOException)
                throw (java.io.IOException) t;
            if(t instanceof RuntimeException)
                throw (RuntimeException) t;
            throw JRunJSPStaticHelpers.handleException(t, pageContext);
```

LISTING 2.2   Continued

```
        } finally {
            __jspFactory.releasePageContext(pageContext);
        }
    }

    private static final String[] __dependencies__ = {"/Hello.jsp",null};

    private static final long[] __times__ = {951454006000L,0L};

    public String[] __getDependencies()
    {
        return __dependencies__;
    }

    public long[] __getLastModifiedTimes()
    {
        return __times__;
    }

    public int __getTranslationVersion()
    {
        return 13;
    }

    public void init(ServletConfig config) throws ServletException
    {
        this.config = config;
        this.application = config.getServletContext();
        super.init(config);
        this.page = this;
        this.__jspFactory = JspFactory.getDefaultFactory();
    }

    public void destroy()
    {
        super.destroy();
    }
}
```

Resin

Resin is a JSP and servlet container from Caucho Technology (http://www.caucho.com). It's free for non-commercial use. Its source is open and licensed under the QT license. Resin 1.1 is lightweight, fast, and easy to configure.

The following is the output from Resin 1.1. Resin 1.1 is smart—I had to trick it into creating this servlet code. Since our example doesn't contain any Java or JSP syntax, Resin just saves the static content as a text file in its work directory and serves the contents of that file without going to the trouble of creating a Java servlet from the JSP. To get the following output, I used a special JSP statement called an *expression* (covered in the next chapter under "Using Expressions") in my example page (Hello.jsp). Listing 2.3 is a somewhat artificial example of Resin's simplest JSP page.

LISTING 2.3   Resin Java Source Example

```
/*
 * Resin(tm) generated JSP
 */

package _jsp;
import java.io.*;
import javax.servlet.*;
import javax.servlet.jsp.*;
import javax.servlet.jsp.tagext.*;
import javax.servlet.http.*;

public class _Hello__jsp extends com.caucho.jsp.JavaPage{

  public void
  _jspService(HttpServletRequest request,
            HttpServletResponse response)
    throws IOException, ServletException
  {
    PageContext pageContext =
        JspFactory.getDefaultFactory().getPageContext(this, request, response,
        null, true, 8192, true);
    JspWriter out = (JspWriter) pageContext.getOut();
    com.caucho.jsp.ByteWriteStream _jsp_raw_out;
    _jsp_raw_out = (com.caucho.jsp.ByteWriteStream) out;
    ServletConfig config = getServletConfig();
    Servlet page = this;
    HttpSession session = pageContext.getSession();
    ServletContext application = pageContext.getServletContext();
    try {
      out.print(( "<html><title>Hello World</title><body><h1>Hello World</h1>
          </body></html>" ));
      _jsp_raw_out.write(_jsp_string0, 0, _jsp_string0.length);
    } catch (Exception e) {
      pageContext.handlePageException(e);
    } finally {
```

LISTING 2.3 Continued

```
      JspFactory.getDefaultFactory().releasePageContext(pageContext);
  }
}

private java.util.ArrayList _caucho_depends;
private java.util.ArrayList _caucho_cache;
private com.caucho.java.LineMap _caucho_line_map;

public boolean _caucho_isModified()
{
  if (com.caucho.util.CauchoSystem.getVersionId() != 986842079)
    return false;
  for (int i = 0; i < _caucho_depends.size(); i++) {
    com.caucho.jsp.Depend depend;
    depend = (com.caucho.jsp.Depend) _caucho_depends.get(i);
    if (depend.isModified())
      return true;
  }
  return false;
}

public long _caucho_lastModified()
{
  return 0;
}

public com.caucho.java.LineMap _caucho_getLineMap()
{
  return _caucho_line_map;
}

public void _caucho_init(HttpServletRequest req, HttpServletResponse res)
{
  res.setContentType("text/html");
}

public void init(ServletConfig config,
                 com.caucho.java.LineMap lineMap,
                 com.caucho.vfs.Path pwd)
  throws ServletException
{
  super.init(config);
  _caucho_line_map = new com.caucho.java.LineMap("_Hello__jsp.java",
                                                 "/Hello.jsp");
  _caucho_line_map.add(1, 1);
  _caucho_line_map.add(1, 28);
```

LISTING 2.3   Continued

```
    _caucho_depends = new java.util.ArrayList();
    _caucho_depends.add(new com.caucho.jsp.Depend(pwd.lookup("/C:/RESIN1.1/doc
➥ /Hello.jsp"),
      956553206000L));
  }

  private static byte []_jsp_string0;
  static {
    _jsp_string0 = "\r\n".getBytes();
  }
}
```

NOTE

Resin 1.1 is tricky in another respect. It quietly created a directory called caucho under C:\temp on my Windows computer. Resin creates and uses C:\temp\caucho\work and C:\temp\caucho_jsp to store its working files (including the Java source of its translated JSPs).

The Jakarta Project

The Tomcat JSP and servlet container is part of the Jakarta Project (http://jakarta.apache.org/), managed by the Apache Software Foundation. Sun cooperated with the Apache Software Foundation to handle the responsibility of creating the reference implementation (a working version of the specifications) of Sun's Servlet and JSP specifications. This has been the case since servlet 2.2 and JSP 1.1. The Jakarta Project includes Tomcat, the servlet and JSP engine, and Watchdog, a set of specification compliance tests. As you might expect of the Apache Software Foundation, the source code of the Jakarta Project is freely available under the same license as the Apache Web server. Listing 2.4 shows how Tomcat 3.1, the latest (at this writing) public release of the Sun reference implementation, translates Hello.jsp.

LISTING 2.4   Tomcat Java Source Example

```
import javax.servlet.*;
import javax.servlet.http.*;
import javax.servlet.jsp.*;
import javax.servlet.jsp.tagext.*;
import java.io.PrintWriter;
import java.io.IOException;
```

LISTING 2.4 Continued

```java
import java.io.FileInputStream;
import java.io.ObjectInputStream;
import java.util.Vector;
import org.apache.jasper.runtime.*;
import java.beans.*;
import org.apache.jasper.JasperException;

public class _0002fHello_0002ejspHello_jsp_0 extends HttpJspBase {

    static {
    }
    public _0002fHello_0002ejspHello_jsp_0( ) {
    }

    private static boolean _jspx_inited = false;

    public final void _jspx_init() throws JasperException {
    }

    public void _jspService(HttpServletRequest request,
                            HttpServletResponse  response)
        throws IOException, ServletException {

        JspFactory _jspxFactory = null;
        PageContext pageContext = null;
        HttpSession session = null;
        ServletContext application = null;
        ServletConfig config = null;
        JspWriter out = null;
        Object page = this;
        String _value = null;
        try {

            if (_jspx_inited == false) {
                _jspx_init();
                _jspx_inited = true;
            }
            _jspxFactory = JspFactory.getDefaultFactory();
            response.setContentType("text/html;charset=8859_1");
            pageContext = _jspxFactory.getPageContext(this, request, response,
                    "", true, 8192, true);

            application = pageContext.getServletContext();
            config = pageContext.getServletConfig();
            session = pageContext.getSession();
            out = pageContext.getOut();
```

LISTING 2.4   Continued

```
        // HTML // begin [file="C:\\Hello.jsp";from=(0,0);to=(6,0)]
            out.write("<html>\r\n<title>Hello World</title>\r\n<body>\r\n
                    <h1>Hello World</h1>\r\n</body>\r\n</html>\r\n");
        // end


    } catch (Exception ex) {
        if (out.getBufferSize() != 0)
            out.clearBuffer();
        pageContext.handlePageException(ex);
    } finally {
        out.flush();
        _jspxFactory.releasePageContext(pageContext);
    }
  }
}
```

Now you've seen the behind-the-scenes view of what goes into translating even the simplest JSP. Note that much of the code we saw in each example, such as import statements, class declarations, and error handling routines, is the foundation for every JavaServer Page. While it seems like a lot of work for our simple example, it should diminish proportionally in the larger JSPs we'll work on later. One lesson to take from this is that it's not wise to use JSPs to serve static content like plain HTML. That's what Web servers excel at. JSP is meant to serve up dynamic content. That is what JSP excels at.

Understanding Access Models

Now let's look at some design principles and patterns that you will inevitably hear tossed around when people discuss JavaServer Pages. The idea is to bring up the concepts and terms now and refer back to them later. Throughout this book we will be using these terms and concepts when we talk about the design and implementation of JSP-based applications. The two design models we will discuss will help you in thinking about how to design a Web application using JSPs and will also give you a toehold in discussion groups, at your work, the pub, and any other place you discuss your JSP development.

When the JSP 0.91 specification draft came out, it included a brief overview of two principal ways to make use of JavaServer Pages in Web development. They became known as Model 1 and Model 2 *access models*. Neither model is inherently good or bad. They are just two different ways of designing a site. Which model you choose should depend on your site's particular needs and size. Don't feel locked into these terms, by the way. They are just part of the JSP vernacular that you ought to be aware of. Also, be aware that perfect adherence to either of these models is not necessarily desirable. A mix-and-match approach might best suit your needs.

Model 1

Model 1 describes the situation in which your Web site is designed so clients access it directly through a JavaServer Page or pages. The JSP(s) would contain business logic written in Java (or other scripting languages supported by the JSP engine, potentially), which it would use to access server-side components such as JavaBeans, Enterprise JavaBeans, or a database with, for example, JDBC code right in the body of the JSP. The main merit of this approach is that it keeps all the coding logic associated with the application in a single location—the JSP page. The main detraction of this approach is that it makes for JSPs that are difficult to maintain, since there is a heavy mix of static content (HTML, JavaScript) and scripting code.

Model 2

Model 2 is for situations in which JSPs are used only to format the presentation of the output sent back to the client. Initial requests are handled by a servlet (usually), which then interacts with other server-side components to handle business processing. The results are forwarded or otherwise made available to a JavaServer Page, which then outputs a response to the client. The main advantage to this approach is that it makes for more maintainable and readable JSP pages. The main goal of Model 2 is clean separation of presentation layer and business logic. The main detraction of this model is that it's been difficult to realize until JSP 1.1, with which business logic can be entirely encapsulated in custom tags, thus completely removing scripting code from the JSP if so necessary. We will cover custom tags later in this book.

Understanding the Model-View-Controller (MVC) Pattern

The Model-View-Controller (MVC) design pattern is related to Model 1 and Model 2. Like the previous terms, MVC is useful when analyzing the structure of a Web site (from the developer's, not the client's, perspective) or thinking about the design of a Web site.

The Model-View-Controller design pattern has an interesting history that's worth a little side trip.

A Quick History Lesson on MVC

Java was built from the bottom up, but its design was deeply influenced by existing programming languages. Smalltalk was one of them. Smalltalk was originally developed in the 1970s by Xerox at its Palo Alto Research Center (PARC) and was one of the first truly object-oriented programming languages (Simula-67 was the first). It was also the language in which the first multi-window, mouse-based GUI was written. Model-View-Controller was the paradigm for creating user interfaces in Smalltalk. The *Model* can be virtually any object that encapsulates data or behavior that you want the user to access. The *View* is the visual interface displayed to the user, such as a button, a table, an image, or a check box. The *Controller* is the intermediary between the View and the Model, interpreting user input and commanding the Model to change state or behavior, and passing information from the Model back to the View.

WYSIWYG Example

A good, simple example of MVC is any WYSIWYG ("What You See Is What You Get") word processing program, such as Word or StarOffice. Here we will break down the broad conceptual components of a WYSIWYG editor.

View

The primary View is the page that you are typing on (other parts of the View include the toolbars and drop-down menus of the word processing program itself). The program gives you a visual onscreen representation of what the page would look like on paper.

Model

Behind the scenes, invisible to you, there's a Model that contains all the information you've typed in, including the text you've typed, the font(s) you've selected, the color of the background, your margin settings, any sections of text that have special processing instructions such as bold or italic, and so on. Each time you type in a new line, select a section to be underlined, or delete a section of text, the Model has to be updated so that when you print out this page or send it to someone in an email, you get the expected results.

Controller

The Controller is the component that manages the interaction between the Model and the View, telling the Model to save your changes, undo something, and so on. When you re-open your file the next day, the Controller transmits the state of the document saved in the Model to the View, which re-creates the visual representation of the page on your screen.

Web Application Example

I have found explanations and discussions of the MVC paradigm to be confusing and vague, so I hope this overview helps you understand it. Now let's apply the MVC paradigm to an analysis of a server-side application involving JSP and other components.

Let's say we have a JSP-generated HTML frontend to the order-taking section of our Web site. Users are invited to order merchandise online through our site. When a user first enters our order page, we present him (via JSP) with a sidebar with a list of categories for his shopping and an empty table in the main body of the page that represents an empty shopping cart. This is the primary View that we present, and it is generated from a JSP.

Behind the scenes is an Enterprise JavaBean (EJB) that is a Session Bean (the different types of Enterprise JavaBeans and their uses will be covered in Chapter 13, "Interacting with Enterprise JavaBeans"). This stores the state of the shopping cart and the categories in which the user is shopping. The EJB is the Model. As soon as the user starts clicking on categories and selecting items to purchase, his choices need to be transmitted to the EJB so that they can be saved for the duration of the session (until we get his credit card number and commit the order to our database).

We can't submit an HTTP request directly to an EJB, so we have to use a middle component, a Controller that knows how to mediate. We use a servlet. Each time the user submits a selection that requires an update to the EJB's state, our servlet can accept the HTTP request and transmit the relevant data via Remote Method Invocation to the Session Bean. (We will mention Remote Method Invocation (RMI) again in Chapter 13; briefly, it is a Java-specific term that refers to one of the primary protocols clients used to communicate with EJBs.)

The servlet can also forward the updated selections to our original JSP page, which reformats itself every time it gets new information. For example, the JSP can dynamically add another table row to represent another item in the user's shopping cart. In this case, the servlet is the Controller.

This is a fairly typical design in the new world of application servers and Java-based Web applications. Later, when we get into XML representations of data, you will see even better examples of MVC in which the Model is completely independent of the View (thanks to XML), and a Controller can be used to transform data via XSL to totally different View on-the-fly.

Now that we've seen the backend translation of a JSP and covered the conceptual foundations for JSP application development, I think we're ready to get into coding pages. I will remind you where appropriate to refer back to these pages. The MVC paradigm will come up again and again. And as you learn more about Java, you may be more interested in the behind-the-scenes representation of JSPs that we looked at earlier.

We'll start by introducing JSP syntax. By the end of the next chapter we will have covered the core syntax of JSP.

Directives

JSP has pre-processing directives that can be used to specify attributes of the JSP response or provide information needed by the JSP engine to accurately translate and compile the JSP. JSP has three directives: `page`, `include`, and `taglib`.

The page Directive

The page directive has many attributes. For now, we will just go over a couple of the most commonly used ones.

One common use of the page directive is to import classes and packages needed for use in the JSP. Packages and classes were introduced in Chapter 1, "Understanding JSP." In the JSP 1.0 specification, there weren't explicit standards for which Java packages should be imported automatically by the JSP engine. You will find that some JSP 1.0 implementations import all of java.io or all of java.util for you, while others do not. Either way, performance isn't affected at all. If you want to see what's imported automatically in a JSP 1.0 implementation, create a simple JSP (like the one we looked at before) and request it via a browser. Then look at the Java source and see which packages were imported for you.

In JSP 1.1, a standard set of imports is made. The packages imported in JSP 1.1 implementations are

- java.lang.*
- javax.servlet.*
- javax.servlet.jsp.*
- javax.servlet.http.*

That isn't much. The Java Virtual Machine imports all of java.lang by default, anyway. The packages listed above are just the barebones necessary for the creation of the JSP servlet itself. We'll assume in the rest of this book that you are using JSP 1.1, and we'll include any packages needed for specific classes and interfaces we use.

> **NOTE**
>
> When you import a package with an asterisk (*) after the second period (.), you are importing all the classes in that package so that you can refer to them directly without using their *fully qualified names*. The fully qualified name of a class includes its full package structure—for instance, java.lang.String. See below for examples of different import statements.

Listing 2.5 is a JSP that uses the page directive to import packages and classes needed for getting the current date and formatting it.

2

CREATING A JSP
PAGE

LISTING 2.5 DateFormat1.jsp—Gets and Formats a Date

```
<%@ page import="java.text.*,java.util.Date" %>
<% String date = DateFormat.getInstance().format(new Date()); %>
<p>The date and time is: <em><font color="#aa0000"><%= date %></em></font>
```

Type this code into a plain text file and save the file with a .jsp extension. Put the file in your Web server's document root and request it via a browser. If you have a JSP engine installed and running, you should see the output, which is just the current date and time in a simple format, as shown in Figure 2.1.

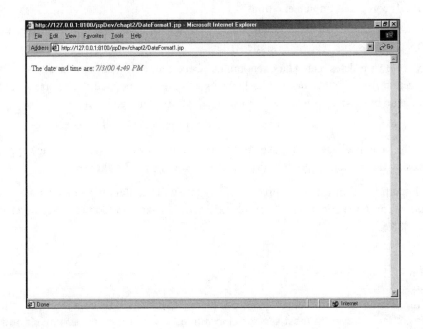

FIGURE 2.1

Output of DateFormat1.jsp *in a browser.*

We could have given the fully qualified names of both classes we needed, in which case we would have used this page directive:

```
<%@ page import="java.text.DateFormat,java.util.Date" %>
```

We could also have imported the full java.util and java.text packages, in which case the import would have looked like this:

```
<%@ page import="java.text.*,java.util.*" %>
```

As you can see, I did one of each. It doesn't matter how you do it as long as you tell the JSP engine which packages and classes it needs to compile your JSP and where to find them. How do *you* know where to find them? You will get to know the Java packages as you go along. I will show you which packages you need for each example. For now, here's a quick reference list for the packages needed for common tasks and classes in Java. For a full listing, get the Java API documentation from Sun. We will revisit these packages and many of their classes in later chapters.

- `java.lang` for common math operations, strings and string methods, and primitive data types such as `int` and `boolean`. Fortunately, this package is imported automatically by all JSP 1.1–compliant implementations.
- `java.io` for file I/O. This package contains classes for all sorts of input streams and output streams, file readers, and file writers.
- `java.util` for dates, calendars, random numbers, properties, string tokenizers, collections (such as vectors and hashtables), and the ever-popular `Enumeration` and `Iterator` interfaces (which we will use much in the coming chapters).
- `java.text` for some formatting and handling of text, dates, and numbers.

These are the main packages that make up the meat of any Java or JavaServer Page application. We'll be using these a lot, so don't worry about learning them all right now.

Another important use of the `page` directive is to specify the content type and character set of the response sent to the client. The default MIME type is `text/html`, and the default character set is ISO-8859-1.

NOTE

The standard Latin character set corresponds to ISO-8859-1. This character set includes all the characters used in most Western languages, including accented vowels and special consonants such as those found in French and Spanish.

Suppose you want to send a Chinese response to your clients, and you have an editor that you've used to create a JSP with Chinese characters. You would use the `page` directive as follows (choosing one of the several possible Chinese character encodings):

```
<%@ page contentType="text/html;charset=Big5" %>
```

Here is the full syntax of the page directive. In the following, if an attribute has a default value, the default is indicated in bold print:

```
<%@ page
      [ language="java" ]
      [ extends="package.class" ]
      [ import="{package.class | package.*}, ..." ]
      [ session="true | false" ]
      [ buffer="none | 8kb | sizekb" ]
      [ autoFlush="true | false" ]
      [ isThreadSafe="true | false" ]
      [ info="text" ]
      [ errorPage="relativeURL" ]
      [ contentType="mimeType [ ;charset=characterSet ]" |
➡      "text/html ;charset=ISO-8859-1" ]
      [ isErrorPage="true | false" ]
  %>
```

As you can see, there are a lot of attributes we haven't covered yet. We will use most if not all of these in the pages ahead. Also, there is a full syntax reference in Appendix A, "JSP Syntax." Here are some pointers on using the page directive.

- The page directive can be positioned anywhere in your JSP and have full effect over the entire page, but it's considered good practice to put it at the top of the page, for the sake of easy visibility. This is unlike ASP, which requires that you put directives *only* at the top of a page.

- page directives exert their influence over any other files that are statically included in a page. We cover static includes in the next section. These differ from dynamic includes, which are covered in a later chapter.

- Multiple page directives can occur on the same page, but each attribute can be used only once. The sole exception is the import attribute, which can be used multiple times. Usually it will make sense just to have a single page directive at the top of the page, with all the attributes needed for that page. This makes for easier readability and code maintenance.

NOTE

Every JSP has a standard translation into a valid XML document. This fact is stated in the JSP 1.0 and 1.1 specifications. For each directive and scripting element we introduce in this book, we will give the XML equivalent after the "shorthand" version. Hand coding JSPs in XML is more time consuming than using the shorthand form of each tag and scriptlet. The XML form of JSP is intended primarily for use with future GUI tools that will write the XML for you. A JSP and its XML equivalent are identical in functionality and efficiency.

The XML equivalent of the page directive is

```
<jsp:directive.page attributes />
```

The `include` Directive

There are a couple of different ways to include another file in a JSP. The `include` directive is one of them. This is used when you want to statically (as opposed to dynamically) include another file in your JSP. Briefly, the other type, the `<jsp:include>` tag, is flexible; it can include files statically or dynamically. A dynamic include is like a roundtrip to another JSP. The dynamic include says "go see this other JSP, execute its contents, and then come back here and include any output from that page." A static include just pulls the contents of the included file into the JSP *at the position where the* `include` *directive is in the page*. Static includes are processed at translation time, that is, when the JSP source is converted to Java code. When the JSP container finishes translating a JSP file into Java source, all static includes have been pulled into its body as if they were all part of the original page.

The syntax of the `include` directive is

```
<%@ include file="relativeURL" %>
```

Not bad, eh? Just one attribute.

NOTE

The XML equivalent of the `include` directive is

```
<jsp:directive.include file="relativeURL" flush="true | false" />
```

Listing 2.6 is an example of a JSP that uses two `include` directives to build a whole page.

LISTING 2.6   `IncludeDir.jsp`—include Directive Example

```
<html>
<%@ include file="inc/head.inc" %>
<%@ include file="inc/body.inc" %>
</html>
```

Listing 2.7 is the head elements of the HTML output (`head.inc`).

LISTING 2.7   `head.inc`—First Included File for the `include` Directive Example

```
<head>
<title>Include Directive Example</title>
<style type="text/css">
<!--
body {background-color: #aa0000; color: #ffffff; }
-->
</style>
</head>
```

Listing 2.8 is the body of the HTML output (`body.inc`).

LISTING 2.8   `body.inc`—Second Included File for the `include` Directive Example

```
<body>
<h1 align="center">Include Directive Example</h1>
<hr />
<p>This is a paragraph in the body of this example.</p>
</body>
```

The file in the `file` attribute of the include must be specified in a relative URL. I put a folder named `inc` in my Web server document root and put `head.inc` and `body.inc` in that folder. I then put `IncludeDir.jsp` in the document root of the Web server and requested it with a browser. The output is shown in Figure 2.2.

The `taglib` Directive

That `taglib` directive is a more advanced feature that we'll cover thoroughly later. Its syntax is as follows:

```
<%@ taglib uri="URIToTagLibrary" prefix="tagPrefix" %>
```

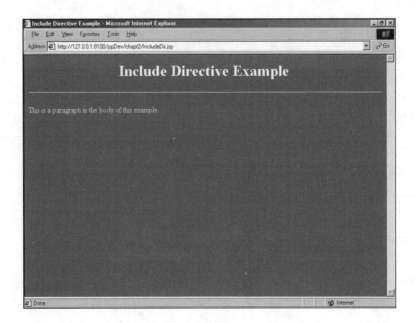

FIGURE 2.2
Output of IncludeDir.jsp *in a browser.*

A custom tag library (taglib) is a very powerful feature introduced in JSP version 1.1. taglibs will become a big part of JSP as tag libraries for common problem domains (such as database interaction and Internet messaging) are standardized. JSP's past is HTML mixed with scripting code. Its future is as an extensible, portable tag language. The present is somewhere in between. This book covers both, with an eye on the future.

NOTE

The XML equivalent of the taglib directive is a bit different from the other directives. Rather than an inline tag, the XML version of the taglib directive is as an xmlns: (XML namespace) attribute of the JSP XML file's root element. Below is an example of the JSP root element with the default XML namespace attribute and a dummy attribute for a user-defined taglib:

```
<jsp:root xmlns:jsp="http://java.sun.com/products/jsp/dtd/jsp_1_0.dtd"
          xmlns:taglib info>
</jsp:root>
```

Commenting Your Code

In JSP there are two types of comments: those that are sent in the response to the client and those that aren't. Each type has its uses.

Source Comments

Comments that are visible to the user when he selects View Source in his browser are just like regular HTML comments:

```
<!-- . . . -->
```

The only difference in JSP is that you can put a JSP *expression* inside the comment. We used an expression in the first page directive example, and we will cover expressions in detail in the next chapter. For now, just know that they are a shorthand way to output string data into your response. Suppose you want a comment to be viewable by the client in the source of the HTML that tells the client what time it was when the response was generated. Listing 2.9 illustrates how you would do this.

LISTING 2.9   Comment1.jsp—Source Comment Example

```
<html>
<head>
<title>Comment with Expression</title>
<body>
<p>View my source and see the comment!</p>
<!--This page was generated on <%= (new java.util.Date()).
➥toLocaleString() %>-->
</body>
</html>
```

Now go to your browser and select View Source. You will see the comment in the source sent to the client in the response, as in Figure 2.3.

Note that we avoided the use of the page directive here by specifying the fully qualified name of the Java class, java.util.Date. If we had explicitly imported its package using the import attribute of the page directive, we could have referred to Date by its class name only.

Another use of the HTML-style comment in a JSP is to include copyright or author information in your response to the client. This information is visible only if the client views the source of your response.

2

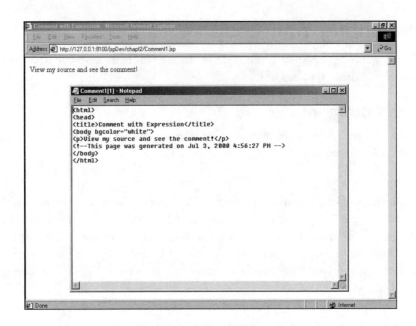

FIGURE 2.3
Output of Comment1.jsp *in a browser.*

Hidden Comments

The second type of JSP comment is the hidden comment. The hidden comment looks like this:

```
<%-- . . . . --%>
```

The JSP engine ignores hidden comments at translation time. Hidden comments are useful in development when you want to comment out a piece of code for testing purposes, to stub out lines of code to isolate a bug, or to view the output of specific portions of code while squelching others. They can also be used to comment the source of a JSP for your own or others' future reference.

Listing 2.10 gives a quick example.

LISTING 2.10   Comment2.jsp—Hidden Comment Example

```html
<html>
<head>
<title>Comment with Expression</title>
<body>
<p>View my source and don't see the comment!</p>
```

LISTING 2.10   Continued

```
<!--
<%--
This page was generated on <%= (new java.util.Date()).toLocaleString() %>
--%>
-->
</body>
</html>
```

Now go to your browser's command menu, select View Source, and note that the comment was not included in the response sent to the client, as shown in Figure 2.4. If you look in the Java source file generated by the JSP container, you will not see the comment. The JSP container completely ignores hidden comments at translation time.

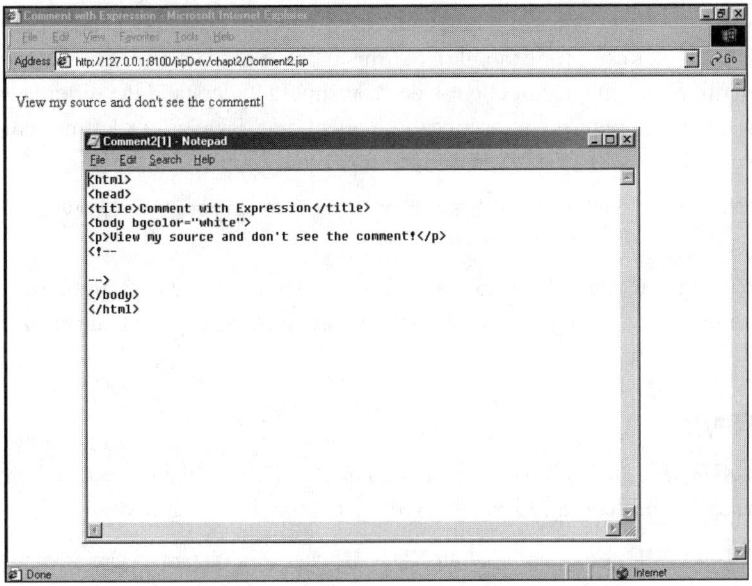

FIGURE 2.4
Output of Comment2.jsp *in a browser.*

Coding Tips

Here are some coding tips to keep in mind as we continue with JSP coding in the pages ahead.

Use Cascading Style Sheets (CSS)

Use cascading style sheets (CSS) whenever and wherever possible. You will see me using them throughout this book. CSS makes formatting HTML much simpler and shorter than it used to be. Future generations of Web browsers will definitely support full CSS1 and at least part of CSS2. (Mozilla, the next-generation browser coming from the AOL/Netscape alliance, is almost finished. At the time of this writing, AOL had just announced that its 6.0 browser would be based on Mozilla.) Since JSPs already contain a mix of HTML, Java, and scripting elements, it makes even more sense to use CSS wherever possible, to simplify the readability and maintainability of pages. To learn more about CSS, go to `http://www.w3.org/Style/CSS/`.

Keep JavaScript and JSP Uncluttered

Import JavaScript files by using links to `.js` files rather than mixing JavaScript with the code on the page. One of the neat features of JSP is that other scripting languages can be used instead of Java if the JSP container supports them. Some JSP containers already support JavaScript (JRun and Resin, for example), but this is JavaScript as a general-purpose server-side scripting language, not client-side. You should understand the difference. And remember that you can reduce clutter by calling client-side JavaScript files into your code by using the `src` attribute of the HTML `<script>` tag. For example

```
<script language="JavaScript1.2" src="myScript.js" type="text/javascript">
</script>
```

This `<script>` tag is regular HTML and is used to include a long JavaScript library in the output sent to the client. Using this tag is another way to help keep the code clean and readable.

Use XHTML

Be aware of XHTML, the XML-compliant version of HTML. I like to try to adhere to the XHTML standard when coding JSP and HTML for a couple of reasons:

- XHTML is XML compliant, and an XHTML page can instantly take advantage of XML technologies such as XSL and XML editors. These technologies will improve and become more prevalent in the future.

- XHTML imposes a stricter standard on HTML coding practices. Granted, if everyone coded according to the HTML 4.0 specification, there would be better Web pages out there. But adhering to the XHTML standard is even easier. Practicing while you code HTML could pay off in the future when you need good XML coding habits.

Throughout this book, I adhere to the XHTML coding guidelines given at the W3C's XHTML Recommendation at `http://www.w3.org/TR/xhtml1/`.

Using Scripting Elements

IN THIS CHAPTER

There are three broad categories of scripting elements in JSP:

- *Expressions*   Useful shorthand for printing out strings and contents of variables.
- *Declarations*   Useful for declaring page wide variables and methods (Java) or functions (JavaScript).
- *Scriptlets*   Open up the JSP for anything you want as long as the scriptlet code is valid for the scripting language being used in the JSP.

JSP, like ASP, is scripting language independent. Java is the default, and part of the JSP specification says that any spec-compliant JSP container *must* support Java scripting. Java is an excellent language to use. Nevertheless, other useful scripting languages are available and may be more familiar to the majority of JSP adopters. The most likely alternative to Java for the initial adopters of JSP is JavaScript. JavaScript is very similar to Java in its core syntax, is much simpler overall than Java, and is already known by thousands of Web programmers. The latest version of JavaScript (1.4 at this writing) is already supported by some of the leading JSP containers (such as JRun and Resin).

In the chapters that follow we will use Java and JavaScript, though the major emphasis will be on Java, since that is the universally supported JSP scripting language. Java is also much more powerful and complex than JavaScript, so it demands closer coverage. At this writing, JavaScript 1.5 is in beta. JavaScript 2.0 will follow soon after 1.5 becomes final. JavaScript is worth paying attention to because it is fast becoming a full-featured scripting language. Features planned for JavaScript 2.0 at this time include classes, packages, types, and other features supported by more featureful object-oriented languages such as C++ and Java. For more information on JavaScript's latest developments and future directions, check it out at the Mozilla Organization's Web site: `http://www.mozilla.org/js/`.

When you are done with this chapter you will be familiar with the core syntax of JavaServer Pages and scripting elements, and you will be well on your way to coding your own JSP-based Web applications.

Using Expressions

Let's get the basic syntax out of the way. A valid JSP expression is of this form:

`<%= expression %>`

> **NOTE**
>
> The XML equivalent of a JSP expression is
>
> ```
> <jsp:expression> expression </jsp:expression>
> ```

Any valid expression of the scripting language you are using can go in a JSP expression.

> **TIP**
>
> A key thing to remember when using expressions is that *JSP expressions never use semicolons*. This is a little annoyance of JSP: Scriptlets and declarations must use semicolons as required by the page's scripting language, whereas expressions never do.

This is important because any valid JSP expression can also be a scriptlet (a more general-purpose scripting element covered later in this chapter), and scriptlets must use semicolons where the scripting language says they should.

So what is a Java expression? An *expression* is any syntactically valid series of method calls, operators, and variables that returns a single value when executed. In the wild, expressions are usually no more than a single line of code, and they don't include any flow control operators such as `if`, `while`, or `until`. When you start adding flow control and longer lines of code, then you are talking about *statements*.

The *Java Language Specification* (the "official," very dry and technical document that describes the grammar of the Java language), by James Gosling, Bill Joy, and Guy Steele, describes several kinds of expressions. The following are excerpts from Chapter 15, "Expressions," of the online edition of the *Java Language Specification* (JLS):

Primary Expressions   Primary expressions include most of the simplest kinds of expressions, from which all others are constructed: literals, field accesses, method invocations, and array accesses. A parenthesized expression is also treated syntactically as a primary expression.

Class Instance Creation Expressions   A class instance creation expression is used to create new objects that are instances of classes.

Method Invocation Expressions   A method invocation expression is used to invoke a class or instance method.

3

USING SCRIPTING ELEMENTS

These are not the only Java expressions (there are postfix, cast, array access, and other expressions in Java), but these are the most important ones and the ones we will be using in this chapter. The entire Specification document can be found at `http://java.sun.com/docs/books/jls/html/index.html`.

Using Strings in Expressions

There is one cardinal rule of JSP expressions that makes them special and stricter than expressions in the general, programming language sense: *Every JSP expression must wind up as a string.*

A string is pretty much any sequence of characters, including spaces, numbers, and anything else you can type into a computer. A string in Java is an object of type `java.lang.String`. Remember that all the types (*aka* classes) in the `java.lang` package are imported for you by default.

JSPs consist of scripting code and template text (though we've seen in the previous chapter that a valid JSP can contain only template text). The most commonly used template text for JSP is HTML. Another likely choice is XML. One could also use WML, VRML, XHTML, or just about anything, since all non-JSP code should be completely ignored by the JSP container. All of the template text you type into your JSPs gets turned into a string (or strings, if there is scripting code separating the template text). For example, the HTML-only `Hello.jsp` from the previous chapter looks like this in JRun:

```
out.print("<html>\r\n<title>\r\nHello World\r\n</title>\r\n<body>\r\n<h1>Hello
➥ World</h1>\r\n</body>\r\n</html>");
```

That line of Java code (see Listing 2.2 for the full source listing) is a command to print out a string to the JSP container's output stream. Everything between the double quotation marks is part of a single string (the \r and \n are special escape characters representing carriage returns in the JSP source).

Some types of things that are easily converted to strings are character data, dates, variables in Java or JavaScript, and Java data types such as `int` and `boolean` (which are converted to strings for you automatically when put in expressions). Of course if your expression is starting out as a string and doesn't change, then it meets the criterion that all expressions must wind up as strings. For example, the expression

```
<%= "Hello, I'm a String" %>
```

is a valid expression that starts and ends its life as a string.

NOTE

Note the double quotes in the string above. You must put strings in double quotes or the JVM thinks you are referencing a variable (or multiple variables if it encounters spaces between words) of some kind.

Expressions are fairly easy to use and understand, so let's get started with a few interesting examples. Later we'll integrate expressions with other scripting elements.

Using Methods and Constructors in Expressions

The example below shows some expressions that might come in handy: getting the current time, getting the last modified date of a file, and environment information such as the name of the JSP container and the client's user agent make and model. Listing 3.1 (`Expressions.jsp`) shows how to do these things in Java. The output of `Expressions.jsp` (see Figure 3.1) shows the expressions' results as processed by the JSP container.

3

LISTING 3.1   `Expressions.jsp`—Several JSP Expressions in Java

```
<%@ page import="java.util.Date, java.text.DateFormat, java.io.File" %>
<html>
<head>
<title>Express Yourself</title>
<style type="text/css">
<!--
body { background-color: #ffffff; }
h1   { text-align: center; color: #008888; }
u { color: #ff0000; }
table { margin-left: 10%; margin-right: auto; }
tr td { font: smaller; }
p { margin-left: 5%; font-family: sans-serif; }
-->
</style>
</head>
<body>
<h1>Expressions</h1>
<p>Some basic expressions:</p>
<table>
<tr>
 <td>call for an unformatted java.util.Date() returns:</td>
 <td><u><%= new Date() %></u></td>
```

LISTING 3.1   Continued

```
</tr>
<tr>
 <td>call for the real path to the root of this JSP returns:</td>
 <td><u><%= application.getRealPath("/") %></u></td>
</tr>
<tr>
 <td>call for the URL path and name of this JSP returns:</td>
 <td><u><%= request.getServletPath() %></u></td>
</tr>
<tr>
 <td>call for the file path and name of this JSP returns:</td>
 <td><u><%= new File(application.getRealPath(request.getServletPath())) %>
 </u></td>
</tr>
</table>
<p>If we add some other methods and combine some of the above we get nicer
    output:</p>
<table>
<tr>
 <td>The current time is:</td>
 <td><u><%= DateFormat.getTimeInstance().format(new Date()) %></u></td>
</tr>
<tr>
 <td>This page was last modified:</td>
 <td><u><%= DateFormat.getInstance().format(new Date(new
File(application.getRealPath(request.getServletPath())).lastModified())) %>
 </u></td>
</tr>
</table>
<p>More expressions using readily available data:</p>
<table>
<tr>
 <td>This site is running <u><%= application.getServerInfo() %></u></td></tr>
<tr>
 <td>Your Web browser is <u><%= request.getHeader("USER-AGENT") %>
 </u></td></tr>
<tr>
 <td>This page was served from <%= request.getServerName() %>, and you used
     the <%= request.getProtocol() %> protocol to access the server on port
     <%= request.getServerPort() %></td>
</tr>
<tr>
 <td>The value of a non-existent header is:
    <u><%= request.getHeader("NO_SUCH_THING") %></u>
```

LISTING 3.1 Continued

```
  </td>
</tr>
</table>
</body>
</html>
```

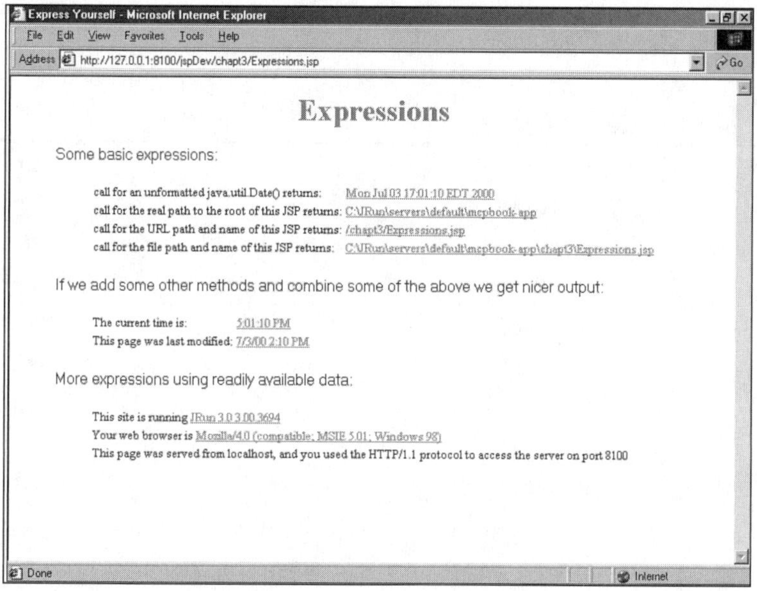

FIGURE 3.1

Expressions.jsp's *result, showing dynamically generated output.*

Let's go through the code in Expressions.jsp (Listing 3.1).

First we use the page directive at the top to import the special classes used in the JSP. I imported the classes using their fully qualified names so that you can see exactly where each is from. After some basic setup of the HTML page and CSS formatting, we get into the first expression, which is a call for a plain vanilla Date object:

```
<%= new Date() %>
```

The word new is a *keyword* in Java, and it must be used when instantiating a class instance (for example, an object). Here we are telling the Java Virtual Machine to instantiate an instance of the java.util.Date class. The JVM does this by allocating memory for the Date object and initializing the object with the time it was allocated. The JVM measures time, as most UNIX systems do, as the number of milliseconds elapsed since midnight, Greenwich Mean Time, January 1, 1970.

> **NOTE**
>
> Keywords in a programming language are *reserved*, meaning their use in the language is restricted by the rules of the language's grammar. The important thing to remember about keywords in Java is that they cannot be used to name variables, classes, or methods. They can be used only where the language says they can. Table 3.1 shows a list of all of Java's keywords. Don't memorize them now. Just be aware of them.

TABLE 3.1   Java Keywords (as of Java 1.2)

abstract	default	if	private
this	boolean	do	implements
protected	throw	break	double
import	public	throws	byte
else	instanceof	return	transient
case	extends	int	short
try	catch	final	interface
static	void	char	finally
long	strictfp	volatile	class
float	native	super	while
const	for	new	switch
continue	goto	package	synchronized

Handily, the `Date` class has a built-in `toString()` method, which is what the JSP container will invoke on our expression to convert the `Date` object into a string of text.

Next we used the `getRealPath()` method of the `javax.servlet.ServletContext` class to get the actual file path of the JSP application. The application in this case is just a single JSP, but you can have many JSPs and other files combined to create an application. JSP provides a built-in object for you to use when you want to refer to the application itself. The class of the object is `javax.servlet.ServletContext`, and the provided reference name for the object is simply `application`. The `getRealPath()` method takes a string as an argument (which for our purposes means you must put the argument in double quotes), and the string it takes must be a URL representing a file or virtual directory on the server. Here we are asking it to return the real path of the Web server's document root, `"/"`:

```
<%= application.getRealPath("/") %>
```

The `application` object (previously discussed) and the `request` object (discussed later in this chapter) are two of nine so-called *implicit objects* that are available for scripting in every JSP. Implicit objects are covered in the next chapter.

Note that `getRealPath()` returns a string so, unlike the `Date` object, there's no extra step involved in getting a string from the method return type.

Next we use the `getServletPath()` method of the `java.servlet.ServletRequest` class (actually it is a subclass of `ServletRequest`, but that's not important here) to get the name of the servlet being invoked. This method was obviously intended and named for use with servlets, but it works just as well for JSPs. What the method really does is get the part of the request URL that contains the name of the JSP. It returns a string representing the JSP's filename (not the path or name of its compiled servlet, as one might think).

```
<%= request.getServletPath() %>
```

Note that the previous two expressions did not use `new` to create instances of the classes whose methods were being called. This is because the JSP container already instantiates these classes for us automatically. Not so for the next expression, which uses `new` to create an instance of the `java.io.File` class:

```
<%= new File(application.getRealPath(request.getServletPath())) %>
```

As you can see, this expression consists of three nested expressions. This is perfectly legal. You can use one expression within another as long as the return type of the inner expression(s) can be used as valid arguments to the outer expression(s). As the JSP container evaluates our JSP expressions and returns results to the client, so too the Java Virtual Machine evaluates Java expressions and returns the results. This is an example of how one of these nested expressions is evaluated:

1. The JVM evaluates the nested expression from the inside out, so the first one evaluated is `request.getServletPath()`, which returns the string `"/Expressions.jsp"`.

2. The return from the first evaluated expression is what the second expression sees, instead of the unevaluated Java code we typed in. So the second expression evaluates `application.getRealPath("/Expressions.jsp")`, which returns the string `"C:\RESIN1.1\doc\Expressions.jsp"`. As we saw above, `getRealPath()` takes a URL string representing a file or virtual directory as an argument.

3. Now the last expression can be evaluated. Since the first two have finished, the actual expression being evaluated is `new File("C:\RESIN1.1\doc\Expressions.jsp")`. We are

using new and the java.io.File class's *constructor* to instantiate an instance of class java.io.File. The constructor is like a special method used to create an instance of a class. What we get as a result is a File object, which here is an abstract representation of the Expressions.jsp file.

4. The JSP container calls the toString() method of the File object, which returns a string representing the pathname of the File object, in this case, "C:\RESIN1.1\doc\Expressions.jsp". This ends evaluation of the nested expression, and we can see the result in the response sent to the browser.

NOTE

All Java objects inherit the toString() method from the super class of all classes, the Object class. Nevertheless, it is up to each class to *override* the toString() method to provide an implementation of it that is appropriate for the data in that class.

The next expression in our Expressions.jsp is a nested expression that uses multiple method calls:

```
<%= DateFormat.getTimeInstance().format(new Date()) %>
```

The java.text.DateFormat class is *abstract*, which, among other things, means that you never instantiate it with new. We call the DateFormat class directly and then call its getTimeInstance() method, which returns a time format object. Then we call the format() method of the time format object, passing it the evaluated result of the inner expression new Date(), (which is, as we've seen, a Date object representing the current date and time). When the format() method of the DateFormat object evaluates the Date object, it returns a string representing the current time: "8:49:14 PM".

The *coup de grace* is where we put it all together in the next expression to print out the date and time when the Expressions.jsp file was last modified. Sometimes it's useful to know when a Web page was last modified, particularly if there's any time-sensitive data on the page, like a schedule or calendar. Here's the expression:

```
<%= DateFormat.getInstance().format(new Date(new
File(application.getRealPath(request.getServletPath())).lastModified())) %>
```

The expressions are evaluated left to right and inside to outside by the JVM. We will do our trick with the DateFormat object, but there's nothing for it to format until all the expressions nested in the format() method are evaluated. The only new things here are the lastModified() method of the File object and the passing of an argument to the Date object's constructor. This is a built-in method of the java.io.File class. After the two nested expressions in the `File` constructor are evaluated, the remaining nested expression would look like this to the JVM:

```
(new Date(new File("C:\RESIN1.1\doc\Expressions.jsp").lastModified()))
```

So the first thing the JVM has to do is execute the `lastModified()` method call on the `File` object. This completes evaluation of the nested expression in the `Date` constructor. The return from the `lastModified()` method is a number (a `long`, to be precise—Java's primitive data types will be covered later) representing the time and date that the `Expressions.jsp` file was last modified, expressed in the number of milliseconds since midnight, January 1, 1970, GMT.

If we printed out the string representation of one of these `long` times, it would look something like this:

```
951623040000
```

That's about a quarter to 11 p.m., EST, 2/26/2000. But we want to print out a nicely formatted date for our client, not a count of milliseconds since 1970! So the next step is to pass the `long` returned from `lastModified()` to the `Date` constructor. This is legal because the syntax for the `Date` class's constructor says it can optionally take a `long` number as an argument. When it does, instead of creating a `Date` object that represents the current date and time, it creates one that represents the time you gave (again, that's in milliseconds since midnight, January 1, 1970, GMT). Now that we have a `Date` object to format, we pass it to the `DateFormat` object's `format()` method. And the end result is something like this:

```
2/26/00 5:09 PM
```

Next we have a few more method invocation expressions just to wrap up the examples. The first one, `getServerInfo()`, is another method of the implicit `application` object. This just returns a string containing information about the JSP container. The information provided is implementation dependent. Usually you get the product name of the JSP container, plus some version information:

```
<%= application.getServerInfo() %>
```

Next is the `request.getHeader()` method. You can pass any standard (and sometimes non-standard, depending on the JSP container) CGI header name as a string to the `getHeader()` method, and it will return the value of that header. Here we got the value of the USER-AGENT header. Appendix A, "JSP Syntax," has a full listing of the standard CGI variable names, with examples of typical return values:

```
<%= request.getHeader("USER-AGENT") %>
```

Finally, here is an example showing how expressions can blend seamlessly with the text in your HTML while providing dynamically generated content (refer to Figure 3.1 for a view of

3

the output in a browser). Like the `getServerInfo()` method, none of these methods take any arguments. You just invoke them and they return strings of data:

```
<%= request.getServerName() %>
<%= request.getProtocol() %>
<%= request.getServerPort() %>
```

Using Declarations

JSP declarations are used to introduce variables or methods (in JavaScript methods are called *functions*, but they are the same concept) for use in a page. Declarations have scope over the JSP they are in, and any static includes (see Chapter 1, "Understanding JSP," for a discussion of static includes) that the page has. The syntax of a JSP declaration is

```
<%! declaration; [ declaration; ] %>
```

The bracketed *declaration* above indicates that multiple declarations are optional but possible. You can have any number of Java or JavaScript declarations in a JSP declaration. You can also have multiple JSP declarations in a page.

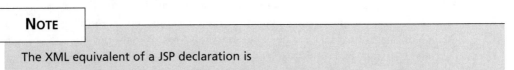

NOTE

The XML equivalent of a JSP declaration is

```
<jsp:declaration> declaration </jsp:declaration>
```

Typically, declarations are used to create a variable for use throughout a JSP, or for a method that you want to use in a JSP without having to declare it every time you use it. Whatever you put in declarations in a JSP goes outside the `service()` method of the compiled servlet. The `service()` method is the main method that services the requests from your page by generating responses to them. Scriptlets, (in the next section) go in the JSP Servlet's `service()` method. Declarations are for variables and methods that you want to reference in the `service()` method but that you want to keep independent of any particular request data or operations.

Java's Primitive Data Types

Before going any further, let's get some more Java syntax out on the table. We'll need to use Java's operators and data types.

Java has eight data types, a few of which you'll see and use frequently. The basic ones you see used most often are `boolean`, `char`, `int`, and `long`, but you should know about all of them. Table 3.2 shows all the primitive Java data types and the values each can contain.

TABLE 3.2 Java's Primitive Data Types

Type	Minimum Value	Maximum Value
boolean	(1-bit) true or false	(1-bit) true or false
byte	-128	127
short	-32768	32767
int	-2147483648	2147483647
long	-9223372036854775808	9223372036854775807
char	\u0000 (0)	\uffff (65535)
float	32-bit IEEE754	32-bit IEEE754
double	64-bit IEEE754	64-bit IEEE754
void	---	---

In most cases if you need a number, you use an int. If you need a floating point for monetary calculations, use a float. For truth checking, use boolean, and for single characters use char.

Java's Operators

For operations on data, you use Java's operators, which are pretty similar to those used in any programming language. We'll introduce them as we go along. Table 3.3 is a listing of the most frequently used operators in Java. If we ever use an odd or unusual operator, we'll mention it. Of the 37 operators in Java, most people only use these few. For a full listing and discussion, get a reference for the Java language.

TABLE 3.3 Java's Common Operators

Operator Type	Operators
Arithmetic	* / % + -
Relational	> < >= <= == !=
Increment/decrement	+ + --
Logical	&& ||
String concatenator	+
Assignment	= += -=

Now let's get into some examples of declarations. Let's also combine some declarations with expressions.

3

Creating a Hit Counter in JSP

Each listing in the rest of this chapter will use the same CSS formatting, so I am going to use the CSS `import` statement to import the style sheet from a separate file. That portion of the code is the same for every page. I put `JSPstyle.css` in the same directory as its calling page, so there is no path prefix specified for the URL to the style sheet. If you put yours in another directory, change the relative URL accordingly. Remember that this has nothing to do with the Java keyword `import` but is a part of the CSS1 standard syntax:

```
<style type="text/css">
<!--
@import url(JSPstyle.css);
-->
</style>
```

Here's Listing 3.2, the source for the `JSPstyle.css` sheet:

LISTING 3.2 JSPstyle.css—The Cascading Style Sheet Used in This Chapter

```
body { background-color: #ffffff; }
h1   { text-align: center; color: #008888; }
h2   { text-align: left; color: #005555; }
u    { color: #ff0000; }
table { margin-left: 10%; margin-right: auto; }
tr td { font: smaller; }
p    { margin-left: 5%; }
span { color: #ff0000; }
```

The idea is to practice formatting our JSP but keep it uncluttered and focused on the code. Listing 3.3 is a simple hit counter in JSP.

LISTING 3.3 Counter.jsp—A Simple JSP Hit Counter

```
<html>
<head>
<title>JSP Declarations</title>
<style type="text/css">
<!--
@import url(JSPstyle.css);
-->
</style>
</head>
<body>
<h1>Declarations</h1>
```

LISTING 3.3 Continued

```
<%! int j = 0; %>
<h2>Counter</h2>
<p>This page has been hit <span> <%= ++j %> </span> times since it was
   first loaded.</p>
</body>
</html>
```

After setting up our HTML and style, we set up a variable to keep track of our page hits using a JSP declaration:

```
<%! private int j = 0; %>
```

The keyword `private` describes the *access level* for the member variable `j`. Access levels are an important concept in Java. For now, just know that declaring a method or variable `private` makes it accessible only within the class in which it is defined. So in our case, the variable `j` is accessible only to this JSP. We could define it as `public`, which would make it available to any other Java class that extended our JSP, but we know that's not going to happen.

There is another access level called `protected`, which is somewhere between `private` and `public`. We could also leave the variable without specifying an access level for it, in which case it takes the default access level, which is `package`. The `package` access level leaves access to this variable open to other classes in the same package. This JSP probably won't even be defined in a package (though that is an implementation-dependent issue). No one's going to extend our JSP's servlet class, either, so it doesn't matter. For a JSP like this and most basic-to-intermediate–level JSPs, it will not matter what access level you use to define your variables or classes. When the issue becomes relevant later in this book, we'll bring it up again. Feel free to use `public`, `protected`, or `private` or just leave the access level undefined so that it defaults to `package`.

The keyword `int` specifies the type of the variable being defined. You must always specify a type for Java variables. In JavaScript this is unnecessary. In Java it is mandatory. There are two basic types of variables in Java: *primitive types* and *reference types*. Primitive types are those integer, character, and truth variable types laid out in Table 3.2. Reference types are *arrays*, *classes* (such as `Date` and `File`), and *interfaces* (such as `java.util.Enumeration`).

Finally, a variable must have a name, so I named this one `j` for no particular reason. By convention, a Java variable name starts with a lowercase letter and is descriptive unless it's just a straightforward counter or coordinate. This is just a counter, so a single-character name is fine.

After an HTML heading announcing the counter, there's a line of code that makes up our counter:

```
<p>This page has been hit <span> <%= ++j %> </span> times since it was first
loaded.</p>
```

The resulting output is shown in Figure 3.2.

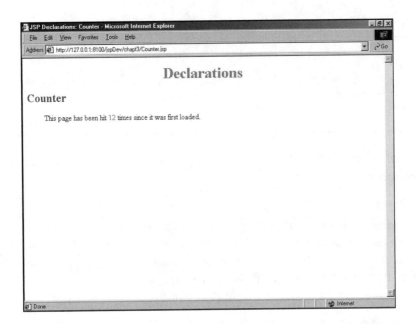

FIGURE 3.2
Counter.jsp *after 12 reloads.*

As you may have guessed, the counter itself is represented by the JSP expression `<%= ++j %>`. The ++ operator is a pretty common one to find in most programming languages. It's called an *auto-incrementor*, and it essentially means "increment the following variable by one *before* you evaluate this expression." So every time we hit Reload on this JSP, the variable j will be incremented by one and printed. The other auto-incrementor is also ++, but it is put after the variable name, like this:

```
<%= j++ %>
```

This auto-incrementor essentially means, "increment the variable that's attached to my back *after* you evaluate this expression." We want the first one because we want to print out the count that includes our request each time. Otherwise we'd be printing out the value of the variable j after the last guy accessed the page, rather than after we accessed it. Note that there is also an auto-decrementor. It works the same as the incrementor, except it subtracts one before or after, and it looks like this: `--`.

A better counter would be one that incremented the counter only for new sessions, rather than for every raw hit. If you count sessions, you are counting the number of browser sessions

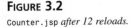

during which the page was accessed. Counting sessions would make it so that each time some-one came to your page, he would be counted only once, even if he hit Reload 100 times. A session-aware hit counter is included in Chapter 5, "Using Beans."

Another feature to improve this simple counter would be a file on the server that stored the counter's state between server restarts. As it stands, its data will be lost any time the JSP container is stopped.

Creating a Table Using a JSP Declaration

We've seen a simple variable declaration and used it in an expression to keep track of the requests made to a JSP. Now we'll do a method declaration and use the method in an expression to build a table of request headers and values (Listing 3.4, `makeTable.jsp`).

Overview of the Page

We're going to use the `java.util.Enumeration` interface in this JSP, so first we import that class using the `page` directive:

```
<%@ page import="java.util.Enumeration" %>
```

Next we do our HTML setup, and we'll throw in the counter from the last example, too. Last time we used the `private` access level, primarily just to introduce access level modifiers. This time let's use the default `package` access level.

```
<html>
<head>
<title>JSP Declarations</title>
<style type="text/css">
<!--
@import url(JSPstyle.css);
-->
</style>
</head>
<body>
<h1>Declarations</h1>
<%! int j = 0; %>
```

We could declare the j variable in the declaration that follows, but to make it clear that we're adding a set of variables for a completely different example, I decided to keep the declarations separate.

> **TIP**
>
> As far as the JSP container is concerned, it doesn't matter whether you declare all your variables in a single declaration or not. The only thing that really matters is that you declare them before you use them or refer to them in your JSP. For example, you're not allowed to put all your declarations at the bottom of the page just to keep them out of the way. You can declare them all at the top of the page, since you won't have used them there. For now we're defining them in proximity to where they're used, just for the sake of clarity.

Now we declare several `String` objects for use later on, in an expression where we'll use them to construct the table:

```
<%!
String table = "<table border=\"1\" cellpadding=\"2\">";
String th = "<th>Header</th><th>Value</th>";
String tr = "<tr><td>";
String trC = "</td></tr>";
String tableC = trC + "</table>";
%>
```

A few things to notice in these `String` declarations are

- The `String`s are declared in the same style that primitive data types are. Note the lack of a new keyword or a constructor method. This is a special feature of `String` literal declarations. On the other hand, you can declare a `String` object as you would any other reference type:

  ```
  String str = new String("Here is a String.");
  ```

  But you can also take advantage of the special feature of `String`s and just declare them without a constructor, assigning the value of whatever quoted text is on the right side of the assignment operator.

- Certain characters can be given special meaning in string literals by *escaping* them. To escape characters in a Java string literal, put a backslash (\) directly before it. Since a literal is defined within double quotes, if you want to use any double quotes as part of your string literal, you must escape the double quote character. This tells the JVM which double quote is actually supposed to end the string literal. That is what we did in this line:

  ```
  String table = "<table border=\"1\" cellpadding=\"2\">";
  ```

- Understanding the `String` concatenator versus the addition operator is a potentially confusing issue, but don't let it be. Basically, the JVM knows when it should add two variables that are numbers and when it should concatenate two string literals instead of trying to add them as integers. You don't have to do anything to tell it how to do this. In one of the declarations above, I created one `String` by concatenating one predefined `String` object with a new string literal. This is perfectly OK. The JVM knows what I am trying to do:

```
String tableC = trC + "</table>";
```

Next we have our counter section, just as in the previous example (Listing 3.3):

```
<h2>Counter</h2>
<p>This page has been hit <span> <%= ++j %> </span> times since
 it was first loaded.</p>
```

And now our method declaration, which we will use just a little way down the page to construct our table:

```
<%!
private StringBuffer makeTable(HttpServletRequest request)
{
  StringBuffer sb = new StringBuffer();
  Enumeration enum = request.getHeaderNames();
  while (enum.hasMoreElements())
  {
    String name = (String) enum.nextElement();
    String value = request.getHeader(name);
    if (value != null)
    {
      sb.append("<tr><td>" + name + "</td>" + "<td>" + value + "</tr>");
    }
  }
  return sb;
}
%>
```

Declaring a Method in Java

Java method declarations have access level modifiers, too. Just as with our counter variable before, it doesn't matter which modifier we use, because we'll use this method only in this JSP. For kicks I used `private`, but you can use anything or nothing, just as before. After the access level modifier, if you choose to have one, you can have one or more of several keywords such as `static`, `final`, `synchronized`, and so on, but we won't go into that right now. At this point, we'll just cover the basics of any method declaration in Java: the return type, method name, parameter list, and body.

Here's how any Java method must be declared:

```
returnType methodName(parameterList)
{
  body
}
```

The return type requires some thought. What's going to pop out of this method when it's done its work? If it's nothing, then the return type should be void. If it's something, then you must provide a primitive type or a reference type as the returned value.

What we're really concerned with is whether there's anything that the JVM needs to know about being returned from the method. Whatever is returned is returned to the JVM. If, for example, this were a method that only wrote a log message directly to System.out (standard output), then there would be nothing returned to the JVM. The data would be written out from the JVM within the method, and the return type would be void.

But we are often going to be getting a value or values back for further use in our JSPs, so the JVM is going to be interested in that. For example, I want this makeTable() method to create a StringBuffer object named sb, which I plan to use later on in an expression. In order for me to do that, the JVM has to be told that my makeTable() method is going to return something for future use. I could use System.out to write my table to a log file, but I want to send it back to the client along with the rest of the response on the client output stream. To do so I must get an object of a particular type returned from the method, tell the JVM about it, and then ask for it again later. That's the idea. And that's the way most of your JSP methods are likely to work; you'll be getting Strings or StringBuffers returned with post parameters, or ints derived from invoice calculations, or boolean values from testing some condition.

Naming the Method

By convention, Java methods are given action names, using verbs wherever possible. Thus our makeTable() here, getHeader(), getServerInfo(), and so on elsewhere. Interestingly, toString() is verbless, but I guess the alternative would have been something like doToString() or Stringify(). Another Java naming convention is that when you have two or more words in a Java entity name, you make the first word lowercase and the first letter of subsequent words uppercase (unless one of the words is an acronym, such as URL, XML, or HTML). Since methods are verbs, you may have guessed that classes are conventionally defined with noun names, always beginning with an uppercase letter, such as String, Date, and File.

NOTE

JavaSoft maintains a document of recommended Java coding conventions. The document is called *Code Conventions for the Java Programming Language*. It covers conventions for class, interface, method, package and variable naming, commenting conventions, recommended flow control statements, and so on. You can get a copy of it at http://java.sun.com/docs/codeconv/index.html. Just a reminder—use the conventions where they make the most sense and where they fit with your practices.

Now let's define this method. I am using a class called StringBuffer, which is the only other string class in Java. Generally you use Strings for immutable literals, and you use StringBuffers for strings that you want to modify on-the-fly. StringBuffers can also be more efficient and realize better performance than Strings, especially when you can use StringBuffer's append() method to append a whole bunch of string data into a single StringBuffer and write that to output rather than writing out a ton of individual Strings (the reason being that when you concatenate Strings, StringBuffers are used behind the scenes in the JVM to do the concatenation). So I define the method's return type and give the method a good verb-based, descriptive name:

```
private StringBuffer makeTable(HttpServletRequest request)
```

The parameter list for the makeTable() method contains one argument: HttpServletRequest request. The argument(s) in a method's parameter list defines how you can pass data into the method. Data that's passed into the method is used by the method to perform its function. The makeTable() method takes an object of type HttpServletRequest and name request as its argument. This is like a miniature variable declaration; there's no constructor or initialization, but there is a specification of the type of object allowed to be passed in here and what its name must be. So if we can get hold of an object of type HttpServletRequest somewhere in our JSP, and if it can be given the identifier name of request, we can pass it to the makeTable() method as an argument. We know there's an implicit object available to us in JSPs called request, and we know that it's a subclass of ServletRequest (namely, HttpServletRequest), so we should be OK passing that implicit object in from our next expression.

> **NOTE**
>
> The JSP implicit objects (request, application, and more—see the next chapter) are not directly available to JSP declarations. The only way to get them into declarations is to have them passed in as arguments by using an expression or a scriptlet.

We have a return type, a method name, a parameter list or one argument; now we just need the method *body*. The body is the actual Java statements that make up the method. Here we go:

```
{
  StringBuffer sb = new StringBuffer();
  Enumeration enum = request.getHeaderNames();
  while (enum.hasMoreElements())
  {
    String name = (String) enum.nextElement();
    String value = request.getHeader(name);
    if (value != null)
    {
      sb.append("<tr><td>" + name + "</td>" + "<td>" + value + "</tr>");
    }
  }
  return sb;
}
```

We open the method body with a curly brace. Then we declare a new, empty `StringBuffer` object using the `StringBuffer` class's constructor. We then instantiate another object, named enum, which we can tell from the type shown is an object of type `java.util.Enumeration` (remember the `import` we did in the `page` directive at the beginning of this JSP):

```
{
  StringBuffer sb = new StringBuffer();
  Enumeration enum = request.getHeaderNames();
```

Using the Enumeration Interface

The `Enumeration` class is a special kind of class, called an interface. We are using it here because we know that the `getHeaderNames()` method of the `HttpServletRequest` object returns an `Enumeration` of its contents. This is because `HttpServletRequest` implements the `Enumeration` interface. I knew this, by the way, because I checked the Servlet API documentation to see what `getHeaderNames()` was going to return.

> **TIP**
>
> As a JSP programmer, you will definitely need to become familiar with the Servlet API. We go over it in some detail in the next chapter. There is also an appendix in the back of this book that will help with the Servlet API calls. Appendix C, "Using Java Methods to Retrieve CGI Environment Variables," has a list of the standard CGI headers and examples of their values. You can also get documentation for the Servlet APIs on the Web at `http://java.sun.com/products/servlet/download.html`.

`Enumeration` is the standard interface for accessing a series of objects contained in so-called *collection*s classes such as `Hashtables` and `Vectors`. In Java 1.2 (*aka* Java 2), there is a new `Iterator` interface that has some improvements over `Enumeration`. For now we'll stay backward compatible and use the `Enumeration`. The `Enumeration` interface has just two methods, both of which are used whenever you use the `Enumeration` interface:

- hasMoreElements()
- nextElement()

The `hasMoreElements()` method is typically used to control a loop. It tells you if there are more elements in the collection being enumerated or if we've gone through them all. The `nextElement()` method grabs the next element out of the collection and returns it, if the last one hasn't been grabbed already. Now we will set up the loop that we'll run until there are no more elements in the collection (that is, until `hasMoreElements()` returns the `boolean` for false):

```
while (enum.hasMoreElements())
  {
    String name = (String) enum.nextElement();
    String value = request.getHeader(name);
    if (value != null)
    {
      sb.append("<tr><td>" + name + "</td>" + "<td>" + value + "</tr>");
    }
  }
```

The syntax for the keyword `while`, which is used to establish a `while` loop, is as follows:

```
while (expression returns true)
{
  execute statement
}
```

As you know from our earlier method calls, the enum.hasMoreElements() call will be evaluated and returned into the parentheses (as boolean true or false) before the keyword while will execute the statement in braces. Each time the enum.hasMoreElements() call returns true, the following events will happen:

1. A new string called name will be created by calling the enum.nextElement() method and *casting* the returned object of type java.lang.Object to type java.lang.String. To *cast* an object of one type to another is to *convert* it. Sometimes you can cast objects to other types, and sometimes you cannot. There are many rules that apply to class casting in Java. The one we are applying here is the rule that it is OK to convert a class to a more specific type as long as the conversion is made to a subclass of the class being converted. String is a subclass of Object, so the class cast is allowed. This is a so-called *narrowing reference* conversion. For all the conversion rules and a good description of class conversion details in Java, see the *Java Language Specification*, Chapter 5, available at http://java.sun.com/docs/books/jls/html/5.doc.html#27529.

2. The next line passes the string name we got in the previous line into the getHeader() method of the request object (which, remember, we will be passing as an argument to the makeTable() method). The getHeader() method will return the CGI header value associated with the CGI header specified in name and will assign it to the appropriately named variable value.

3. Now we enter an if statement that's nested inside the while statement, and which uses the name and value variables we get each time we loop through the while statement:

```
if (value != null)
    {
        sb.append("<tr><td>" + name + "</td>" + "<td>" + value + "</tr>");
    }
```

Just like the while statement, this if is checking the truth value of an evaluated expression. What it is doing is saying "if the variable named value is not equal to null, then go ahead and execute this statement." This just makes the loop skip a table row if there's a header with a null value.

4. The line of code being executed in the if statement is the line that creates table rows. The String concatenates a bunch of Strings with the StringBuffer object's append() method. Each time through the loop, if while and if return true, another table row is concatenated and then appended to the StringBuffer named sb.

5. The last few bits finish up the method:

```
    }
    return sb;
}
```

The first brace closes the `while` loop. The keyword `return` returns the `StringBuffer sb` to the JVM, and the last brace closes the method, which is done once `hasMoreElements()` returns `false`.

Calling the Method

The last line of JSP in this example is the expression we use to call the `makeTable()` method and print out the result:

```
<%= table + th + makeTable(request) + tableC %>
```

We use the `String` concatenator operator to piece together some of the string literals we declared above, namely the HTML code we need to neatly open and close the HTML table and add two header cells. In the middle we call `makeTable(request)`, passing as an argument the implicit JSP `request` object. When the method returns, the JSP container can print out the result. The resultant JSP, after requests to make the counter increment a couple of times, looks like Figure 3.3.

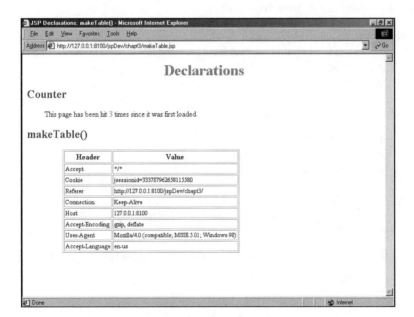

FIGURE 3.3
`makeTable.jsp` *showing request headers and their values below the simple hit counter.*

The complete `makeTable.jsp` is in Listing 3.4.

LISTING 3.4 `makeTable.jsp`—Creates a Table Using a JSP Method Declaration

```jsp
<%@ page import="java.util.Enumeration" %>
<html>
<head>
<title>JSP Declarations</title>
<style type="text/css">
<!--
@import url(JSPstyle.css);
-->
</style>
</head>
<body>
<h1>Declarations</h1>
<%! int j = 0; %>
<%!
String table = "<table border=\"1\">";
String tr = "<tr><td>";
String trC = "</td></tr>";
String tableC = trC + "</table>";
String th = "<th>Header</th><th>Value</th>";
%>
<h2>Counter</h2>
<p>This page has been hit <span> <%= ++j %> </span> times since
    it was first loaded.</p>
<h2>makeTable()</h2>
<%!
private StringBuffer makeTable(HttpServletRequest request)
{
  StringBuffer sb = new StringBuffer();
  Enumeration enum = request.getHeaderNames();
  while (enum.hasMoreElements())
  {
    String name = (String) enum.nextElement();
    String value = request.getHeader(name);
    if (value != null)
    {
      sb.append("<tr><td>" + name + "</td>" + "<td>" + value + "</tr>");
    }
  }
  return sb;
}
%>
```

LISTING 3.4 Continued

```
<%= table + th + makeTable(request) + tableC %>
</body>
</html>
```

Using Scriptlets

There is an ongoing debate in the server-side Java programming world about scripting elements and JSP in general. Briefly, the debate is over whether there should be any scripting code in JSPs, or whether it should be all tag based. I think it is great to have the accessibility of Java in JSP whenever I want it. But we'll see later in the book that JSPs can get uglier the more you mix HTML, JSP tags, and scripting code. So it's nice to have the availability of custom tags to hide away the code implementation. We needn't take a hard line one way or the other. Let the situation prescribe the methods used. If it makes sense to put a little scripting code in a JSP, then do it. If the scripting is taking the majority of the page content, and if you have tag libraries, beans, and servlets available to offload heavy coding, then you should definitely use them. As JSP technology advances (with things like a standard tag library and widely available custom tag libraries), it will become more practical to keep the scripting to a minimum.

The cool thing about scriptlets is that you already know how to write them. The basic syntax for scriptlets is as simple as this:

```
<% scriptlet code %>
```

> **NOTE**
>
> The XML equivalent of a JSP scriptlet is
>
>   <jsp:scriptlet> scriptlet code </jsp:scriptlet>

Several of the declarations and expressions we've looked at in this chapter would make valid scriptlets. Scriptlets are the general-purpose glue for JSP coding. They can contain any code fragment that's valid in the page scripting language. What that means, though, is sometimes complicated. What's valid really depends on context. For example, an open brace is never valid by itself: `<% { %>`. But if there is an appropriately placed, corresponding closing brace further down the page, then the opening brace makes sense: `<% } %>`.

On the one hand, scriptlets are like declarations in that they always use semicolons to end statements and expressions. They can have multiple expressions and statements as long as each is ended with a semicolon. But declarations are used to declare global variables and methods, which are initialized when the JSP is initialized (first compiled and loaded into the JVM). Scriptlet code goes into the service method of the JSP's compiled servlet, which means it is executed only when a request is actually serviced by the JSP. The same is true of expressions. The difference can be summed up in a sentence:

> *Declarations are executed at initialization time; expressions and scriptlets at request time.*

On the other hand, scriptlets are like expressions in that they have full access to the implicit objects of JSP. These implicit objects are covered in full in the next chapter. But unlike expressions, which always write something to the default output stream, scriptlets may or may not write anything out, depending on their code.

When you use an expression in a scriptlet, it will not automatically be converted to a `String` and printed out for you. To print a Java expression in a scriptlet, use the implicit JSP `out` object, and invoke its `print()` method like this:

```
<% out.print( new java.util.Date()); %>
```

We will use scriptlets extensively throughout this book. Again, they are the all-purpose glue that's used (if needed) to tie things together in a JSP.

By now you should be familiar with Java basics, and you have links to resources for further investigation. Java is a massive, powerful programming language with APIs in a wide range of areas, from cryptography to 3D graphics, from email to EJB. No one is an expert in all of it. It takes a long time to learn Java well, so take it easy on yourself if you're frustrated or overwhelmed sometimes. In the next chapter, we'll be dealing with JSP's implicit objects, which are pretty friendly. We'll also be mixing and using scriptlets, expressions, and declarations, so there will be plenty more of what we've covered in this chapter in those that follow.

Using Available Objects

IN THIS CHAPTER

Now we have seen some sample JSPs, learned a lot about Java syntax and terminology, and covered the basics of JSP syntax. Next we will cover some general concepts and history of object-oriented programming, which will come in handy as you learn Java and JSP. The main goal in this chapter is to learn and understand *implicit objects* in JSP. The JSP implicit objects are going to be your friends. You will use them often. They should be the foundation of almost any JSP you write.

If you are not familiar with object-oriented programming (OOP) and you are not interested in it, you can probably ignore the fact that JSP is built on an object-oriented language and that scripting in Java and JavaScript is inherently object oriented. But if you are interested, this chapter is for you. This chapter also covers all of the JSP implicit objects.

Understanding Objects

There are two categories of available objects in JSP. The objects available to you in every JSP, regardless of the scripting language used, are

1. The nine implicit JSP objects: `application`, `config`, `exception`, `out`, `page`, `pageContext`, `request`, `response`, and `session`.

2. When you are using Java as the scripting language, any and all classes that you import using the `import` attribute of the `page` directive (as shown in Chapter 2, "Creating a JSP Page") are available to be instantiated as objects, as are all classes in the packages imported for you by the JSP container (`java.lang.*`, `javax.servlet.*`, `javax.servlet.jsp.*`, and `javax.servlet.http.*`).

Objects are instances of a class. A class is the principal programming unit of OOP. We've been using objects and classes all along, but now it is time for an explanation of what they are. If you are already familiar with the concepts and terminology of OOP, you can skip this section unless you feel like a review. This is an incomplete crash course in computer programming history and theory. If programming history and theory interest you at all, don't rely on this quick-and-dirty summary. Visit the Web, the library, or the bookstore for full-length explorations of these topics.

All computer programming has the goal of giving a computer instructions to execute. The earliest computer programming was done in machine language, that is, binary code. Then a slightly abstract language was developed, called Assembly, which was one step removed from writing programs in ones and zeroes. Lots of other languages were developed over the years, moving further from the ugly, purely binary machine code to languages with recognizably English verbs, nouns, and prepositions.

Very early on there were object-oriented languages such as Simula and SmallTalk. But the mainstream programmers wrote most of their code in procedural languages such as COBOL,

BASIC, FORTRAN, and C. In procedural programming, the programmer is primarily focused on writing procedures that will be translated into machine code. The main purpose of creating programming languages is to make it easier for the programmer to tell the computer what to do. But even though it relied on English vocabulary and human-language concepts, procedural programming always focused more on the machine's way of doing things than the person's. Object-oriented programming was conceived as a better way to program computers.

In object-oriented programming, the programmer thinks of the problem in terms of objects and behaviors instead of procedures. The end goal is the same as ever: to make the computer do what you want. But rather than conform to the computer's mechanical, procedural structure, object-oriented programming languages force you to think in terms of the problem to be solved, to focus on developing abstract objects that model the properties and behaviors of the real world. This adds another layer of abstraction between the programmer and the raw physical layer of the hard drive's tracks and cylinders, the CPU's registers, and other physical devices. The physical or logical parts of the computer (or other real-world objects) can be represented in an OOP language, but usually in a much friendlier way than was possible in the world of procedural languages. The main idea is to let the programmer think about the objects involved in the problem and solution at a more conceptual level and let the computer (or in the case of Java, the Java Virtual Machine and the computer) handle the work of translating everything into bits and bytes.

Every object in OOP is an instance of a class. Every class has methods and variables. Classes are like nouns. If you are trying to solve a real-world problem in an object-oriented programming way, think of the things (*objects*) that are involved with the problem and would be involved with the solution. The things are what you want to design as classes. Think of the *actions* that these things should perform or be able to perform to solve the problem. The actions are the methods (in C, Perl, and other languages, these are called *functions*). Think of the attributes or properties of these objects. Those are the *variables* (things such as color, length, width, or speed).

So how does this relate to JSP? JSP is a Java-based technology, and the JSP container itself is written in Java (usually as a servlet named `JSPServlet` running in a servlet container). Java is the OOP language *par excellence*, designed from the ground up as an OO (object-oriented) language for the Internet. The more you know about Java and OO, the more you can apply that knowledge in your JSPs (not to mention other Java contexts related to JSP, such as EJB, servlets, performance tuning for server-based Java applications, and so on). You can take full advantage of Java when you do scripting in JSPs and, if you ever want to code custom tags for your JSPs, you'll have to do it in Java. Finally, JavaScript is also an OOP language, and it is likely to be supported in many major JSP containers as an alternative scripting language.

4

USING AVAILABLE OBJECTS

Understanding JSP's Implicit Objects

JSP's implicit objects are a standard set of classes pre-instantiated for you by the JSP container. To *instantiate an object* in OO-speak means to create an instance of a class in memory. Java class definitions are what programmers write and compile (in the case of Java) into byte code. JSPs become Java class definitions when the JSP container translates them into Java source.

We will go over all the implicit JSP objects in the rest of this chapter and show you how to find out which methods and variables are automatically available to you for each of them. We will use some features of the `java.lang.reflect` package to create a JSP that describes these objects for us. And we'll relate each of the objects to its appropriate scope in a Web application. Along the way we will cover some concepts of OOP, such as inheritance, introspection, and encapsulation.

Understanding Object Instantiation

As you know, Java programs are executed by loading them into the JVM. Whenever the JVM sees the keyword `new` in a program, it looks for the class definition of the type being created with `new` (for example, `String` or `Date`) and uses that definition to create an object in memory. The Java platform comes with a whole set of standard class definitions, such as the packages `java.util`, `java.lang`, `java.sql`, and so on, and extends the standard core with libraries of APIs like the `javax.rmi`, `javax.servlet`, and `javax.ejb` packages.

As you have seen, we instantiate a class by using the keyword `new` and assigning the object instance a name:

```
Date now = new java.util.Date();
```

Now you understand why we import these package and class names. We need to refer to their definitions so we can use them and instantiate objects based on them. If we didn't have the rich set of classes provided to rely on, we would have to write our own class definitions for everything.

Now we come to a special feature of JSP's implicit objects, which is that you never have to instantiate them yourself. The JSP container does it for you as one of the services it provides. For example, for the `out` object, the JSP container does something like this for you:

```
JspWriter out = new javax.servlet.jsp.JspWriter();
```

The `out` object has been assigned a name and instantiated using the constructor for the class `JspWriter`, saving you the trouble.

Relating JSP to Servlets, CGI, and HTTP

You have already seen some of the objects because we've been using some of them here and there to illustrate other points. It should come as no surprise that the nine objects chosen to be pre-instantiated for every JSP would be practical and useful for a variety of tasks related to Web application programming. All of them have their roots in the Java Servlet specification, which itself is rooted in the world of CGI and Web programming, which is further rooted in the Hypertext Transfer Protocol (HTTP). HTTP is further rooted in TCP/IP and other things, but we'll stop there, since HTTP is as far as we need to go for the basis of JSP and servlet programming.

HTTP describes a text-based standard for linking, sending/receiving requests, and sending/receiving responses for resources on the Internet. All standard HTTP requests and responses carry with them a lot of information about themselves, their origins, and their destinations.

When programmers began extending the functionality of existing HTTP servers (daemon processes that simply served up static HTML documents in response to HTTP requests), they began paving the road toward dynamic, extensible server-side technologies such as CGI, ASP, JSP, and servlets. They didn't know it at the time, of course.

The easiest way to extend the functionality of an HTTP server was to write a utility that ran separately from the Web server but that acted as a slave to special processing requests from the server. A protocol was built around that concept, with the intention of making the interface between the server and its extensions standard and portable. It was called common gateway interface (CGI). CGI programs ruled the Web for several years (and still do in many places). They grew from hit counters and server-side includes to major backend applications processing credit card purchases and making huge inventories of merchandise searchable via attractive, dynamically generated Web interfaces.

Soon Web server vendors opened APIs to the proprietary interfaces of their Web servers, allowing other vendors and programmers to write extensions directly for their servers. These extensions could run in-process with the Web server, bypassing the CGI protocol, and thus responding faster and more efficiently to requests. In similar fashion, Sun's Java Web Server, an HTTP server written in Java, was extended by small, specialized Java programs that came to be called "servlets." JSP, like ASP, ColdFusion, PHP, and other dynamic, Web-based scripting languages, was developed as an alternative, "friendlier" way to write specialized server extension objects. Since JSP is entrenched in this world of request and response and is really a way to script servlets, it makes sense that the two most fundamental objects of every servlet are represented in JSP by two implicit objects: request and response.

We can find out more about these objects by consulting the JSP documentation (see the references and appendixes in the back of this book, for example), but we can also query the objects themselves by using the Java Reflection API.

Understanding the Java Reflection API

The Reflection API was introduced in Java 1.1, partly as a complement to the JavaBeans API for reusable software components, which was also introduced in Java 1.1. The Reflection API is made up of classes in the package `java.lang.reflect` and the class `java.lang.Class`. The API is all about looking into Java objects loaded in the JVM and getting information about their methods, variables, inheritance hierarchy, and so on. The process of querying objects for information about their attributes is called *introspection*.

NOTE

One of the original motives of the Reflection API was to make it easy for GUI Java IDEs (Integrated Development Environments), such as Visual Age for Java and Visual Café, to introspect arbitrary JavaBeans. The IDEs used the introspected data to present graphical dialogues, which listed the methods and variables of the JavaBeans, to programmers. JavaBeans were originally used and intended for programming widgets for GUI applications written in Java. But JavaBeans have outlasted and outgrown their original role and are now used for all sorts of programming tasks. JSP has several tags, especially for use with JavaBeans. We will be covering those tags and JavaBeans in Chapter 5, "Using Beans."

We are going to use the Reflection API to introspect the inheritance hierarchy, methods, return types, and parameter types of the JSP implicit objects. Consider this an exercise in using more of the core Java APIs and learning the OO concept of inheritance, while also getting to know the implicit objects of JSP. First, let's start with the `request` object and just look at the classes from which it inherits. We don't need any of the `java.lang.reflect` classes for that, just the `java.lang.Class` class.

Listing 4.1 declares a `getAncestors()` method that we will use to get the information about the classes the `request` object inherits from.

LISTING 4.1 `reqInherits.jsp`—To Get the Inheritance Tree of the JSP request Object

```html
<html>
<head>
<title>Prints JSP implicit object class hierarchy for JSP container</title>
<style type="text/css">
<!--
@import url(css/JSPstyle3.css);
-->
</style>
</head>
<body>
<h1>JSP Implicit Objects</h1>

<%!
public static StringBuffer getAncestors(Object obj)
{
    StringBuffer sb = new StringBuffer();
    Class clazz = obj.getClass();
    sb.append("<ul>");
    do
    {
        sb.append("<li>").append(clazz.getName());
        clazz = clazz.getSuperclass();
    }
    while (clazz != null);
    sb.append("</ul>");
    return sb;
} %>
<p>In the <%= application.getServerInfo() %> JSP container: </p>
<p><em>request</em> has an inheritance tree of: <%= getAncestors
➥(request) %></p>
</body>
</html>
```

Let's break it down. Some of this is review from the previous chapter, and some is new. First we set up some HTML and CSS code, which I won't repeat (the CSS pages for all the examples in this chapter are included with the resources for this chapter on the CD-ROM accompanying this book). Then we start a JSP declaration for the method that will look up the classes that the response object inherits from.

The method declaration is `public` and `static`. Remember that `static`, `private`, and `final` methods can be faster than others because of the way they are put into the byte code of class files. We specify a return type of `StringBuffer` since we'll be creating a `StringBuffer` in the method and returning it. Then we specify the argument for the method, which states that it takes one argument named `obj`" of type `java.lang.Object`:

```
public static StringBuffer getAncestors(Object obj)
```

Then we initialize a couple of objects for use in the method. We create an instance of the `StringBuffer` class, which we can use to create a string of HTML text to return from the method.

```
StringBuffer sb = new StringBuffer();
```

Next we create an instance of `java.lang.Class`, using the `getClass()` method of `java.lang.Object` to get a reference to the already instantiated `response` object. This is not only a handy method, but it is also a necessary one because `java.lang.Class` has no public constructor.

```
Class clazz = obj.getClass();
```

You might think it would be nice to use the name `class` for our instance of `java.lang.Class`, but we can't, because `class` is a keyword in Java. Remember that keywords are *reserved* and cannot be used as variable names.

Now add an HTML tag for an unordered list to our `StringBuffer`:

```
sb.append("<ul>");
```

> **NOTE**
>
> The other way to get a reference to an instance of the `Class` representation of a particular Java class is to explicitly load an instance of the desired class into the JVM. This is done using the `forName()` method of `java.lang.Class`. We will use `Class.forName()` later in the book, when we get into JDBC and need to load database drivers.

Code listing 4.1 features another of Java's flow control statements, which uses two Java keywords, `do` and `while`. As you can see, `do` and `while` can be used to loop through a statement until an expression returns `false`.

> **NOTE**
>
> Most of Java's flow control statements are similar or identical to standard ones used in other programming languages, so if you've done any programming you've seen them before. We've already seen `while`, `if`, and `return` statements (though we haven't seen `else` or `then-else` clauses of `if` statements yet). The remaining flow control statements are `break`, `continue`, `switch`, `synchronized`, `throw`, and `try`. You can see some of them used throughout this book, and you can look them up in any basic Java syntax reference. Although `goto` is reserved as a Java keyword, it's not implemented. Java has no `goto` or `until` statements, unlike some other languages.

The `do...while` loop that follows uses the `getName()` method of `java.lang.Class`, which returns a `String` containing the fully qualified name of the `Class` object, `clazz`. The first time through the loop, the `clazz` reference is equal to the `request` object that was passed into the method. So the first fully qualified Java class name we see in the HTML response will be the class the JSP container instantiated as `request` for us.

```
do
{
    sb.append("<li>").append(clazz.getName());
    clazz = clazz.getSuperclass();
}
while (clazz != null);
```

Subsequent recursions through the loop get the name of `clazz`'s super classes. Each time through, the `clazz` variable is set to refer to the next class up the chain of inheritance. When the class hierarchy has been fully described, there are no more super classes to get. At that point, `clazz.getSuperclass()` will return `null` and the `while` expression return `false`, thereby completing the loop.

Finally we close the unordered list with the appropriate tag and use `return` to exit from the method with the `StringBuffer` object. Then we close the declaration with a right curly brace:

```
sb.append("</ul>");
return sb;
} %>
```

We can see that each JSP container has its own implementation of the `request` object. We'll first print out the JSP container's name and version using the implicit `application` object (don't worry, it's covered later) and one of its available methods, `getServerInfo()`:

```
<p>In the <%= application.getServerInfo() %> JSP container: </p>
```

4

USING AVAILABLE OBJECTS

All that's left is to call `getAncestors()` in an expression and pass the implicit `request` object reference then close the HTML document:

```
<p><em>request</em> has an inheritance tree of: <%= getAncestors(request) %>
</p>
</body>
</html>
```

Next we're going to look at the output of this JSP from a couple of different JSP containers.

> **CAUTION**
>
> All JSP implicit objects must be spelled exactly as shown in this chapter. All of them are lowercase, except for pageContext. You will get errors if you do not use the proper case.

Figures 4.1 and 4.2 show the output of `reqInherits.jsp` from two different JSP containers, Resin 1.1 and JRun 3.0.

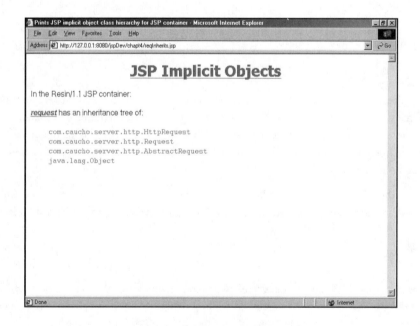

FIGURE 4.1

The response generated from Resin 1.1, showing the class of which request *is an instance, followed by the superclasses it extends.*

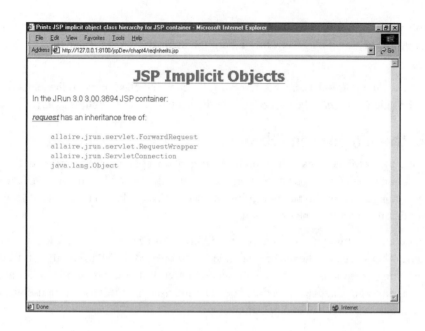

FIGURE 4.2
The response generated from JRun 3.0, showing the class of which request *is an instance, followed by the superclasses it extends.*

Understanding Inheritance

Inheritance is the term used to describe the technique of deriving a class's state and behavior from another class. When a class inherits another class's state and behavior, it is said to be a *subclass* or to *extend* the parent, which is the *superclass*. The state and behavior are inherited in the form of variables and methods that are defined in the superclass. The Java keyword extends is used in a class declaration when creating a new class that inherits from another class. For example

```
public abstract class javax.servlet.http.HttpServlet extends
➥ javax.servlet.GenericServlet
```

4

> **NOTE**
>
> In case you're wondering, there is no such thing as lateral or "sibling" inheritance. Also, in C++ there is a notion of multiple inheritance. In Java, a class can inherit a successive chain of parent classes, but only one at each successive level. Multiple inheritance was purposefully omitted from Java to make the language easier to use.

An important thing to remember is that in Java, all classes are subclasses of `java.lang.Object`, so all classes in Java inherit the methods of `java.lang.Object`, such as `toString()`.

As you can see in Figures 4.1 and 4.2, the last fully qualified class name in the `request` object's class hierarchy (*aka* the root of its inheritance tree) is `java.lang.Object`.

Using the `exception` Object

You can use the `getAncestors()` method in the `reqInherits.jsp` page to print out the inheritance tree of any object, with one exception (pun intended). The odd man out is the `exception` object. You can get the `exception` object instantiated for you only if one of your JSPs has a Java error that throws a runtime exception.

The `exception` object will be an instance of a different Java exception class each time it is instantiated. That's because the `exception` object is to be used in JSP primarily for debugging and for catching exceptions before they are sent to a user. With the `exception` object and a couple of attributes of the `page` directive, you can send users any JSP as a response when an exception occurs. Listings 4.2 and 4.3 show how:

LISTING 4.2 `illegal.jsp`—Throwing a Java Exception by Making an Illegal Statement

```
<%@ page errorPage="exceptInherits.jsp" %>
<html>
<head>
</head>
<body>
<% int i = 1 / 0; %>
</body>
</html>
```

The first thing we did in `illegal.jsp` was use the `page` directive to declare that there is an `errorPage` available should any Java exceptions occur during the processing of this JSP. That's what the `errorPage` attribute is for. Once you specify an `errorPage` for a JSP, you have to make sure you create the JSP that corresponds to the URI you put in the `errorPage` attribute. The `errorPage` is what is served to the client should an error occur on this page. It's good to use this feature to make your site look professional and to respond to errors by catching them and handling them in the `errorPage`.

Then we have a quick scriptlet that tries to assign the value of 1 divided by 0 to `i`. Dividing by zero is an illegal math operation in any computer language. It's just a quick-and-dirty way of generating an exception for our example.

Now let's create the errorPage that will be served when the JSP container tries to handle a request for illegal.jsp. Listing 4.3 shows the errorPage.

LISTING 4.3 exceptInherits.jsp—To Catch and Print an Exception and Print the Inheritance Tree

```
<%@ page isErrorPage="true" %>
<html>
<head>
<title>Class Hierarchy for "exception"</title>
<style type="text/css">
<!--
@import url(css/JSPstyle3.css);
-->
</style>
</head>
<body>
<h1>JSP Implicit Objects</h1>
<%!
public static StringBuffer getAncestors(Object obj)
{
    Class clazz = obj.getClass();
    StringBuffer sb = new StringBuffer();
    sb.append("<ul>");
    do
    {
        sb.append("<li>").append(clazz.getName()).append("\n");
        clazz = clazz.getSuperclass();
    }
    while (clazz != null);
    sb.append("</ul>");
    return sb;
} %>
<p>In <%= application.getServerInfo() %>: </p>
<p><em>exception</em> has an inheritance tree of:
    <%= getAncestors(exception) %></p>
<p>Here is the exception thrown in the calling page:</p>
<br><%= exception %>
</body>
</html>
```

In exceptInherits.jsp (Listing 4.3), the first thing we did was specify that it is an errorPage, setting the isErrorPage attribute of the page directive to true. Now it can serve as an errorPage for any JSP that points its errorPage attribute to the location of this page. By the time exceptInherits.jsp is called, an exception will have been thrown and caught during the processing of illegal.jsp. Once we're in exceptInherits.jsp, we just call getAncestors(), passing the exception object reference. Then we print our detail message for the exception, just to see what the description of the problem is. Figure 4.4 shows the result of trying to call illegal.jsp. Note that the URL in the browser's location bar still says illegal.jsp.

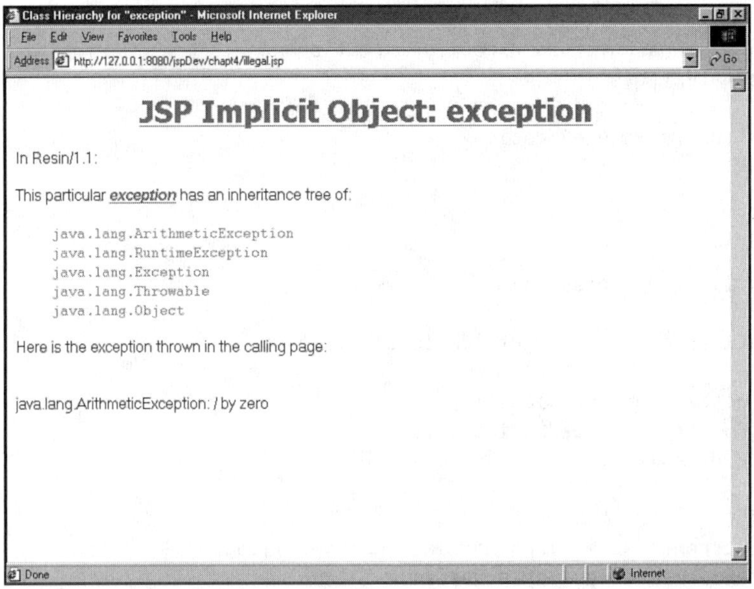

FIGURE 4.3
The response from exceptInherits.jsp *as generated from Resin 1.1.*

NOTE

For more on exception handling in JSP, see Chapter 14, "Handling Errors."

Viewing the Class Hierarchies of All the Implicit Objects

Now let's look at the official set of JSP objects as required by the JSP 1.1 specification. Then we'll beef up reqInherits.jsp and jspInherits.jsp so that they print out all the methods, parameters, and return types of each JSP object.

Table 4.1 lists the JSP implicit objects, their scopes, and the classes they subclass or represent. Note that each commercial JSP implementation may or may not directly subclass or instantiate the exact class listed here and specified in the JSP 1.1 specification. It is enough that the JSP container implement the `javax.servlet` classes and provide all the methods and variables provided in the specification.

TABLE 4.1 A Guide to the JSP Implicit Objects

Object Name	Scope	Class
application	Application	javax.servlet.ServletContext
config	Page	javax.servlet.ServletConfig
exception	Page	java.lang.Throwable
out	Page	javax.servlet.jsp.JspWriter
page	Page	java.lang.Object
pageContext	Page	javax.servlet.jsp.PageContext
request	Request	subclass of javax.servlet.ServletRequest
response	Page	subclass of javax.servlet.ServletResponse
session	Session	javax.servlet.http.HttpSession

Now let's see a full listing of the implicit object class hierarchy as implemented in the Resin 1.1 JSP container. Listing 4.4 shows how to re-use the technique used in reqInherits.jsp to do that. This JSP prints out the inheritance trees for all the implicit objects except exception. The enhancements are trivial. I just added an expression to call getAncestors() for each of the JSP implicit objects and wrapped them all in a table for easy viewing.

LISTING 4.4 jspInherits.jsp

```
<html>
<head>
<title>JSP implicit object class hierarchy</title>
<style type="text/css">
<!--
@import url(css/JSPstyle3.css);
-->
</style>
</head>
<body>
```

LISTING 4.4 Continued

```
<h1>JSP Implicit Objects</h1>
<%!
public static StringBuffer getAncestors(Object obj)
{
    StringBuffer sb = new StringBuffer();
    Class clazz = obj.getClass();
    sb.append("<ul>");
    do
    {
        sb.append("<li>").append(clazz.getName());
        clazz = clazz.getSuperclass();
    }
    while (clazz != null);
    sb.append("</ul>");
    return sb;
}
%>
<p>In the <%= application.getServerInfo() %> JSP container: </p>
<table>
<tr><td>
<p><em>out</em> has an inheritance tree of: <%= getAncestors(out) %></p>
<p><em>request</em> has an inheritance tree of: <%= getAncestors(request) %>
</p>
<p><em>response</em> has an inheritance tree of: <%= getAncestors(response) %>
</p>
<p><em>pageContext</em> has an inheritance tree of:
   <%= getAncestors(pageContext) %></p>
</td>
<td>
<p><em>session</em> has an inheritance tree of: <%= getAncestors(session) %>
</p>
<p><em>application</em> has an inheritance tree of:
   <%= getAncestors(application) %></p>
<p><em>config</em> has an inheritance tree of: <%= getAncestors(config) %></p>
<p><em>page</em> has an inheritance tree of: <%= getAncestors(page) %></p>
</td></tr></table>
</body>
</html>
```

Figure 4.4 shows the output of jspInherits.jsp, using JRun 3.0 as the JSP container.

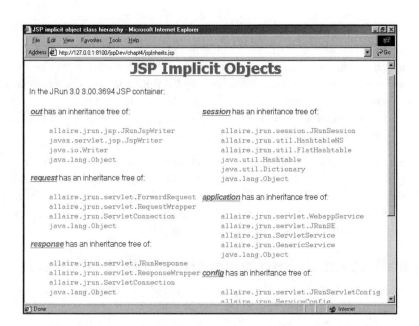

FIGURE 4.4

The response generated from JRun 3.0, showing the class of which each implicit object is an instance, followed by the superclasses it descends from.

Understanding Encapsulation

Before we move on, I want to cover the OO concept of *encapsulation*. It's not going to make or break you as a JSP coder to know the term, but understanding the concept will get you a step closer to grasping the OOP paradigm and Java.

Encapsulation describes nothing more than the fact that data and related behavior are packaged together in object-oriented languages into units called classes. I say "related" behavior because in OO, the behavior (methods) associated with data should be appropriate to the type of data being manipulated. For example, the Servlet API defines a bunch of classes with methods for dealing with HTTP headers and URLs. These classes take HTTP headers and URLs (encapsulated in objects like `HttpServletRequest` and `HttpServletResponse`) and get them, set them, enumerate them, and so on. The encapsulation of variables and methods in OO languages helps programmers hide the implementation of their classes from users, for both security and simplicity. All that needs to be made known to the user of a class is the variable and method names and parameters he can use. The programmer need not understand (usually) or worry about how a class works internally to be able to use it. Encapsulation also helps force programmers to think about solving problems by using virtual objects, which is the whole point of OO programming.

Consider as a fairly simple example the java.lang.Class class we've been using in this chapter. When we call getName() on a Class object, how exactly does it retrieve the class's name? It doesn't matter, as long as we know how to use it to get what we want, right? We don't need to know, for example, that java.lang.Class is compiled from a Java source file made of over 1300 lines of code (mostly comments), that it imports several classes from java.lang.reflect, or that it relies on a native (non-Java) program running in the Java Virtual Machine for getting the names of classes when getName() is called.

Encapsulation emphasizes the value of Java's documentation. Java is wonderfully self-documenting if you put the right comments in your code, which Sun has done with all its Java classes. There is a tool in the JDK (*aka* JSDK, the Java Software Development Kit) called *javadoc* that reads Java source files that have the right comments and spits out documentation in the form of HTML files, complete with CSS for formatting.

Using Reflection to Introspect the Implicit Objects

The next and final step is to use the java.lang.reflect.Method class to get more information about these implicit objects. I am going to use the config object for the example here. This is just for space-saving purposes. There is a fully commented printObjects.jsp file in the Chapter 4 section of the CD-ROM provided with this book. You can use that to print out the data for all these objects and any others, if so desired. The config object can illustrate our point as well as any other object, and it has the briefest list of methods of any of the implicit objects.

Listing 4.5 shows the contents of printConfig.jsp, which we will use to print the config class hierarchy (just as we did in reqInherits.jsp and jspInherits.jsp), followed by a table containing all the methods available for use on the object. Along with each method is listed the method's return type and the parameter type(s).

LISTING 4.5 printConfig.jsp

```
<%@ page import="java.lang.reflect.Method" %>
<html>
<head>
<title>JSP's config object</title>
<style type="text/css">
<!--
@import url(css/JSPstyle2.css);
-->
</style>
</head>
<body>
<h1>JSP Implicit Objects: config</h1>
```

LISTING 4.5 Continued

```
<%!
public static StringBuffer getAncestors(Class c, StringBuffer s)
{
    sb.append("<ul>");
    do
    {
        s.append(c.getName()).append("<br />\n");
        c = c.getSuperclass();
    }
    while (c != null);
    sb.append("</ul>");
    return s;
}%>

<%!
public static StringBuffer describeObj(Object obj)
{
    StringBuffer sb = new StringBuffer();
    Class clazz = obj.getClass();
    sb = getAncestors(clazz, sb); //Call getAncestors and pass clazz and sb

    sb.append("<table>\n<thead><tr>\n");
    sb.append("<th>Method Name</th><th> . . . of Class</th><th>Return type</th>
➡<th>Parameter type(s)</th>\n");
    sb.append("</tr></thead>\n");

    Method[] methodsArr = obj.getClass().getMethods();
    for (int i = 0; i < methodsArr.length; i++)
    {
        String methodName = methodsArr[i].getName();
        String declClass = methodsArr[i].getDeclaringClass().getName();
        String returnType = methodsArr[i].getReturnType().getName();

        sb.append("<tr><td><tt>").append(methodName).append("()</tt></td>");
        sb.append("<td><tt>").append(declClass).append("</tt></td>");
        sb.append("<td><tt>").append(returnType).append("</tt></td>");

        Class[] parameterTypes = methodsArr[i].getParameterTypes();
        if (parameterTypes.length >= 1)
        {
            sb.append("<td>");
            for (int j = 0; j < parameterTypes.length; j++)
            {
                String parameterString = parameterTypes[j].getName();
                sb.append("<tt>").append(parameterString).append(
➡"</tt><br />\n");
```

4

LISTING 4.5 Continued

```
            }
            sb.append("</td>");
        }
        else
        {
            sb.append("<td>--</td>");
        }
        sb.append("</tr>\n");
    }
    return sb.append("</table>");
}
%>
<p>In the <%= application.getServerInfo() %> JSP container: </p>
<p><em>config</em> has an inheritance tree of: <%= describeObj(config) %></p>
</body>
</html>
```

The first thing to note in this listing is that we are importing the java.lang.reflect.Method
class using a page directive:

```
<%@ page import="java.lang.reflect.Method" %>
```

The next thing to notice is that there's a modified version of the getAncestors() method. I
wanted to re-use that method here, but I am going to call it from within the describeObject()
method instead of calling it directly from an expression:

```
<%!
public static StringBuffer getAncestors(Class c, StringBuffer s)
{
    s.append("<ul>");
    do
    {
        s.append("<li>").append(c.getName());
        c = c.getSuperclass();
    }
    while (c != null);
    s.append("</ul>");
    return s;
}%>
```

> **NOTE**
>
> As you can see, the method now requires two arguments, a `StringBuffer` object, and a `Class` object. An important rule to remember about Java methods is that method arguments must be passed in the same order they are defined in the parameters section of the method signature. They must match the number of parameters defined in the method signature. And they must either be the same type as those defined in the signature or be convertible without an explicit cast (for example, no cast is required when converting from a `char` to an `int` or an `int` to a `long`).

Also note that there are no objects instantiated in the method. I moved the object instantiation into the `describeObj()` method below. We'll create the `StringBuffer` and `Class` objects there and pass them to `getAncestor()` for processing.

The next method is where we do the bulk of the processing. We first declare the method's *signature*, specifying that it should take an object of class `java.lang.Object` as its only argument:

```
public static StringBuffer describeObj(Object obj)
{
```

Then we create the `StringBuffer` and `Class` objects:

```
    StringBuffer sb = new StringBuffer();
    Class clazz = obj.getClass();
```

And now call the `getAncestors()` method, passing it the instances of `java.lang.Class` and `StringBuffer` that we just instantiated. The assignment operator is used to assign the result, which is a `StringBuffer` named s, as you can see in the `return` statement of `getAncestors()`, to `StringBuffer sb`:

```
    sb = getAncestors(clazz, sb);
```

Now we need some basic HTML code appended to the `StringBuffer`. I put in a Java newline character (\n) for each HTML line just so that if you want to view the HTML source in a browser, it won't appear as one long, giant string. This is purely cosmetic and has no impact on the functionality of the JSP:

```
    sb.append("<table>\n<thead><tr>\n");
    sb.append("<th>Method Name</th><th>Return type</th><th>Parameter type(s)
➥</th>\n");
    sb.append("</tr></thead>\n");
```

4

USING AVAILABLE
OBJECTS

Now we create an array of Method objects, named methodsArr, by calling the getMethods() method of the clazz object. Remember, clazz is a reference to the Class object created from the config object passed into decribeObj():

```
Method[] methodsArr = clazz.getMethods();
```

> **NOTE**
>
> An *array* is a standard construct found in most programming languages. An array is an ordered collection of other values. It can contain primitive values or objects, including other arrays. Just keep in mind that the values in an array must all be of the same kind. To declare an array in Java, you use the left and right brackets after the type you want to create an array of, for example
>
> ```
> int[] i; //declares an Array of ints
> String[] s; //declares an Array of Strings
> char[] c = new c[26];
> //declare and instantiate an Array that can hold 26 chars
> ```
>
> After an array is created, its size is fixed. For more on arrays, see a basic Java syntax, such as Sun's online Java Tutorial at http://java.sun.com/docs/books/tutorial/index.html.

The getMethods() method of the Class class returns an array of Method objects. The Method objects returned here represent all the public methods of the config object, including all the methods the config object inherited from its superclasses. The Method class is a class of java.lang.reflect. It has methods that will allow us to ask for information about each Method object in the array. Since an instance of java.lang.reflect.Method represents a method of a particular class, it has been designed so that it has a bunch of handy methods you can use to find out properties of the method in the class, such as its return type, its parameter types, exception types, access modifiers, and the class that originally declared it. You can even invoke the method represented by the Method object instance, using the invoke() method. But we won't do that here.

The methods of java.lang.reflect.Method that we are going to use in this example are listed in Table 4.2:

TABLE 4.2 Useful Methods of `java.lang.reflect.Method`

Method Name	What It Does
getDeclaringClass()	Returns a `Class` object representing the class that originally declared the method represented by `Method[i]`.
getName()	Returns a `String` with the name of the method represented by `Method[i]`.
getReturnType()	Returns a `Class` object representing the return type of the method represented by `Method[i]`.
getParameterTypes()	Returns an array of `Class` objects that represent the parameter types, in the order they are declared, of the method represented by `Method[i]`.

NOTE

In Table 4.2, I used the array reference notation to represent the current `Method` object. You should read `Method[i]` as something like "the `Method` object at index `i` in the array." The standard way of referencing a value at a particular location in an array is by creating a variable, usually named `i` for *index* or `n` for *number*. The index variable is created just so you can set it equal to a number and then stick it in the brackets after the array name when you want to reference the nth member of the array. This technique is frequently used when looping through an array of items, as we do here.

Now we set up a loop to run through the object representations of all the methods of the `config` object. Remember that `methodsArr` now contains a collection of `Method` objects that represents all these methods. We set up a `for` loop, which will return when the expression in parentheses after the `for` keyword returns.

```
for (int i = 0; i < methodsArr.length; i++)
{
```

We refer to the array itself for its quantity of members by using the array's `length` field. It almost looks like we used a method there, but we didn't. All arrays have a single constant field named `length` that just stores the length of the array. The way to read that expression is something like this: "For as long as `i` is less than the number of objects in the `methodsArr` array, do this loop. And increment `i` by one each time we do the loop."

Now the first part of the loop just declares some `String`s and assigns them values corresponding to the name, declaring class, and return type of the `Method` currently being run through the loop (the `methodsArr[i]` `Method` object). Then we append those values to our `StringBuffer` and include some HTML formatting:

```
String methodName = methodsArr[i].getName();
String declClass = methodsArr[i].getDeclaringClass().getName();
String returnType = methodsArr[i].getReturnType().getName();

sb.append("<tr><td><tt>").append(methodName).append("()</tt></td>");
sb.append("<td><tt>").append(declClass).append("</tt></td>");
sb.append("<td><tt>").append(returnType).append("</tt></td>");
```

Now we are going to create another array, just like above, only this time it's an array of `Class` objects:

```
Class[] parameterTypes = methodsArr[i].getParameterTypes();
```

Now we set up an `if` statement to run through the parameter types for the current method. We need an `if` statement because it's likely that a method has from zero to many parameters. We didn't need an `if` statement or a loop for the method name, return type, or declaring class, because we know there's going to be one and only one of each of those. The `if` statement will be executed if its expression is `true`. The expression makes use of the `length` field of the `parameterTypes` array:

```
if (parameterTypes.length >= 1)
{
```

NOTE

We could have achieved the same result in this expression by checking to see if the `parameterTypes` array is `null`, like this:

```
if (parameterTypes != null)
```

If there is at least one element in the array, we enter the `if` statement's body, which is

```
sb.append("<td>");
for (int j = 0; j < parameterTypes.length; j++)
{
    String parameterString = parameterTypes[j].getName();
    sb.append("<tt>").append(parameterString).append(
➡"</tt><br />\n");
}
sb.append("</td>");
```

We wrap the whole body between two `StringBuffer.appends()` so that whatever comes out of the nested `for` loop will be put into an HTML table data cell. The nested `for` loop is identical in function to the `for` loop we created earlier. Here we are interested in going through the loop until we've generated `String`s for every parameter type that the current method accepts. We stick them onto the end of our `StringBuffer`, along with some HTML, each time we get one.

If the method accepts no parameter types, then the `parameterTypes` array would be empty and the `if` expression would return `false`. In that case, we have an `else` clause that just appends a `String` consisting of an HTML table data cell with a couple of dashes to indicate there are no parameter types for this method:

```
else
{
    sb.append("<td>--</td>");
}
```

Then, no matter whether any parameter types were found, each time we go through this loop we have finished getting information about one `Method` object, so we close the table row in the HTML as the last step each time we do the loop:

```
    sb.append("</tr>\n");
}
```

When the first `for` loop finishes (that is, the loop that runs for as long as `i` is less than the length of `methodsArr`), we exit the loop, append a `String` consisting of a closing table tag for the HTML, and then exit the `describeObj()` method.

The result is shown in Figure 4.5. You can see the nine methods inherited from `java.lang.Object` listed first. Then there are four methods specific to the `ServletConfig` class, of which `config` is an instance.

4

USING AVAILABLE
OBJECTS

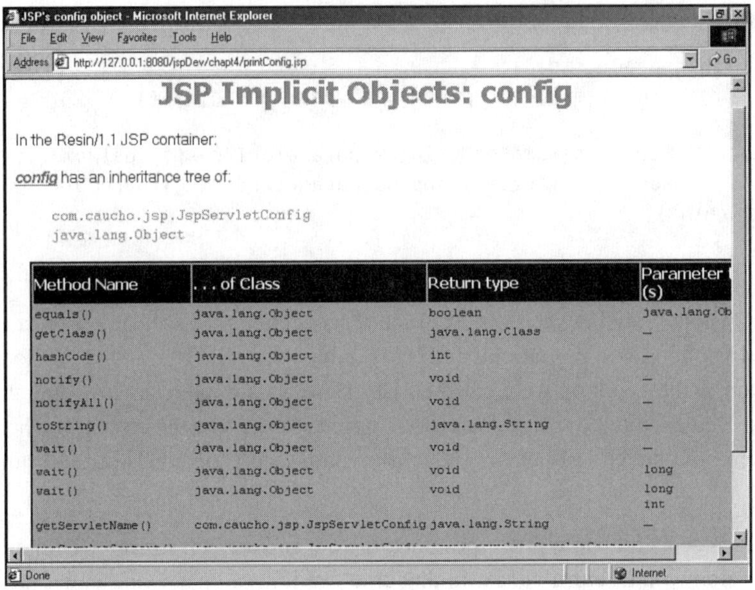

FIGURE 4.5

The response generated from Resin 1.1.

> **NOTE**
>
> You will have noticed that there are three methods named `wait()` for
> `java.lang.Object`. Why is that? The answer is in the OOP concept of method over-
> loading. To *overload* a method is to define multiple methods with the same name in
> the same class, but with different parameter lists. There is an initial `wait()` method
> with no parameters, an overloaded `wait()` that takes a `long` for a timeout, and a sec-
> ond overloaded `wait()` that takes a `long` and an `int` for a different kind of timeout.
> The Java compiler determines which method you mean according to the arguments
> you pass to the method in your code.

The key here is to understand what the implicit objects are, what they have to offer, and how
they inherit methods from other classes. The important thing to remember is that these implicit
objects make all their methods available to you as a JSP programmer. You should refer to other
resources for a full description of the methods available via JSP's implicit objects. To that end,

we have provided an appendix in the back of this book. Appendix C, "Using Java Methods to Retrieve CGI Environment Variables," focuses on the methods of the `request` object used to retrieve CGI environment variables. The example JSP for that appendix, `serverVars.jsp`, is an excellent resource with a link to the Servlet 2.2 API at the top. I will put a reference to the Servlet 2.2 API here, because it's a resource so crucial to our work as JSP developers: `http://java.sun.com/products/servlet/2.2/javadoc/index.html`.

Understanding Scope

Scope, in server-side applications, refers to the validity domain of particular objects. Every JSP object has a defined scope. There are excellent reasons behind this scheme. For example, if no scope restrictions were enforced, there would be no way to ensure that one client's credit card transaction did not suddenly apply to all the users currently visiting the transaction application on your site. If no scope restrictions were enforced, a user might have to log in again every time he visited another page on your site, or he might never have to log in when he should.

Understanding the Scope of the JSP Implicit Objects

As shown in Table 4.1, reproduced here as Table 4.3, every JSP implicit object has a predefined scope.

TABLE 4.3 A Guide to the JSP Implicit Objects

Object Name	Scope	Class
application	Application	javax.servlet.ServletContext
config	Page	javax.servlet.ServletConfig
exception	Page	java.lang.Throwable
out	Page	javax.servlet.jsp.JspWriter
page	Page	java.lang.Object
pageContext	Page	javax.servlet.jsp.PageContext
request	Request	subclass of javax.servlet.ServletRequest
response	Page	subclass of javax.servlet.ServletResponse
session	Session	javax.servlet.http.HttpSession

4

Page Scope

An object with Page scope is accessible only within the page where it was created. All references to these objects are released as soon as one of two things happens:

1. The response is completed and sent to the client.

2. The current request is forwarded to another JSP prior to the response being sent.

Page scope is the strictest scope in JSP.

An object with Request scope is accessible as long as a client request is still being processed, including any forwards to other JSPs. So if object 0 was instantiated in JSP 1, and the request was forwarded to JSP 2, the second JSP would have full access to 0. Request scope is broader than Page scope, but not as broad as the next two scopes.

Session Scope

An object with Session scope is accessible for as long as the client maintains a session with the server, or until the session times out. Therefore, multiple requests for one or more JSPs in the same browser session all share the same session object for a particular client. Your JSP container will timeout sessions after a certain time if they are inactive. Usually there is a way to configure this timeout. Another way to invalidate sessions is to do so explicitly using the invalidate() method of the session object (as per Table 4.3; see the API documentation for the javax.servlet.http.HttpSession class, since this is the class represented by session). This is what programmers do to kill a session after a user explicitly logs out, for example. Since there's no reliable way to find out whether a user has just closed his session by closing his browser, it's necessary to timeout sessions after a reasonable amount of time.

Session-awareness can be disabled in JSP using the session attribute of the page directive. The default is for JSPs to be session aware. To disable the use of sessions for a particular JSP, you would use the page directive like this:

```
<%@ page session="false" %>
```

Application Scope

An object with Application scope is accessible from any JSP in a Web application. This is the broadest type of scope. At this level you can have global variables that apply to everyone on your site.

I think it is easy to visualize the various types of scope as an increasingly restrictive domain of Web events and entities. For example, at the application level, you have lots of clients accessing your Web site, each with its own session, which may maintain user preferences, an authentication flag, or something else. These sessions come and go throughout the day, but as long as your server is up, the application and its objects remain.

At a finer level, within every session that is initiated with your Web application there are usually multiple requests. Some users may come and go after looking at a single page. But most who came with the purpose of browsing your e-commerce site for a piece of merchandise or to place an order, or to your search engine to look something up, are going to make at least a couple of requests before surfing elsewhere. At the finest level, you have individual pages being requested each time the user clicks on a link or hits Submit on a form.

We've now gone over the basics of Java and JSP syntax, object-oriented programming, and the JSP implicit objects. These first few chapters are intended to get you started with Java and JSP programming as quickly as possible. I highly recommend following up on the links and other resources mentioned in these chapters and getting yourself a decent Java reference. It will come in handy as you learn and use Java more.

In the chapters that follow, we will build on the introductory material that has been covered up to now. Everything we've been working on will serve you well as you move forward in this book and in your development as a JSP expert. You are now ready to start doing more advanced and complex JSP programming. The next several chapters fill out more of the JSP landscape by introducing ways to use and write JavaBean objects in your JSPs (Chapter 5, "Using Beans") and mix HTML and JSP effectively to get data from users on the Web (Chapter 7, "Working with Forms"). There are other chapters on the more advanced and specialized subjects of security and authentication, email, custom tags, and Enterprise JavaBeans.

Using Beans

IN THIS CHAPTER

This chapter delves into the development and use of JavaBeans with JSPs. We will develop a few Beans and see how they and their properties are used with standard `<jsp:useBean>` and related JSP tags or *standard actions*. We will discuss how the use of JavaBeans with JSP illustrates the Model 2 application design approach introduced in Chapter 2, "Creating a JSP Page." And of course we will learn some more Java along the way.

Understanding JavaBeans

First and foremost, a JavaBean is a generic Java class that is coded according to a few naming and design conventions. The term *JavaBean* is a cute play on the whole coffee theme that runs through Java marketing and PR, but the name itself is not descriptive of anything special about how a JavaBean looks or what it does.

JavaBeans are Java's formal approach to reusable components. They were introduced in Java's GUI-development heyday, back when everyone was using Java primarily for applets and GUI applications (a day that may return, but lately server-side Java is where it's at). A reusable component is not a concept unique to Java or to software (think of any household object you reuse for a specific task on a regular basis, such as a can opener or doorknob). The Beans concept in Java was that software components could (and should) be designed in such a way that each one could be specialized and interchangeable *and* could be introspected by tools using standard means.

In everyday English, *introspection* refers to self-reflection or self-examination. In Java, *introspection* is a technical term specific to the JavaBean technology. According to Chapter 8 of the JavaBeans Specification (`http://java.sun.com/beans/spec.html`)

> At runtime and in the builder environment, we need to be able to figure out which properties, events, and methods a JavaBean supports. We call this process *introspection*.

Its implementation depends on the Reflection API, which we covered in Chapter 4, "Using Available Objects." Its meaning in Java is closer to the general meaning of "to look into." The `Introspector` class in the core `java.beans` package has as its principal function to analyze, inspect, or "introspect" JavaBean classes and return information about their methods, properties, and events. The trick is that it only works right if you code your JavaBeans according to the conventions it expects, which we cover below.

So the original emphasis in JavaBean development was on GUI components and development using GUI "application builders." The original Beans were applet buttons, canvases, and other widgets. Nowadays you can find whole spreadsheet applications implemented as JavaBeans.

From a coding perspective, the main thing that set JavaBeans apart was a set of naming and design conventions, used when a JavaBean was written, that enabled it to be prepared for use by tools as an introspectable JavaBean. This allowed tools to use standard naming conventions for a Bean's methods and other formal properties. (Use of the term "conventions" is somewhat misleading. There is a small set of conventions that every Java programmer must use in order to write a JavaBean that behaves and can be used like a JavaBean, so they might as well be called *standards*.)

JavaBeans were designed to use the Java Reflection API (discussed and used in Chapter 4). The Reflection API was designed partly to simplify development with arbitrary, interchangeable JavaBeans, so that a JavaBean could be used without requiring a programmer to decipher its internal workings or even have its source code. Introspection can access and describe the public methods of any properly coded JavaBean loaded into your IDE. In GUI development, most major Java IDEs allow you to drag and drop JavaBean class files onto a GUI panel, whereupon they are instantiated and displayed visually by the IDE.

JavaBeans have persisted beyond their original role as reusable GUI widgets (in truth, they have never been restricted to any particular use by anything but the programmer's imagination). Most recently they have become an important part of the highly componentized server-side J2EE world. They are particularly useful as utility or helper classes with JSPs and servlets, as we shall see. The custom tag API that we cover in Chapter 12, "Developing Custom Tags," is also implemented using the JavaBean architecture, so it's something you'll be seeing a lot of. Most Java code that you would put in a JSP can be put into a JavaBean (later we'll see how custom tags can also be used to keep JSPs free of Java code). Using Beans with JSP is in keeping with the Model 2 approach because it separates the view and business logic into separate components: JSP and JavaBeans.

Accessor/Mutator Methods and the No-Argument Constructor

The most salient features of JavaBeans are their special methods. There are three special methods used in JavaBeans. Two of them are called *accessor* methods because they are used to access the properties of a JavaBean. The other special type is called a *mutator* method because it is used to change the properties of a JavaBean. JavaBeans are all about private properties and public accessor/mutator methods. If you have those, then you have JavaBeans. JavaBeans can have other methods as well, but it's the coding conventions applied with private properties and corresponding accessor and mutator methods that make a Bean a Bean. We will cover these special methods and their corresponding JSP actions in the following sections.

A JavaBean must also be written so that it defines a non-abstract class (because abstract classes cannot be instantiated) with a public, no-argument constructor. The rationale for this convention is also given, with examples.

5

`public void setPropertyName(PropertyType arg)`

When you write a Bean, you can specify methods for setting its properties. A property is just a variable that's been declared in the Bean. The form of a method signature for a settable property is important. It must be of the form

```
public void setPropertyName(PropertyType arg)
```

There are reasons for everything in the naming conventions. The method must be declared `public` so that other classes can invoke the method in the Bean. Recall that if we make a method `private`, it can be accessed only from within the same class. That's no good, because Beans are meant to be open to introspection and reuse from potentially any source. That's why other restrictive access-level modifiers such as `package` (the default) and `protected` are no good for Bean properties.

The method is declared `void` because it will not return any value. `set` methods are write-only.

The name of the method must begin with the word `set` in lowercase, followed by an uppercase letter that begins the property name. The corresponding property variable defined in the Bean need not begin with a capital letter, nor need it even have the same name as the mutator method from which it is set.

`PropertyType` must be specified as an argument to the method because a `set` method is always going to take some value and set it in the Bean.

Examples of valid `setProperty` declarations are

> `public void setMyString(String s)`
>
> This method sets a property called `MyString`. It takes an argument called `s` of type `String`, which will be used to set the value of `MyString` in the method.
>
> `public void setI(int i)`
>
> This method sets a property called `I`. It takes an argument called `i` of type `int`, which will be used to set the value of `I` in the method.

Note that there is a pattern to corresponding `set` and `get` methods: The property type passed in the argument to the `set` method is always the same as the corresponding return type in the `get` method:

```
public void setPropertyName(PropertyType arg)
```

```
public PropertyType getPropertyName()
```

JavaBeans do not have to have both `set` and `get` methods for every property. If a Bean has only a `get` method for a particular property, then that property is read-only. If there's only a `set` method, then it's a write-only property.

public *PropertyType* getPropertyName()

When you write a Bean, you can write accessor methods for reading its properties. The form of a method signature for a readable property is important. It must be of the form

```
public PropertyType getPropertyName()
```

As with `set` methods, there are reasons for everything in the naming conventions. The method must be declared `public` so that other classes in potentially any package can invoke the method in the Bean.

PropertyType must be specified because a `get` method is always going to return some value. This is the nature of any Java `get` method, not just those in Beans.

The name of the method must begin with the word `get` in lowercase, followed by an uppercase letter that begins the property name. The property variable defined in the Bean need not begin with a capital letter nor even have the same name as the accessor method from which it is called (this may be confusing at first, but we'll see some examples). But the `get` and `set` methods must uppercase the property name, regardless.

Some valid `getProperty` declarations are

```
public String getMyString()
```
This method retrieves a property called `MyString`, which must be a `String`.
```
public int getI()
```
This method retrieves a property called `I`, which must be an `int`.

public boolean isProperty()

The `isProperty` method is an optional variant of the `getProperty` accessor method, as you may have noticed from the signature. The only essential difference between `isProperty` and `getProperty` methods is that an `isProperty` method must always return a `boolean` value. Its only real use is as a recognizable marker that the value of the property in question must be `true` or `false`.

Public, No-Argument Constructor

To review what a constructor is, recall that Java classes are like templates for objects. When you want to use a class, you must first instantiate an instance of the class and give it a name. Most classes have one or more special methods called *constructors* whose sole purpose is to be called with the `new` keyword when an instance of the class is created.

> **NOTE**
>
> You can always create an instance of a JavaBean in a JSP using a Bean's constructor in a scriptlet. Anything you do with a Bean in a JSP using standard actions you can also do using scriptlets and straight Java code, but it's easier to take advantage of the tags and other features provided by JSP containers for working with Beans. Consider the JSP container to be like a knowledgeable Java programmer working behind the scenes. Among other things, it knows how to instantiate Beans with minimal information. These conventions of public, no-argument constructors and standard get and set methods make the JSP container's work easier.

Since JavaBeans are meant to be easy to instantiate on-the-fly from any non-privileged application, their constructors must be declared public. Since JavaBeans are meant to be easy to instantiate on-the-fly with no foreknowledge of requirements for their construction (such as objects or other parameters needed for construction), their constructors should require no arguments. An example of a public, no-argument constructor is

```
public HelloBean(){}
```

For contrast, this is an example of a public constructor requiring arguments (one of the three constructors for the java.io.File class):

```
public File(String pathname){}
```

Now that we've covered the conventions and rules of writing JavaBeans, Listing 5.1 shows an example of a complete but very simple JavaBean named FirstBean:

LISTING 5.1   FirstBean.java—A Simple JavaBean to Illustrate Bean Conventions

```java
public class FirstBean
{
    private String stringVar;

    //public PROPERTY_TYPE getPROPERTY_NAME()
    public String getStringThing()
    {
        return stringVar;
    }

    //public void setPROPERTY_NAME(PROPERTY_TYPE arg)
    public void setStringThing(String foo)
    {
        stringVar = foo;
    }
```

LISTING 5.1 Continued

```
    public FirstBean()
    {
        stringVar = "";
    }
}
```

Note that `FirstBean` has matching `get` and `set` methods for a property called `StringThing`, following the conventions we laid out earlier. It doesn't matter which method is defined first. The class variable we've defined is declared `private`. That's not necessary, but it's good practice, since we want only to modify and access it from within this Bean (by calling the Bean's public `get` and `set` methods). Note that all the `getStringThing()` method does is return (using the keyword `return`) the value represented by the `StringThing` property. That's all a `get` method should do. Finally, note that there is no necessary relationship between the name of the private class variable `stringVar` and the name of the Bean's `public` property. Since the general public has access only to the Bean's methods, not to the variable itself, there does not need to be one-to-one correspondence of variable name and property name. There's really no reason to make the names distinct, but I want you to see that there is no necessary connection.

Writing Your Own JavaBeans

JavaBeans can be as simple or as complex as you need them to be. As a result, there may be some situations in which you as a JSP developer are comfortable writing a simple Bean and others in which you are better off using JSP tags to invoke a Bean's methods. The same issue will be confronted when using custom tags. Are JSP developers primarily glorified HTML programmers, are they Java developers, or are they something in between—sometimes called "scripters"? The question will have to be answered as JSP technology develops in the future. I think JSP lends itself to all those levels. Where you place yourself depends on your skill and comfort level and possibly on the development team you are working with.

The source code for the JavaBeans shown in this book is provided and discussed for those who are interested in pursuing that middle-to-advanced scripter/Java developer level. The Beans themselves are provided as source and class files on the CD-ROM accompanying this book. The class files are provided so that you don't need to figure out how to compile them in order to get started. Eventually, to become proficient at developing JavaBeans, you'll have to know how to set up your Java development environment and compile your Java programs from an IDE or from the command line. To compile or modify and recompile these JavaBeans, you'll typically need a Java compiler, which you can obtain as part of the Java SDK from Sun (`http://java.sun.com/j2se/1.3/`). Read the `README` and `INSTALLATION` files to make sure you install the SDK properly. Then use the javac tool to compile the Bean source files.

An alternative to running the compiler yourself is to obtain a JSP container that compiles classes for you. Caucho's (`http://www.caucho.com`) Resin 1.1 is the only container with this feature at this time. Look for other containers to implement auto-recompiling in the near future (perhaps by the time this book hits the shelf). If you get Resin and a Java SDK (the SDK is needed because it provides the compiler), you can just put your JavaBean classes in the default `WEB-INF/classes` directory and Resin will auto-detect changes to the JavaBeans and recompile them for you. It's a nice feature.

Using JSP Standard Actions and JavaBeans

A *standard action* is a JSP tag that the JSP container must recognize regardless of implementation version or vendor-specific server differences. JSP provides several standard actions for instantiating JavaBeans and invoking their `get` and `set` methods.

> **NOTE**
>
> The JSP standard actions for JavaBeans already conform to valid XML syntax, so there is no separate XML form.

`<jsp:useBean>`

The first tag you need to know in order to work with JavaBeans in JSPs is the `<jsp:useBean>` tag, which instantiates an instance of the Bean class you want to work with. You must create an instance of the Bean before using any of the other tags or doing anything else with a Bean.

You can instantiate a Bean from a class file or from a serialized Java object file. *Serialization* lets you save Java objects in a form that enables you to re-instantiate them later. To make a Bean eligible for serialization, all you need to do is add the words `implements java.io.Serializable` after the Bean's class declaration.

You can serialize the state of a Bean's properties along with the Bean. Bean serialization is inherent because of Beans' GUI history. GUI development with Beans requires the capability to serialize them so that developers can customize properties and save them in their customized state.

JavaBeans used with JSP could also benefit from automating this feature, but there is no support for it in the JSP or servlet specification. There are two reasons for this:

1. The use of Beans in GUI development is logically different from the use of Beans in JSP runtime. GUI development primarily takes advantage of the public methods of a Bean to customize the Bean with the state it will retain at runtime. In JSP and servlets, Beans are used primarily so that their properties can be dynamically modified and accessed at runtime.

2. JSPs will often use Beans that have a lifetime of only a single page or one user request, in which case it makes no sense to store a Bean's state. If a Bean is being used with session scope, then it will be serialized automatically if there's a server shutdown in the middle of a live session, but then so will everything else in the session. The only time JSP containers might auto-serialize a Bean's state is when you use a Bean with application scope.

Currently, no JSP container has a feature that makes it easy to turn on serialization of application-scope Beans. You can write your own Java code in a servlet or another Bean to serialize you application-scope Beans when the server shuts down (which is a third reason for not making it a required part of a specification). One instance in which this would make sense is with a hit counter. Rather than increment a number and write it to a file every time a user accesses a Web page, you could just serialize a Bean that does the counting. Then, whenever the server stops or starts, the hit count can be stored to and retrieved from the Bean itself.

This explanation of serialization is to introduce the full `<jsp:useBean>` syntax and account for the option of instantiating a Bean from a `.ser` serialized object file. Also, implementing the Serializable interface is a standard part of JavaBean development in the GUI development world.

```
<jsp:useBean
    id="beanInstanceName" scope="page | request | session | application"    {
        class="package.class" [ type="package.class" ] |
        type="package.class" |
        beanName="{ package.class | <%= expression %> }" type="package.class"
    }
{ /> | > other elements </jsp:useBean> }
```

The syntax shows that there are three ways to instantiate a Bean. The syntax follows Sun's convention of indicating a list of exclusive options (requiring a choice of one) between curly braces ({}). A vertical pipe (|) separates each option. An optional attribute is listed between brackets ([ ]). Note that when the beanName attribute is used, an expression can be evaluated to the Bean's type or filename. However, the simplest and most common form of instantiating a JavaBean is to specify an id for the Bean, leave the scope set to the default page, and give the class name of the Bean:

```
<jsp:useBean id="pickAnyName" class="HitCountBean" />
```

This is a typical JSP Bean instantiation for a Bean that will only persist for the life of the current page. If you want to set a Bean's properties to an initial value, then you can use one or more <jsp:setProperty> tags and have a closing tag:

```
<jsp:useBean id="lucy" class="HitCountBean" >
<jsp:setProperty name="lucy" property="prop1" value="pickles" >
</jsp:useBean>
```

The beanName and class attributes are exclusive—if you use the beanName attribute, you won't have a class attribute and vice versa. The difference between using class and using beanName is academic (the beanName version *requires* the type attribute, whereas the class version does not) unless you are instantiating a Bean from a .ser file, in which case you must use the beanName form.

The type attribute can be used alone to give a local name to a Java object that's already been defined and instantiated in another JSP or a servlet. When instantiating a Bean for use in a JSP, you typically want to use either the class or beanName technique. You use class with the optional type attribute only if you want to instantiate an instance of a Bean and cast it to the type specified in the type attribute. Again, this is useful information but not typical. These are more advanced techniques, available for special uses.

There are two features provided for the <jsp:useBean> tag that prevent you from running into exceptions you might otherwise encounter if you are always trying to instantiate Beans using scriptlets. The first is that the <jsp:useBean> tag causes the JSP container to attempt to instantiate a Bean instance only if there's not already an instance of the Bean with the name specified in id and in the specified scope.

The second feature is that the same holds true of <jsp:setProperty> tags in the body of a <jsp:useBean> tag; if the Bean has already been instantiated in that scope with that id, then the <jsp:setProperty> tag(s) will have no effect. This allows you, for example, to use application-scope Beans in any JSP and not worry which one did the instantiating. Whichever one was hit first in the application would have caused the Bean to be instantiated.

<jsp:setProperty>

There are two somewhat self-explanatory standard actions in JSP 1.1 for getting and setting a JavaBean's public properties: <jsp:setProperty> and <jsp:getProperty>. These methods specify the instance name of a Bean that's been instantiated and named with the id attribute in a <jsp:useBean> tag. Then they name the property you want to set or get and give it a value for setting or getting. The full syntax of <jsp:setProperty> is as follows:

```
<jsp:setProperty name="beanInstanceName"
    {
```

```
         property= "*"   | [sr]
         property="propertyName" [ param="parameterName" ]   | [sr]
         property="propertyName" value="{ string | <%= expression %> }"[sr]
    }
/>
```

Once again, there is some flexibility about how a Bean's properties can be set from a JSP. Note that the name attribute must match the corresponding id attribute of the Bean you introduced with a <jsp:useBean> tag. There are three ways to set a Bean's properties.

Setting All Properties from the request Object

The first property-setting method (with the asterisk) should be used when you want to pass *all* the values you've gotten from a user request to corresponding Bean properties. User properties are typically entered via an HTML form submitted to a servlet or a JSP and encapsulated in the JSP implicit request object. HTML forms are commonly used to submit name/value pairs to the server for processing. JavaBeans and JSPs are perfect for manipulating these name/value pairs via logic in the Beans and JSP standard actions. If there's no matching property in the Bean to set, no problem: The container will skip it and look for a match for the next one until all the request parameters have been tried.

Setting a Single Property from a request Parameter

The second property-setting method is convenient for setting a Bean property to the value of a single request parameter. Suppose you have an HTML form with a name/value pair of userid=user'sID, where user'sID would always be set to whatever the user submitted via the form. Then you could pass the value of the userid parameter to the Bean like this:

```
<jsp:setProperty name="beanName" property="userid" />
```

The JSP container parses the form parameters for you and sets the Bean's userid property (accessed by a public method in the Bean called setUserid()) to the value of the userid request parameter. If the request parameter and Bean property have different names, then you must specify the param attribute. Here is an example of that, assuming a public method of setWhoLoggedIn() in the Bean and a request parameter of userid submitted via an HTML form:

```
<jsp:setProperty name="beanName" property="whoLoggedIn" param="userid" />
```

Setting a Single Property from a String or an Expression

The third technique of setting Bean properties is to use a string or a runtime-evaluated expression. Both of these techniques use the value attribute of <jsp:setProperty>.

5

You should note that all property values you send using any of these three <jsp:setProperty> techniques will be sent as strings. What if you have a property whose set method takes an int or a long as an argument? Good question. What the JSP container does is use some tricky methods of the java.lang package to try and convert whatever strings you sent into an appropriate value for the set method being accessed. So, for example, if the set method takes a Boolean as an argument because the property type is a Boolean, then the JSP container will note that and attempt to get the Boolean equivalent of the string it received for that method. The standard chart of allowed conversions and how they are done is shown in Table 5.1:

TABLE 5.1 <jsp:setProperty> String Conversion Methods

Property Type	String Is Converted Using
boolean or Boolean	java.lang.Boolean.valueOf(String)
byte or Byte	java.lang.Byte.valueOf(String)
char or Character	java.lang.Character.valueOf(String)
double or Double	java.lang.Double.valueOf(String)
int or Integer	java.lang.Integer.valueOf(String)
float or Float	java.lang.Float.valueOf(String)
long or Long	java.lang.Long.valueOf(String)

<jsp:getProperty>

The easiest Bean-oriented JSP standard action to use is the <jsp:getProperty> tag. All you do is supply the name of the Bean you want to access (which must first have been instantiated using the <jsp:useBean> tag, of course) and the name of the property on which you want to invoke the corresponding public get method in the Bean. The full syntax of <jsp:getProperty> is as follows:

```
<jsp:getProperty name="beanInstanceName" property="propertyName" />
```

Whatever returns from the Bean get method named in the property attribute will be displayed in the output of the JSP at the location where the <jsp:getProperty> tag was used. Listing 5.2 is a basic JSP that uses all the tags we've just covered to instantiate and access the FirstBean JavaBean class.

LISTING 5.2 FirstBean.jsp—A Simple JSP to Illustrate <jsp:useBean> and Related Tags

```
<jsp:useBean id="fb" class="FirstBean" />
<jsp:setProperty name="fb" property="stringThing" value="Hello World" />
<html>
<head><title>First Bean JSP</title></head>
```

LISTING 5.2   Continued

```
<body>
The value of FirstBean's stringThing property is:
<br />"<jsp:getProperty name="fb" property="stringThing" />"
</body>
</html>>>>>
```

Figure 5.1 shows the browser output of `FirstBean.jsp`.

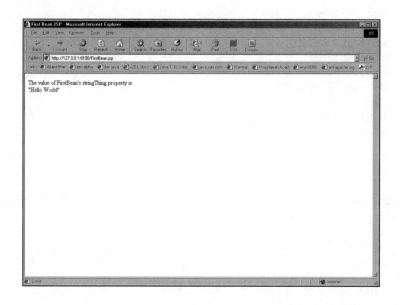

FIGURE 5.1
`FirstBean.jsp`'s *HTML output in a browser.*

Using JavaBeans in JSP

Now that we've covered the basics of coding conventions and syntax for JavaBeans and JSP's special tags for working with them, let's see some Beans in action. The rest of this chapter presents several JavaBeans and complementary JSPs that do some typical server-side tasks: a session hit counter, a random quote generator, and an online message board/suggestion box. The goal here is to show how JSPs and JavaBeans can be used to do some typical, fairly simple tasks that any competing server-side technology can do.

Before moving ahead, let me show you the style sheet and JSP `errorPage` used throughout these examples, so that you have to see each only once. Listing 5.3 is the style sheet used throughout, and Listing 5.4 is the JSP `errorPage`.

LISTING 5.3   `JSPstyle6.css` —The CSS Used Throughout the Examples in This Chapter

```
body    { background-color: #ffffff;;
          font-family: sans-serif;
          text-align: left; }
h1      { text-align: center;
          color: #cc0000;
          text-decoration : underline; }
h2      { font-style: italic; }
h3      { margin-left: 1em;
          color: #aa0000;
          text-decoration : underline; }
em      { font-weight: bold;
          color: #cc0000;
          text-decoration: underline; }
ul, li { font-family: monospace;
          color: #008888;
          list-style-type: none; }
table, td { border: none;
            vertical-align: top; }
```

LISTING 5.4   `uh-oh.jsp`—A Simple `errorPage` JSP Used Throughout This Chapter

```
<%@ page isErrorPage="true" %>
<html>
<head><title>Uh-oh Page</title></head>
<body>
<h1 align="center">Uh Oh . . .</h1>
<p><font color="red"><%= exception %></font></p>
<p><% exception.printStackTrace(); %></p>
<hr />
<p>Why don't you email the owner of this page and send the error you got?</p>
<p>Here's his email:
    <a href="mailto:userid@yourdomain.net">userid@yourdomain.net</a></p>
</body></html>
```

Creating a Hit Counter in JSP

First we have `HitCountBean`, shown in Listing 5.5. This Bean increments an internal variable every time it's asked to by a JSP that uses it. Note that it implements the `java.io.Serializable` interface. We aren't going to get into how you would write a servlet to serialize this Bean when the server shuts down, but it is a good exercise for further development.

As long as the Bean implements `java.io.Serializable`, it's eligible to be serialized by another component on the server. Note that the Bean has a no-argument constructor, according to the conventions of writing JavaBeans. Also note that the getter and setter methods don't necessarily correspond to the private variables used in the Bean. This is interesting because it points out the object-oriented concept of *encapsulation*, which we covered in Chapter 4. Since the Bean's variables are private, they can remain hidden from the user or application accessing the Bean. The implementation of the variables in the Bean and how they are created or changed or even what they are named are hidden from the outside world. Recall that encapsulation allows a programmer to alter the implementation of a class without affecting anyone (or anyone's code) using the class. As long as the public accessor/mutator methods stay the same, no one's the wiser.

LISTING 5.5   `HitCountBean.java`—Hit Counter JavaBean to Store Session Counts

```java
import java.util.Date;
import java.text.DateFormat;
import java.io.Serializable;

public class HitCountBean implements Serializable
{
    private boolean b;
    private int hitCount;
    private String serverStart;
    private Date date = new Date();

    public String getStartTime()
    {
        return serverStart;
    }

    public int getHits()
    {
        return hitCount;
    }

    public void setNewSession(boolean b)
    {
        b = b;
        if (b)
        { hitCount++; }
    }

    public HitCountBean()
    {
        hitCount = 0;
        serverStart = DateFormat.getDateInstance(DateFormat.LONG).format(date);
    }
}
```

The JSP that uses `HitCountBean` instantiates the `HitCountBean` class, names it `counter`, and specifies its scope as `application`. The reason for this scope is that the Bean is going to serve as a session counter for everyone who accesses the server with a new session. The only way for multiple users to share access to the Bean's state is to declare the Bean with `application` scope:

```
<jsp:useBean id="counter" scope="application" class="HitCountBean" />
```

Next the JSP calls the Bean's `setNewSession()` method and sends a string representation of a Boolean as the value to set. A Boolean value is what is returned from the `HttpSession.isNew()` method. Recall from Chapter 4 that the implicit `session` object in JSP is an instance of `javax.servlet.http.HttpSession`. As such, you can avail yourself of any of the methods contained in the `HttpSession` class by invoking them on the `session` object. The `isNew()` method simply returns `true` if the client has not yet received or acknowledged a cookie from the server.

This trick will work only if the client has cookies enabled and if this JSP is hit upon the client's first access to the server. The best way to use this JSP would be as an include in some subtle location of your site's index page, in which case you should remove the <html>, <head>, and <body> tags as you would with an included HTML file. I would probably include something like this page at the bottom of an `index.jsp` to subtly track and notify interested parties of the number of users accessing the site.

LISTING 5.6   `HitCountBean.jsp`—The Hit Counter JavaBean's Corresponding JSP

```
<%@ page errorPage="uh-oh.jsp" %>
<jsp:useBean id="counter" scope="application" class="HitCountBean" />
<jsp:setProperty name="counter" property="newSession"
                 value="<%= session.isNew() %>" />
<html>
<head><title>Hit Counter</title>
<style type="text/css">
<!--
@import url(JSPstyle6.css);
-->
</style>
</head>
<body>
<h1>Hit Counter</h1>
<p>This page has had <jsp:getProperty name="counter" property="hits" />
user sessions since the server started on <jsp:getProperty name="counter"
                                           property="startTime" />
</p>
</body>
</html>
```

Figure 5.2 shows the browser output of HitCounter.jsp after six separate session hits. The only way to test that this JSP works correctly is to open multiple browser sessions and hit the page. If you open just one browser window, or even multiple windows spawned off the same window, you will see only one session counted. This is because the Bean has application scope and will count your hit only when your session is first established.

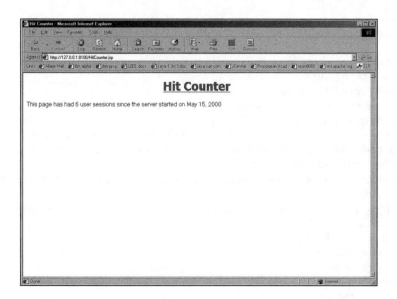

FIGURE 5.2
HitCounter.jsp *after accessing it with six new browser sessions.*

Creating a Quote Randomizer in JSP

The next example is a random quote generator of sorts. It's based on a typical code snippet found in client-side JavaScript for generating a random quote from an array of quotes. For a large number of quotes you would need to do some file I/O or database queries to keep coming up with new quotes. This example lists just ten quotes, only five of which are actually anything interesting. The others are numbered so that you can see that the quote and author arrays are indexed correctly; you will always get the right quote with its matching author.

You don't have to use this idea for literary quotes, of course. You could easily modify it to be about World Series champions and years, car makes and models, movies and directors, or jokes and punch lines. You can add more arrays if you like (for example, add a title array so that you can separately retrieve and format quote, author, and title), but the general idea stays the same. I used arrays of strings because arrays should be faster than similar Java collections objects such as Vector or Hashtable. Arrays are fixed length in Java—once you define an array's length, you can't alter it. So another reason to use `collections` objects would be to take advantage of their flexible capacity, built-in methods, and other features. For a case like this, arrays are fast and easy.

LISTING 5.7   `QuotesBean.java`—A JavaBean Class to Provide Random Quotes for `quotes.jsp`

```java
public class QuotesBean
{
    private String quote;
    private String author;
    private String[] quotes = {
        "Once more unto the breach, dear friends, once more<br />Or close the
    ➥ wall up with our English dead!",
        "Now does my project gather to a head:<br />My charms crack not; my
    ➥ spirits obey,<br>and time Goes upright with his carriage.",
        "The brain is wider than the sky",
        "April is the cruelest month, breeding <br />lilacs out of the dead
    ➥land, mixing",
        "Thou still unravish'd bride of quietness,<br>Thou foster-child of
    ➥silence and slow time,",
        "quote number 6",
        "quote number 7",
        "quote number 8",
        "quote number 9",
        "quote number 10" };

    private String[] authors = {
        "Shakespeare, Henry V, III.1",
        "Shakespeare, The Tempest, V.1",
        "Emily Dickinson, XLIII, The Brain",
        "T.S. Eliot, The Wasteland, I. The Burial of the Dead",
        "John Keats, Ode on a Grecian Urn, I.1-2",
        "author number 6",
        "author number 7",
        "author number 8",
        "author number 9",
        "author number 10" };

    public String getQuote()
    {
        return quote;
    }

    public String getAuthor()
```

LISTING 5.7   Continued

```
    {
        return author;
    }

    public QuotesBean()
    {
        int i = (int) Math.floor(Math.random() * quotes.length);
        quote = quotes[i];
        author = authors[i];
    }
}
```

Note that the Bean defines a couple of string arrays and then uses a simple pseudo-random function to randomize access to the arrays. The Math class is a member of the java.lang package. It has several static methods that you can call without instantiating it. The random() method generates a pseudo-random number (random enough for our purposes here) between zero and one. The floor() method rounds the resultant number down to the nearest whole number. It returns a double, so we have to cast it to an int for use as an array index i.

The multiplication of the random number times the length of the quotes array "magically" gives a number within the limits of the array. (Remember that the length member of every array is a special read-only field, not a method, used to determine an array's length.) This is important, because if we try to access the array at a point longer or shorter than its length, we will get an ArrayIndexOutOfBoundsException. A Java array's first entry is 0, and 0 will be our first quote in the array.

LISTING 5.8   Quotes.jsp—A JSP to Get Random Quotes from QuotesBean

```
<%@ page errorPage="uh-oh.jsp" %>
<jsp:useBean id="quotes" class="QuotesBean" />
<html>
<head><title>Quotes JSP</title>
<style type="text/css">
<!--
@import url(JSPstyle6.css);
-->
</style></head>
<body>
<h2><jsp:getProperty name="quotes" property="quote" /></h2>
<h3><jsp:getProperty name="quotes" property="author" /></h3>
</body>
</html>
```

The JSP is very simple. We instantiate the Bean before we try to use it, and we go with the default page scope because we want to get a different result from the Bean (actually, a new instance of the Bean) on each access. Then we get the public getQuote() and getAuthor() methods, using the coding conventions of the JSP property getter tags.

Figure 5.3 shows an example of the output of Quotes.jsp.

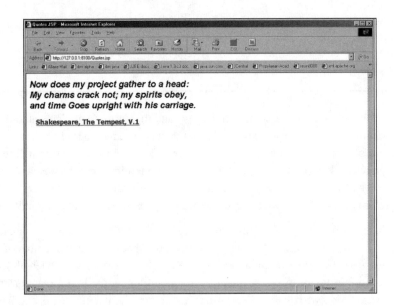

FIGURE 5.3
Sample output from Quotes.jsp.

Creating a Message Board Web Application in JSP

Now we get into a more involved example that makes use of the Servlet 2.2 notion and standards of a Web application. This is a good time to introduce a real, albeit simple, application using JSPs, JavaBeans, and two standard components of any portable Servlet 2.2 Web application: a web.xml deployment descriptor and a WAR file.

I won't go into the details of what these things are, since they are covered in Chapter 1, "Understanding JSP," and Chapter 12. A little refresher in the current context may be appropriate, however.

Using JBoard

Basically, the Servlet 2.2 API introduced a standard descriptor file, using XML, that a Web application can use to configure itself in a standard, portable way. Furthermore, the directory structure of a Servlet 2.2 Web application is also standardized. Listing 5.9 shows the web.xml file for this JSP-based message board application, called *JBoard*. This file must go in the root of the WEB-INF directory for the JBoard application.

LISTING 5.9   web.xml—Servlet 2.2 Standard XML Deployment Descriptor Written for the JBoard Web Application

```
<!DOCTYPE web-app PUBLIC
          "-//Sun Microsystems, Inc.//DTD Web Application 2.2//EN"
          "http://java.sun.com/j2ee/dtds/web-app_2_2.dtd">
<web-app>
  <display-name>JBoard</display-name>
  <description>JBoard Suggestion Board App</description>
  <welcome-file-list>
      <welcome-file>MakeSuggestion.htm</welcome-file>
  </welcome-file-list>
</web-app>
```

Listing 5.10 is the directory structure for the JBoard application, all of which should be archived into a standard Java Web application archive file, called a *WAR* file. The accompanying WAR file and its expanded contents are included on the CD-ROM for your convenience.

Should you want to develop this application on your own, there are a couple of minor things we should get out of the way. First, once you have copies of all the JBoard files, you will also need to create an empty directory called data and arrange it and all the JBoard files into a structure like that shown in Listing 5.10.

LISTING 5.10   JBoardDirectoryListing.txt—Directory Listing for the JBoard Web Application

```
data/
Jboard.css
LogData.jsp
MakeSuggestion.htm
SuggestionLog.jsp
uh-oh.jsp
WEB-INF/web.xml
WEB-INF/classes/JBoardBean.class
WEB-INF/classes/LogDataBean.class
```

Now you can turn this pile of files into a Web application archive (assuming you have the Java SDK installed properly by now) by getting to a command prompt and using the `cd` command to change your current directory to the directory in which you have replicated this file structure. To "WAR up" the files, execute the jar (*Java archive*) tool with the following syntax:

```
jar -cf jboard.war data/ JBoard.css *.jsp *.htm WEB-INF/
```

You might want to come back and try this step after reading the rest of this chapter, but I thought I'd introduce it here to get it out of the way. All we're doing is creating a regular Java archive with a specially named extension and a standard internal directory structure. You could use the syntax

```
jar -cf jboard.war *
```

but only if there's nothing else in the directory that will get sucked into the WAR file. The jar utility will automatically descend into directories to grab all subdirectories and files. To see that you've archived the file correctly, use the `-tf` options of the jar tool to look at a table of contents for the archive. Apart from the addition of a `META-INF` directory and a `Manifest.mf` file put there by the jar tool, you should see the same directory structure in the jar file as shown in Listing 5.10:

```
jar -tf jboard.war
```

To deploy this application when it's all ready to go, just follow the documentation for your servlet/JSP container. Allaire's JRun has a particularly user-friendly admin interface for deploying WAR files. The Jakarta project's Tomcat server has easy-to-follow instructions for deploying WAR files. As the Servlet 2.2–based generation of application servers matures, everyone will have deployment tools for unpacking and installing WAR files easily.

Developing the JavaBeans for JBoard

Listing 5.11 shows a straightforward JavaBean with "classic" getter and setter methods, all taking strings as parameters or returning strings. The only extra is a `Date` that is instantiated when the Bean is first instantiated. You might find it beneficial to create an independent `DateBean` or `CalendarBean` as a utility class for getting a variety of custom date and time formats. For now, we'll get a `Date` and format a string from it right in this Bean.

The `JBoardBean` class is one of two Beans we use in this application. `JBoardBean` is used just for setting and getting `request` parameter values, plus a time stamp (the `date` string) and a property for the `PATH` to the application root's "real path" on the server file system. This `PATH` property is used for locating and saving the log file for the application in a standard platform-independent location. No matter which platform the application runs on, its log file will always be stored relative to the real path of the application's root.

LISTING 5.11   JBoardBean.java—A JavaBean for Use with a Message Board
Implemented in JSP and Beans

```java
import java.text.DateFormat;
import java.util.Date;

public class JBoardBean
{
    private String name, login, date, domain, suggestion, PATH;

    public void setName(String name)
    {
        name = name;
    }
    public void setLogin(String login)
    {
        login = login;
    }
    public void setDomain(String domain)
    {
        domain = domain;
    }
    public void setSuggestion(String suggestion)
    {
        suggestion = suggestion;
    }
    public void setPATH(String PATH)
    {
        PATH = PATH;
    }
    public String getDate()
    {
        return date;
    }
    public String getName()
    {
        return name;
    }
    public String getLogin()
    {
        return login;
    }
    public String getDomain()
    {
        return domain;
    }
```

LISTING 5.11   Continued

```java
    public String getSuggestion()
    {
        return suggestion;
    }
    public String getPATH()
    {
        return PATH;
    }
    public JBoardBean()
    {
        date = DateFormat.getInstance().format(new Date());
    }
}
```

The `LogDataBean` shown in Listing 5.12 is the worker Bean that actually writes a log file to save the user entries submitted to JBoard. As you can see, it wraps a `FileWriter` object in `BufferedWriter`. `BufferedWriter` is used mainly for performance reasons.

The synchronized keyword is introduced here as a new concept and term. Using the synchronized keyword on a block of code or an object makes access to that code or object singlethreaded and therefore thread safe. You want to be careful not to synchronize more than you have to. Since this Bean needs to accept and write a bunch of properties to a file whose integrity must be maintained, I synchronized all the Bean's methods. With today's JVMs, synchronization is highly optimized and much faster than it used to be. Nevertheless, you should put some thought into whether your methods or classes need to be synchronized.

LISTING 5.12   `LogDataBean.java`—A Bean Used in `LogData.jsp` to Write User-Submitted Messages to a Flat File

```java
import java.io.BufferedWriter;
import java.io.FileWriter;
import java.io.IOException;

public class LogDataBean
{
    private BufferedWriter bw;
    private String date, domain, login, logPath, name, suggestion;
    private String fileName = "/data/SuggestionLog.inc";
    private StringBuffer sb1 = new StringBuffer();
    private StringBuffer sb2 = new StringBuffer();
    private StringBuffer emailUrl;
    private String TRuser = "<tr><td id=\"user\">";
    private String TRdata = "<tr><td id=\"data\">";
```

LISTING 5.12 Continued

```
private String TRclose = "</td></tr>";

public synchronized void setSuggestion(String suggestion)
{
    suggestion = suggestion;
    try
    {
        bw = new BufferedWriter(new FileWriter(this.logPath +
                                            fileName, true));

        emailUrl = new StringBuffer("<a href=\"mailto:").append(login).
append("@").append(domain).append("\">").append(name).append("</a>");

        // write out HTML table rows with id hooks for CSS formatting
        bw.write(sb1.append(TRuser).append(date).append(" ").append(
emailUrl).append(" wrote:").append(TRclose).toString());
        bw.newLine(); // write platform independent newline
        bw.write(sb2.append(TRdata).append(suggestion).append(
TRclose).toString());
        bw.newLine();
        bw.close();
        sb1.setLength(0); // truncate the StringBuffers to zero.  If we
        sb2.setLength(0); // didn't do this, then we'd continue appending
                          // to them on every request.
    }

    catch(IOException e)
    {
        System.err.println(e);
        e.printStackTrace();
    }
}

public synchronized void setLogPath(String logPath)
{
    logPath = logPath;
}

public synchronized void setName(String name)
{
    name = name;
}

public synchronized void setLogin(String login)
{
    login = login;
```

LISTING 5.12   Continued

```
    }

    public synchronized void setDate(String date)
    {
        date = date;
    }

    public synchronized void setDomain(String domain)
    {
        domain = domain;
    }

    public LogDataBean() // no-arg constructor
    {
    }
}
```

Developing the Default HTML Page for JBoard

MakeSuggestion.htm (Listing 5.13) is the default document of the JBoard application. It's the default document because it has been specified as such using the standard <welcome-file> tag in the web.xml file for JBoard (seen previously in Listing 5.9):

```
<welcome-file-list>
     <welcome-file>MakeSuggestion.htm</welcome-file>
  </welcome-file-list>
```

MakeSuggestion.htm uses a bunch of HTML form attributes for sending a user's data to the JBoard.jsp file in a post request:

```
<form action="JBoard.jsp" method="post">
```

LISTING 5.13   MakeSuggestion.htm—The Default Document of the JBoard Web Application

```
<html>
<head><title>JBoard Suggestion Box</title>
<style type="text/css">
<!--
@import url(Jboard.css);
-->
</style></head>
<body>
<h1>JBoard</h1>
<p>Use this page to make a suggestion.</p>
```

LISTING 5.13   Continued

```
<p><small>Note: You can use any HTML in the TEXTAREA of this form,
        but please only use the simplest formatting HTML for your
        suggestions, e.g., &lt;br&gt;, &lt;p&gt;, etc.</small></p><br />

<form action="JBoard.jsp" method="post">
<p>
Full Name:
<input type="text" name="name" value="your name" maxlength="25"><br />
User id:
<input type="text" name="login"
       value="userid" maxlength="12"> @: <input type="text" name="domain"
                              value="yourdomain.com" maxlength="20"><br />
Suggestion:<br />
<textarea name="suggestion" rows="8" cols="72">
</textarea><br />
<input type="submit" value="Suggest"><input type="reset">
</p>
</form>
</body></html>
```

Figure 5.4 shows what `MakeSuggestion.htm` looks like. It's just an HTML page with some `form` elements and light CSS formatting. The techniques foreshadowed here with HTML `form` parameters are covered in depth in Chapter 7, "Working with Forms."

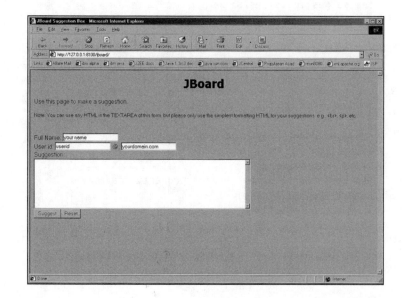

FIGURE 5.4

`MakeSuggestion.htm`, *the initial page of the JBoard Web application, as defined in* `web.xml`.

5

USING BEANS

Developing the JSPs for JBoard

The JBoard.jsp file in Listing 5.14 receives a post from MakeSuggestion.htm and then passes all the properties of the request parameters to JBoardBean in a `<jsp:setProperty>` tag of the following form:

```
<jsp:useBean id="jboard" scope="request" class="JBoardBean" />
<jsp:setProperty name="jboard" property="*" />
```

LISTING 5.14   JBoard.jsp—The Main Action Page of the JBoard Web Application

```
<%@ page errorPage="uh-oh.jsp" %>
<jsp:useBean id="jboard" scope="request" class="JBoardBean" />
<jsp:setProperty name="jboard" property="*" />
<jsp:setProperty name="jboard" property="PATH"
                 value="<%= application.getRealPath(\"/\") %>" />
<html>
<head><title>JBoard Thanks</title>
<style type="text/css">
<!--
@import url(Jboard.css);
-->
</style></head>
<body>
<h1>JBoard: Thank you . . .</h1> <p>
  <b>Hi, <jsp:getProperty name="jboard" property="name" />. <br />
  Thanks for the suggestion.</b></p>
<table>
    <tr>
        <td>From <em>
            <a href="mailto: <jsp:getProperty
                              name="jboard"
                              property="login" />@<jsp:getProperty
                                                   name="jboard"
                                                   property="domain" />">
        <jsp:getProperty name="jboard" property="name" /></a>
        </em><br />
        <em id="red"><small>
        <jsp:getProperty name="jboard" property="date" />
        </small></em>
        </td>
    <tr>
        <td>
            <jsp:getProperty name="jboard" property="suggestion" />
        </td>
    </tr>
</table><br />
```

LISTING 5.14 Continued

```
<%@ include file="LogData.jsp" %>
<a href="SuggestionLog.jsp">Suggestion Log</a>
</body>
</html>
```

Note the static include of the LogData.jsp (Listing 5.15) near the bottom of the JBoard.jsp file in Listing 5.14. This means that the content of the LogData.jsp file is included in the content of the JBoard.jsp file at translation time, so they become part of the same servlet. I split them up for neatness and readability. As far as the JSP container is concerned, they make one file.

LogData.jsp (Listing 5.15) also sets some properties. Note that LogDataBean is instantiated as having application scope. This makes sense because there's no benefit to having two objects try to write to a file simultaneously. Again, since the scope of this Bean is application, it makes sense to synchronize its methods.

Note that one of the properties uses the expression evaluation method of specifying a Bean property:

```
<jsp:setProperty name="logbean"
                 property="date"
                 value="<%= jboard.getDate() %>" />
```

In this case, the logbean instance of LogDataBean invokes the JBoardBean instance named jboard and calls its getDate() method.

LISTING 5.15 LogData.jsp—This JSP Uses a Bean to Log the Entries Made by JBoard Users

```
<%@ page errorPage="uh-oh.jsp" %>
<jsp:useBean id="logbean" class="LogDataBean" scope="application">
<jsp:setProperty name="logbean"
                 property="logPath"
                 value="<%= application.getRealPath(\"/\") %>" />
</jsp:useBean>
<jsp:setProperty name="logbean"
                 property="date"
                 value="<%= jboard.getDate() %>" />
<jsp:setProperty name="logbean" property="*" />
```

Viewing the Output of the JBoard Application

Figure 5.5 shows the output of JBoard.jsp after processing a sample request. The mouse pointer is over the email address link so that you can see the dynamically constructed email address shown in the browser's scrollbar at the bottom of the frame.

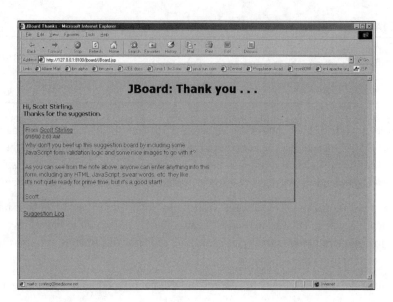

FIGURE 5.5

JBoard.jsp, *the result page of the JBoard Web application, which includes* LogData.jsp.

Listing 5.16 shows the final page, SuggestionLog.jsp, which dynamically includes the Suggestion.inc file into the JSP on each request. It is mostly just HTML and CSS, with a link back to the main page.

LISTING 5.16   SuggestionLog.jsp—The JBoard Log Display Page, with a Link Back to the Main Page

```
<%@ page errorPage="uh-oh.jsp" %>
<html>
<head><title>JBoard Suggestion Log</title>
<style type="text/css">
<!--
@import url(Jboard.css);
-->
</style></head>
<body>
<h1>JBoard: Suggestion Log</h1>
<center>
<table>
<jsp:include page="data/SuggestionLog.inc" flush="true" />
</table>
<p><a href="<%= request.getContextPath() %>">back to main JBoard page</a>
```

LISTING 5.16   Continued

```
</center>
</body>
</html>
```

Figure 5.6 shows the output of SuggestionLog.jsp after a couple of example runs.

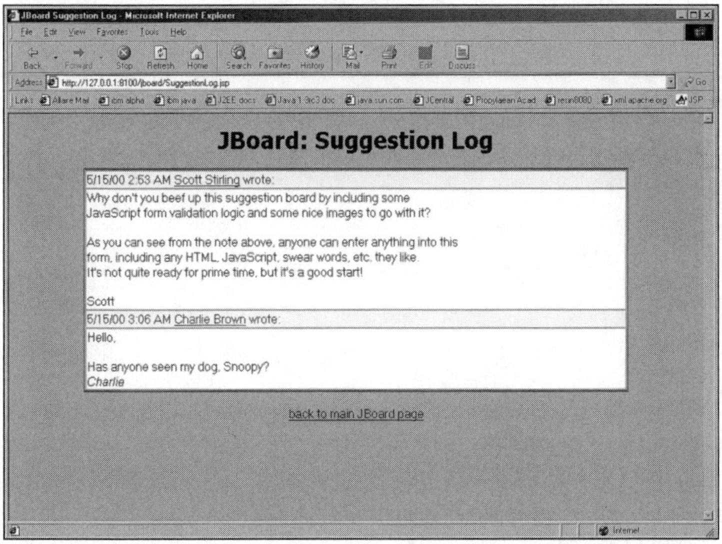

FIGURE 5.6
SuggestionLog.jsp, *the final page of the JBoard Web application, showing the included log file of the suggestion board.*

Auxiliary Pages for the JBoard Application

Finally, for completeness, we have the CSS file (Listing 5.17) and errorPage (Listing 5.18) of the JBoard application. Using CSS keeps the HTML uncluttered. Using an errrorPage presents users with a nicer message than a stark Java stack trace if an exception occurs. I included the Throwable.printStackTrace() method for debugging purposes, but you could remove it or replace it with the shorter output of the Throwable.getMessage() method.

LISTING 5.17   Jboard.css—The Style Sheet Used for the JBoard Web Application

```
body    { background-color: #31CE31;
          font-family: sans-serif;
          text-align: left; }
h1      { text-align: center; }
```

LISTING 5.17   Continued

```
table   { border: thin solid #FF0000;
          width : 80%; }
#user   { background-color: #FFFF63;
          color: #006363; }
#data   { background-color: #FFFFFF; }
#red    { color: #FF0000; }
```

LISTING 5.18   uh-oh.jsp—The JSP errorPage Used for the JBoard Web Application

```
<%@ page isErrorPage="true" %>
<html>
<head><title>Uh-oh Page</title>
<style type="text/css">
<!--
@import url(Jboard.css);
-->
</style></head>
<body>
<h1>Uh Oh . . .</h1>
<p id="exception"><%= exception %></p>
<% exception.printStackTrace(); %>
<hr>
<p>Why don't you email the owner of this page and send the error you got?</p>
<p>Here's his email: <a href="mailto:userid@domain.net">
➥userid@domain.net</a></p>
</body></html>
```

Wrapping Up

Now that we've introduced JavaBeans and the JSP tags for interacting with them and seen some examples of typical Web development uses, I'd like to revisit the design and goals of JSP technology for a minute. Since its inception, JSP has been intended as an easy-to-use technology with a low barrier to entry and a smooth learning curve. The fact of the matter is that, until the middle of this year, JSP has been used primarily by Java programmers. JSP users have been the all-in-one Java programmers (or teams of them) who fill practically every role defined in the J2EE specification rather than compartmentalize the development process as the J2EE model recommends.

The goal of JSP is to bring the power of Java to HTML coders, Java newbies, and the crossover audience migrating from ASP and ASP+, CFML, Perl, and so on. Ideally, JSP coders shouldn't have to write JavaBeans. The first step is for Java developers to write the Beans and provide documentation to the JSP developers that explains how to use the Beans with their JSP tags. The next step is for the GUI development tools of JSP programmers to introspect JavaBeans with drag-and-drop ease and make point-and-click use (auto-generating the `useBean` and `get` and `set` tags) of JavaBeans in JSP a reality. At the time of this writing, JSP is a 1.1 technology, with the first public draft of the JSP 1.2 specification about to hit the development community in August. JSP 1.3 will soon follow in 2001. By the time JSP 2.0 is a reality (if that's how the versioning goes), the original intent of JSP should be fully realized. The advent of JSP custom tag libraries in JSP 1.1 is a huge step in that direction, and we will see how they work in Chapter 12.

Connecting Pages

IN THIS CHAPTER

Armed with the basics to build individual JSP pages, you are now ready to learn how to pass information between them. This chapter covers how to pass information via the query string with name/value pairs. Chapter 7, "Working with Forms," will focus on using form controls as a more interactive way of passing information between pages.

Part of this chapter will look at how browsers and servers interpret a URL. Java methods used to parse a user's request and construct new links will also be covered.

We will conclude the chapter by taking a look at the `<jsp:forward>` directive. This tag allows you to redirect the original request to another resource without changing the URL of the browser, making the transition seamless to the user.

Understanding URLs

A *uniform resource locator* (URL) is the address of an object found on the Internet. This object can be in the form of a text file, an image, an executable, or virtually any other type of file.

For example, if you were to request the original proposal for the URL standard at `http://www.w3.org/History/1995/WWW/Paper/url-spec.txt` with your Web browser, you would be downloading a text file. The browser identifies this file as plain text and does nothing more than display the contents of the file to you. No further downloading or processing is needed with the request.

However, if you download Yahoo!'s home page at `http://www.yahoo.com/index.html`, the browser will know to render this text file via its HTML tags. Upon doing so, the browser will download additional resources such as Java classes, Flash movies, and GIF images as it is instructed by the tags. Each of these items will have its own URL. The browser can also display hyperlinks directing you to other HTML-rendering pages. This simple yet powerful concept of referencing other resources is one of the foundations of the Internet as we know it today.

Constructing a URL

You can refer to the same resource in several ways. For example, Sun Microsystems' official JSP site can be reached at `http://java.sun.com/products/jsp/index.html`. Each of the following URLs will take you to the same place:

- `java.sun.com/products/jsp/index.html`
- `http://java.sun.com/products/jsp`
- `http://java.sun.com/products/jsp/`
- `http://192.18.97.137/products/jsp/`
- `http://java.sun.com:80/products/jsp/index.html#Bottom`
- `http://java.sun.com/products/jsp/index.html?name1=value1`

Notice that in the first example I left out the `http://`. Most browsers will assume that you are using Hypertext Transfer Protocol (HTTP) and will prefix your URL with the `http://` string. Visit `http://www.w3.org/Protocols/` for more information about HTTP.

Let's look at the sections that make up a URL. A reference list of the methods is in Appendix C, "Using Java Methods to Retrieve CGI Environment Variables."

Scheme: `request.getScheme()`

This describes what scheme was used to access a resource. In our examples above, the `http` scheme was used. However, saving the page as an HTML file to our hard drive and viewing the file at a later time would make use of the `file` scheme. Other schemes include `ftp` and `https`.

Server Name: `request.getServerName()`

This value is the actual address of the server on the Web that is delivering the requested resource. The address is represented with four sets of numbers in the range 0 to 255, with each set separated by a dot (`.`). The address might instead be represented by a domain name that is mapped to the number series. The domain name typically runs in the format of `machine.domain.domainType`, where `machine` is the computer name, `domain` is the entity that the machine belongs to, and `domainType` specifies the type of entity the domain is. Typical entity types are `.com` (commercial), `.edu` (educational), `.gov` (governmental), `.mil` (military), `.net` (network), and `.org` (organization).

Port Number: `request.getServerPort()`

Port numbers are used by TCP/IP to allow clients to specify a particular program on the server. The range of values can be from `0` to `65535`, with well-known or reserved ports ranging from `0` to `1023`. The default value of `80` is assumed if no port number is entered in the request.

Script Name: `request.getRequestURI()`

This is the virtual path of the request being made. It is between the first `/` after the server name and the query string `?`. This is commonly used by a form to refer the `ACTION` attribute back to itself.

Filename and Extension: `request.getServletPath()`

This information is included with the script name and can be determined by reading past the last forward slash (`/`). Most resources served by Web servers are HTML files, with an `.htm` or `.html` file extension, but other file types, such as executables, multimedia, and other text formats, can be served as well. If a valid directory is requested without a filename, the Web server will traverse through its default document list and serve the first file it finds in the list. However, if no document is found, the Web server has the option to display the directory listings or deny permission to see the listing.

Query String: `request.getQueryString()`

This will be covered in greater detail later in the chapter. Essentially, a query string helps pass name/value pairs from one request to another.

HTML Anchor: Client-Side Functionality

This is an attribute of the `<A>` tag in HTML. If `#someAnchor` is present in the URL, the browser will look for `<A NAME="someAnchor">` and scroll the page to the location of the tag.

Using the GET Method

HTTP methods such as GET indicate what actions are to be performed on the resource being requested. All the links mentioned in this chapter are GET requests. You might be concerned that the GET method could serve the source code of your JSP file, including sensitive database information, to the browser. Provided that the JSP engine is configured properly, it will process the JSP source code into HTML before the response is ever sent back to the browser. Any information going to a GET method page will be posted in the URL as part of the query string.

Using Query Strings

HTTP provides the capability to append extra information to the end of a URL. This bit of extra information in the URL is referred to as the query string and is flagged by a question mark (?) at the beginning. The query string comes in the form `name1=value1&name2=value2`. `name1` can be any name you assign it so that the request can refer back to retrieve any value in place of `value1`. The ampersand (&) represents the delimiter or separator for the request to start processing the next name/value pair. Typical uses for query strings include feeding search words to search engines, passing non-sensitive client information for form processing, and managing session state (see Chapter 10, "Managing Session States"). In Figure 6.1, you can see the query string `?fruit=watermelon&fruit=mango&fruit=kiwi`, with `fruit=watermelon` as the first name/value pair, `fruit=mango` as the second pair, and `fruit=kiwi` as the third.

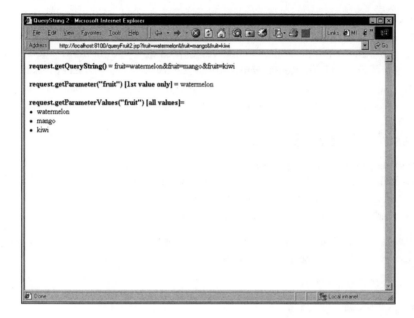

FIGURE 6.1
Recognizing query strings.

Generating Query Strings

To reach the URL in Figure 6.1, all I did was click a link found on the previous request,
`queryFruit1.jsp`. Listing 6.1 shows what the JSP source looks like.

LISTING 6.1   `queryFruit1.jsp` Query String Link

```
<HTML>
<HEAD><TITLE>Query String 1</TITLE></HEAD>
<BODY>

My favorite fruit is
<LI><A HREF='queryFruit2.jsp?fruit=watermelon'>watermelon</A>
<LI><A HREF='queryFruit2.jsp?fruit=mango'>mango</A>
<LI><A HREF='queryFruit2.jsp?fruit=kiwi'>kiwi</A>
<LI><A HREF='queryFruit2.jsp?fruit=watermelon&fruit=mango&fruit=kiwi'>
   [Multiple values] Heck, it's too hard to decide, I like
   watermelon <B>&amp;</B>
   mango <B>&amp;</B>
   kiwi</A>

</BODY>
</HTML>
```

Do you recognize the query string from Figure 6.1 at the fourth <LI> tag? This link reference looks like any other link that you might encounter, except that I have manually appended the query string information to the end. Another way to pass query string information is via the GET method of a form. The name and value from each form <INPUT>, <SELECT>, and <TEXTAREA> tag will be written to the end of the URL as a query string name/value pair. We will discuss working with forms in the next chapter.

Processing Query Strings

Merely passing in the query string as part of the request doesn't necessarily do you any good. If you forcefully request a URL with your own set of name/value pairs and the page doesn't need the names for anything, they are simply ignored. Likewise, passing fruit=kiwi to a page that doesn't read in the fruit name won't affect the page generation.

So how do we read in fruit and its values? Seeing that the query string is part of a request, the Request object fills the need by providing the following methods:

getParameter(String name)

getParameterValues(String name)

getParameterNames()

getParameter(String name)

The getParameter() method requires that you pass in the name of the name/value pair in order to retrieve the value. If you have multiple values passed to the same name, the getParameter() will return only the first value. In the above example, getParameter(fruit) will return only watermelon. Secondly, the value returned will always be of type String or null. For instance, if you wrote

String f = request.getParameter(fruit);

and fruit were nowhere to be found in the query string, the null object would be evaluated and assigned to f. Alternatively, if you had just myNumber= in the query string with no value to the right of the equal sign, an empty string would be returned.

> ### Retrieving Numbers in the Query String
> Passing in myNumber=8 as part of the query string and assigning
> ```
>     int num = request.getParameter(myNumber);
> ```
> will generate a compilation error if you try to run it. It will complain that the left side (int) of the assignment is not compatible with the type on the right side (String). How do we work around this? Essentially, we will use the integer's parseInt(String) method to convert whatever String value we get back.

```
    int num = Integer.parseInt(request.getParameter(myNumber));
or
    int num;
    String tempVal = request.getParameter(myNumber);
    if( (tempVal!=null) && (!tempVal.trim().equals()) ) {
        num = Integer.parseInt(tempVal);
    }
```

getParameterValues(String name)

What if there is more than one value assigned to the parameter? For parameters containing multiple values, calling the getParameter(*some_name*) method will return only the first value in the list. To get all the values associated with a particular name, you will need to use getParameterValues(*some_name*), which returns a String array of all possible values. Listing 6.2 shows the source for queryFruit2.jsp, which handles single- and multiple-parameter values for fruit.

LISTING 6.2   queryFruit2.jsp Processing Parameters

```
<%
// Assign the default value for fruit
String fruit = "";

// Retrieve a String array for all values passed in for "fruit"
String[] fruits = request.getParameterValues("fruit");

// Assign fruits an array size of ZERO so the loop at the bottom
➡ doesn't fail upon null
if( fruits == null ) { fruits = new String[0]; }
%>

<HTML>
<HEAD><TITLE>Query String 2</TITLE></HEAD>
<BODY>

<B>request.getQueryString() =</B> <%=request.getQueryString() %><P>

<B>request.getParameter("fruit") [1st value only] =</B> <%=request.
➡getParameter("fruit") %><P>

<B>request.getParameterValues("fruit") [all values]=</B>
<%// Loop through each of the "fruit" name/parameter received
```

LISTING 6.2   Continued

```
for( int i=0; i<fruits.length; i++ ) { %>
   <LI><%=fruits[i] %>
<% } %>

</BODY>
</HTML>
```

getParameterNames()

Both the getParameter() and getParameters() methods take the name of the parameter in order to retrieve the value. What if you want to process a list of 10, 25, or even 100 name/value pairs passed in from form fields? Performing getParameter() or getParameters() for each field would be very time consuming and inefficient. Fortunately, the Request object is equipped with the getParameterNames() method, which returns an Enumeration object that lets you loop over all the parameter names that were passed in the request. We won't be covering this method much, but here is how you would loop through the parameters to get all the names and associated values.

```
<%@ page import="java.util.Enumeration" %>
<%
// Make sure to import the Enumeration object
for( Enumeration e=request.getParameterNames(); e.hasMoreElements(); )
{
   String name = (String) e.nextElement();
   String[] values = request.getParameterValues( name );
   String valueList = "";
   // Loop through all values associated with this name
   for( int i=0; i<values.length; i++) {
      valueList += values[i] + ", ";
   }
   out.println("<P>" + name + " = " + valueList);
}
%>
```

Escaping URLs

Perhaps we want to insert green grapes as the second choice in our list of favorite fruits. We will need to add it to the list containing all the other fruits. You might be inclined to just cut and paste the first line and swap out watermelon for green grapes. Let's do the swap and insert fruit=green grapes to the query string of the entry with multiple values. After you save your changes as queryFruit3.jsp, your code should look something like that shown in Listing 6.3.

LISTING 6.3   Partial Listing of `queryFruit3.jsp`, with `green grapes`

```
My favorite fruit is
<LI><A HREF='queryFruit2.jsp?fruit=watermelon'>watermelon</A>
<LI><A HREF='queryFruit2.jsp?fruit=green grapes'>green grapes</A>
<LI><A HREF='queryFruit2.jsp?fruit=mango'>mango</A>
<LI><A HREF='queryFruit2.jsp?fruit=kiwi'>kiwi</A>
<LI><A HREF='queryFruit2.jsp?fruit=watermelon&fruit=green grapes
➥&fruit=mango&fruit=kiwi'>
   [Multiple values] Heck, it's too hard to decide, I like
   watermelon <B>&amp;</B>
   green grapes <B>&amp;</B>
   mango <B>&amp;</B>
   kiwi</A>
```

At this point, request the `queryFruit3.jsp` page and click the `green grapes` link. If you have the option, try it on both Microsoft Internet Explorer and Netscape Communicator. The result for Internet Explorer should look like Figure 6.2, and the result for Communicator should look like Figure 6.3.

FIGURE 6.2
Internet Explorer automatically encodes the query string, providing the expected result of `green grapes`.

FIGURE 6.3

Communicator misinterprets the query string because it was not encoded.

You might be surprised by the different values retrieved when performing getParameter(fruit). What's more important is that the value passed by Communicator was misinterpreted, thus only reading green for fruit and stopping at the space. However, what you were expecting was green grapes as the value. The reason for this is that some browsers automatically encode the URL before sending it to the server, while others do not. By URL encoding, I mean that some characters in the URL, such as spaces, ~, /, =, and others, might not be read properly by the request unless they are replaced, or *escaped*, in a Request-friendly format. Table 6.1 provides the characters to escape.

TABLE 6.1   Common Character Encoding

Character	Escape Sequence
space	%20 or + symbol
~	%7E
!	%21
@	%40
#	%23
$	%24

TABLE 6.1 Continued

Character	Escape Sequence
%	%25
^	%5E
&	%26
*	none required
(	%28
)	%29
- (dash)	none required
+	%2B
=	%3D
_ (underscore)	none required
[	%5B
]	%5D
{	%7B
}	%7D
:	%3A
;	%3B
'	%60
"	%22
<	%3C
>	%3E
?	%3F
/	%2F
\	%5C
|	%7C

As you can see, all escape sequences start with a percent sign (%) and are followed by two characters, which represent the character's ASCII hexadecimal equivalent. To avoid processing the wrong values by misinterpreting the query string information, you should try to memorize the entire table above and replace the character with the escape sequence. Sounds unreasonable? It probably is. Fortunately, ever since JDK 1.0, there has been a URLEncoder class that does the escaping for you. This class can be found in the java.net package and contains only one method, encode(String s). The s argument that it takes is any string that you want to encode. In this case (see Listing 6.4), we will insert green grapes so that it can be properly encoded.

LISTING 6.4   queryFruit4.jsp URL Encoding Values

```
<%@ page import="java.net.URLEncoder" %>
<HTML>
<HEAD><TITLE>Query String 4</TITLE></HEAD>
<BODY>

My favorite fruit is
<LI><A HREF='queryFruit2.jsp?fruit=watermelon'>watermelon</A>
<LI><A HREF='queryFruit2.jsp?fruit=<%=URLEncoder.encode("green grapes")%>'>
➥green grapes</A>
<LI><A HREF='queryFruit2.jsp?fruit=mango'>mango</A>
<LI><A HREF='queryFruit2.jsp?fruit=kiwi'>kiwi</A>
<LI><A HREF='/d/queryFruit2.jsp?fruit=watermelon&fruit=<%=URLEncoder.
➥encode("green grapes")%>&fruit=mango&fruit=kiwi'>
    [Multiple values] Heck, it's too hard to decide, I like
    watermelon <B>&amp;</B>
    green grapes <B>&amp;</B>
    mango <B>&amp;</B>
    kiwi</A>

</BODY>
</HTML>
```

Notice that you need to manually import the URLEncoder class for use in this page, because by default JSP imports only the packages java.lang.*, javax.servlet.*, javax.servlet.jsp.*, and javax.servlet.http.*. Netscape Communicator will now properly pass the query string information for green grapes for both links. Figure 6.4 shows the result of selecting the last link of queryFruit4.jsp.

You may wonder why not bypass the hassle of importing the URLEncoder class altogether and simply insert a + sign between green and grape, since we know that the space needs to be escaped. If you know exactly what the query string will look like, then you are welcome to do so. You must remember that it's not just a matter of converting spaces into plus signs.

Imagine a case in which your strings are dynamically generated via a database (see Chapter 8, "Interacting with Databases"). You may not know if all the values are alphanumeric. Just to be sure, you have the option to encode them using the URLEncoder class.

FIGURE 6.4

A query string that has been properly passed.

Linking JSP to HTML, JSP, and Servlets with `<jsp:forward>`

The main purpose of `<jsp:forward>` is to direct the request to another resource, such as another JSP page.

Two features you will also find useful are

1. The request is not redirected to the browser. Instead, the original request is flushed and the Response object is reset. However, the query string information will be preserved and can be read by the new destination. The newly forwarded page can also process any `<jsp:param>` parameters that were set when the original request was forwarded. This saves a trip back to the browser.

2. Because of the above, the newly forwarded page will be processed and displayed, but the URL in the browser's address bar will not change. For those who consider this a disadvantage there is `response.sendRedirect( String location );`, which will send the response back to the browser; the newly processed URL will be shown in the Address/Location field of the browser to notify the user that his request was redirected. The advantage of masking the URL might be to conceal direct access to a particular resource such as a servlet, image, or another JSP page.

NOTE

Be careful of relative links in the page you are forwarding to. Because the browser has not changed the URL, it still thinks that relative links in the destination page are relative to the URL. For instance, `/doForward.jsp` performing a `<jsp:forward>` to `/dir/subdir/page1.jsp` will cause any relative link, such as `<A HREF='page2.jsp'>`, to be requested from `/`.

The syntax for the `jsp:forward` standard action is as follows:

```
<jsp:forward page= relativeURLspec />
```

and

```
<jsp:forward page= urlSpec>
   <jsp:param name=" name" value=" value" />
</jsp:forward>
```

The `relativeURLspec` can be any static resource (HTML, text file, image, and so on), JSP page, or Java Servlet that is in the same application context as the current page. Also, recall that the `forward` action allows the `relativeURLspec` to be evaluated at runtime. This means that you do not have to hard-code the page to which the request will be forwarded.

NOTE

Application context refers to the application's working environment. The concept of a WAR (Web application archive) file was introduced in JSP 1.1. This serves as a means of organizing your HTML, JSP, servlets, images, and so on into a single file to be deployed by JSP/Servlet engines such as JRun. During deployment, you will be prompted for the URL root of the application where browsers will be able to access the application. The `<jsp:forward>` tag allows you to forward only to another resource of the same application. Therefore, if you have an application rooted at /myApp1, and another application is rooted on the same server but at /storeApp, then any JSP in the application /myApp1 can forward only to resources defined in /myApp1. Attempting to forward a page in /myApp1 to any resource in /storeApp will result in an error.

Forwarding to HTML and JSP

It is not uncommon for a Web site to redesign its layout several times a year. Usually there is a specific launch date for the new design, and not exposing the location of the new site layout until then is key for some. Let's assume that the new layout is complete and loaded to the production server. The launch date is in five days, but you are set to go on a two-week vacation starting tomorrow. You are the sole control of the Web site and don't trust anyone else to set index.html to redirect to /newSite/new.jsp using the <META> tag, as follows:

```
<META HTTP-EQUIV="refresh" content="0; URL=/newSite/new.jsp">
```

Do you postpone the vacation that was scheduled three years ago? No way! You create a new index.jsp that forwards all incoming requests to the current index.html page up to the second of the launch date and forwards all requests to the new site layout the second the launch date arrives. However, you will need to change the default document of the Web server to load index.jsp if it is not already set up to do so. Listing 6.5 shows what index.jsp would look like.

LISTING 6.5   index.jsp jsp:forward by Date

```
<%@ page import="java.util.*" %>
<%
// Example usage of runtime evaluation of the page being forwarded to
String newSiteLocation = "newSite/new.jsp";

Calendar todayCal = Calendar.getInstance();
Calendar launchCal = Calendar.getInstance();

// Set the date to reveal the new site down to the second
// Mar 25th, 2000 - Arguments: year, month (0 based: Jan=0), date, hour,
➡ minute, and second
launchCal.set( 2000, 2, 25, 0, 0, 0 );

Date todayDate = todayCal.getTime();
Date launchDate = launchCal.getTime();
```

LISTING 6.5   Continued

```
// Compare today with the launch date
// Values returned for compareTo: -1 = before, 0 = same, 1 = after
int compVal = todayDate.compareTo(launchDate);
if( compVal >= 0 ) { // on launch date or after %>
    <jsp:forward page="<%=newSiteLocation %>" />
<% } else { // not launch date yet, go to current index.html page %>
    <jsp:forward page="index.html" />
<% } %>
```

The steps needed to automatically schedule JSP forwarding to a different source are as follows:

1. You will need to import Java's utility package because of the use of the Calendar and Date classes.

2. Set the location of the new site as String variable newSiteLocation. This is mainly to show <jsp:forward>'s flexibility to evaluate the page value during runtime.

3. We now create two Calendar instances, one for the current date and one for the date of the launch.

4. The Calendar object can be manipulated to reference a particular date with its set() method. We will use the full-blown set method that takes the year, month, date, minute, and second arguments.

5. Since the Calendar class doesn't offer a versatile compare method and the Date class does, we need to create two Date objects based on the Calendar objects that we've created and then use Date's compareTo(Date d) method.

6. compareTo returns only one possible int value. A negative value, usually -1, indicates that the argument Date is newer than the Date calling the compareTo method. A value of 0 means that the two Date objects are equal. Any positive value, usually 1, indicates the argument Date has already passed.

The logic we apply in determining which page to forward will be based on the int value returned by the compareTo method. If the current date is on (0) or after (1) the specified launch date, the page will be forwarded to the new layout page.

Forwarding to Servlets

At the time this book is being written, the JSP specification is 1.1 and the current servlet specification is 2.2. This means that servlet development was well on it's way before a complete JSP specification came along.

Picture a company using servlets to build its site because either JSP isn't around at all or JSP 0.92 isn't considered mature enough to use in a production environment. Imagine further that a request for the home page of the site (`www.somesite.com`) can read cookies being sent by the browser to provide personalized content. It is likely that the Web server has a default document of `index.html` that redirects to the `/servlet/Personalize` URI via the `<META>` tag refresh, located in the `<HEAD>` tag.

```
<META HTTP-EQUIV="refresh" content="0; URL=/servlet/Personalize">
```

Enter `jsp:forward`. The second the company installs or upgrades its servlet engine to Servlet 2.2–compliant with JSP 1.0+ support, it can add `index.jsp` as the Web server's top default document and insert the following line in `index.jsp` to forward the request to the personalization servlet:

```
<jsp:forward page="/servlet/Personalize" />
```

This example would be pretty simple to implement. Listing 6.6 shows an example of passing parameters via the `<jsp:param>` tag to a servlet named `WhereAmI`.

LISTING 6.6   `jspForwardServlet.jsp`

```
<jsp:forward page="/servlet/WhereAmI?param2=query string passed from the jsp:
➥forward standard action" >
        <jsp:param name="param1" value="this was passed using the
➥jsp:param standard action" />
</jsp:forward>
```

Note that the URL in Figure 6.5 is `http://localhost:8100/jspForwardServlet.jsp?param3=querystring+of+the+current+URL`, but the actual resource served is `/servlet/WhereAmI`.

Another thing to look at here is the order in which the parameters are read. The `<jsp:param>` parameter seems to take precedence, followed by the query string parameter found in the `<jsp:forward>` tag. Finally, the query string parameter from the URL is processed.

Listing 6.7 is the servlet source code that generated Figure 6.5.

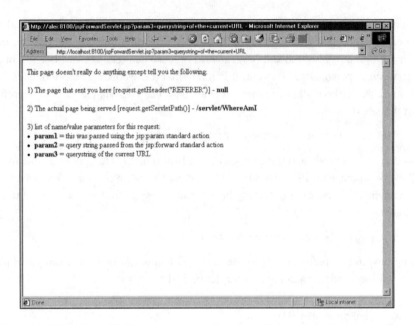

FIGURE 6.5

This JSP is really forwarded to a servlet.

LISTING 6.7   WhereAmI.java Servlet Source Code

```java
import java.io.*;
import java.util.Enumeration;
import javax.servlet.*;
import javax.servlet.http.*;

public class WhereAmI extends HttpServlet {
   public void service( HttpServletRequest request, HttpServletResponse
➡ response )
      throws ServletException, IOException
   {
      response.setContentType( "text/html" );
      PrintWriter out = response.getWriter();

      out.println("This page doesn't really do anything except tell you the
➡following:<P>");
      out.println("1) The page that sent you here [request.getHeader
➡ (\"REFERER\")] - <B>" + request.getHeader("REFERER") +"</B><P>");
      out.println("2) The actual page being served [request.getRequestURI()] -
➡ <B>" + request.getRequestURI() + "</B><P>" );
```

LISTING 6.7   Continued

```
out.println("3) list of name/value parameters for this URI: ");
for( Enumeration e=request.getParameterNames(); e.hasMoreElements(); )
{
    String name = (String) e.nextElement();
    String value = request.getParameter( name );
    out.println("<LI><B>" + name + "</B> = " + value);
}
}
}
```

The compile `WhereAmI.class` file has been included with the book. However, if you modify `WhereAmI.java` and recompile, remember to place the class file in a directory where the JSP/Servlet engine can load it.

Connecting pages and passing information between them can be easily done in JSP. The capability to mask the URL being requested with `<jsp:forward>` comes in handy as well.

Working with Forms

IN THIS CHAPTER

In the previous chapter, we learned how to connect pages by passing data in the query string and processing the data on the following page. However, the mechanisms for doing so were hyperlinks and predefined query strings. This chapter will extend the concept of passing information from one page to another via HTML forms. Forms allow the user to dynamically pass data from one page to another as opposed to presetting the hyperlinks with static query strings. The following items will be covered in this chapter:

- Using Form Controls
- Processing Form Values
- Populating the Form Dynamically
- Considering Frames

Using Form Controls

Forms seem to be a way of life in our society. Ever applied for a driver's license? There was a form that you needed to fill out so that your information is kept on file. Most likely there was a data entry person or scanning software to enter all the information into a centralized database accessible by law enforcement and motor vehicle employees outside of your local area. This way of life has carried over to the Internet, where companies offering online services want you to register for the program to have you on file. You might then be targeted with advertisements, updates, special promotions, and so on.

In addition to the traditional text fields, check boxes, and text areas found on paper, HTML also provides password fields, hidden fields, drop-down menus, and others. All form controls are basically governed by five main HTML tags.

With the introduction of cascading style sheets (CSS) in fourth-generation browsers, both Internet Explorer and Netscape Communicator support the CLASS and ID tag attributes for most form controls. Because our main concern in this chapter is the retrieval and display of form values, we will be focusing only on the essential tag attributes such as TYPE, NAME, VALUE, control state(SELECTED and CHECKED), and a few others.

Many of the code examples we will use for the form controls are taken from car_drawing.jsp, available on the accompanying CD-ROM. Figure 7.1 displays car_drawing.jsp and shows what many of the different controls look like.

<FORM> Tag

This tag is the starting point for all your form controls. Because you can have more than one form per page, you will need to wrap an ending </FORM> tag around all the controls you want to submit for a particular form. For the form for car_drawing.jsp, the <FORM> tag looks like the following:

```
<FORM NAME='form1' ACTION='car_drawing.jsp'>
```

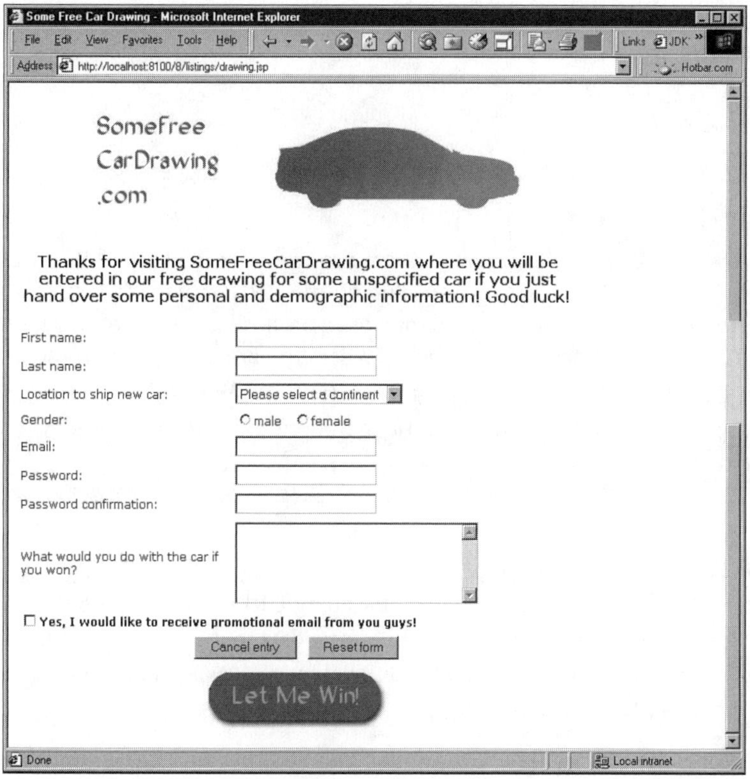

FIGURE 7.1

car_drawing.jsp *demonstrating the use of multiple form controls.*

ACTION **Attribute**

This attribute defines where to submit the form values for processing. The value for this attribute is usually a URL, such as a servlet, JSP, or email address. The following are some examples of this:

```
<FORM ACTION="/servlet/ProcessSomeForm">
<FORM ACTION="/cart.jsp">
<FORM ACTION="/cart.jsp?function=add&x=val2">
<FORM ACTION="<%=request.getRequestURI()%>">
<FORM ACTION="mailto:me@myEmail.com">
```

In the third example, notice the additional query string information that we are passing in the URL. This is completely valid and extremely useful when you want to pass information along to the processing page. The fourth example demonstrates using an expression to evaluate the

URL. When using an email ACTION, resulting email will simply have all the form controls listed in a name=value format, such as the following:

```
item=fries
size=SuperDuperBig
```

Set It and Forget It!

Using the request URI is a very common practice to create portable JSP forms. The portability is found when copying or renaming the JSP. This way, the ACTION is directed to itself, no matter what the name of this form, because it is evaluated at runtime. This saves a lot of development headaches when you are trying something new but keep getting the wrong results because you are submitting to the incorrect ACTION.

The catch is that this only works if you have designed the form to display and process on the same page.

ENCTYPE Attribute (Optional)

Encoding was covered to some degree under "Escaping URLs" in Chapter 6, "Connecting Pages." The default encoding format for sending form data to the server is *application/x-www-form-urlencoded*. This covers any additional query string parameters you might have specified in the ACTION attribute as well.

Just about the only time you will have to explicitly specify the ENCTYPE is when you are dealing with file uploads. In this case, you will need to set the following:

```
<FORM ACTION="/servlet/SomeFileUpload" ENCTYPE="multipart/form-data"
➥METHOD="post">
```

METHOD Attribute (Optional)

This attribute tells the browser how to send the form data to the server. The default method is GET, and it simply appends all form data to the ACTION URL as query string name/value pairs to be sent all at once. The other method is POST, which sends the form data in a separate transmission after a successful contact with the ACTION URL. When dealing with the following situations, I suggest using the GET method:

- Only a couple of fields need to be passed in the submission, such as a search engine word. The amount of data is an issue because some browsers will not support more than 255 characters in the URL, while others support up to 32,000 characters. If you know in advance that a large sum of data needs to be passed to the server, use the POST method instead.
- When you need to view what is actually being passed without writing a debug servlet or JSP. Being able to quickly pick out what was passed in the URL is a nice option to have.

- You should only use GET when security is not an issue. The GET method allows anyone viewing the screen to see all the data that has just been submitted. To keep passwords confidential, the POST method should always be used when submitting login forms.

NAME Attribute (Optional)

As you will see, most form controls that deal with transmitting data will need a NAME so that you can perform a request.getParameter("name") to extract the value for processing. However, the FORM sets this attribute as optional.

TARGET Attribute (Optional)

Use this attribute to define which frame cell should be used to display the results of the form submission. The default is to display the results to itself. We will be covering uses for this attribute in the "Considering Frames" section of this chapter.

> **NOTE**
>
> Netscape will be really picky and will not render any of your form items at all if you don't have the <FORM> tag.

<INPUT> Tag

You will be using this for the majority of your forms because <INPUT> encompasses a good portion of the controls. To distinguish one control from the next, you will need to provide a required TYPE attribute. The available types are covered in the following sections. Another required attribute for all INPUT tags is the NAME attribute. This needs to be supplied so that the server can retrieve the value associated with the name. The basic INPUT syntax should look like the following:

```
<INPUT TYPE='someType' NAME='someName' ATTRIBUTE1='someAttribute'>
```

Controls with additional required attributes will be covered on an individual basis. Unlike most HTML tags, the closing </INPUT> tag is not required.

Buttons

This control allows you to create a pushbutton that is primarily used for client-side script triggering. Clicking this type of button will not necessarily submit the form unless you have scripted the button to do so using JavaScript's document.formName.submit() function via the onClick attribute.

Common uses for this control include the following:

- Providing a control for the user to cancel the current form and return to one location before encountering the form using onClick='history.back(-1);'.

- Same as the previous use, except that you send the user to a specific location, such as /home/index.jsp.
- Mimicking the Submit button and writing your own function, such as validate(), which checks the form before calling the document.formName.submit() function.

The typical syntax for buttons is as follows:

```
<INPUT TYPE='button' NAME='notPassedToServer' VALUE='someDisplayValue'
➥onClick='JavaScript_function()'>
```

We use a button to cancel out of the car_drawing.jsp form as follows:

```
<INPUT TYPE='button' VALUE='Cancel entry' onClick='history.back(-1);'>
```

VALUE (Required)

The VALUE attribute determines the caption that shows up on the button. The button will still work without it, but a button without a caption telling what it does is pretty much useless.

onClick (Optional)

This is the most common event-based attribute used for the BUTTON type. onClick instructs JavaScript to be executed when the user clicks the button. Other event-based attributes include onFocus and onBlur.

Check Boxes

Check boxes provide a great interface to the user for checking and unchecking options. You can even group them by giving them all the same NAME attribute. The following code demonstrates how check boxes can be grouped together:

```
<B>Which of the following item(s) interest you?</B>
<BR>
<INPUT TYPE='checkbox' NAME='question1' VALUE='1A'> BIG burger
<INPUT TYPE='checkbox' NAME='question1' VALUE='1B'> Tongue-scalding fries
<INPUT TYPE='checkbox' NAME='question1' VALUE='1C'> Cool Cola
```

For our car drawing, we use a standalone check box to ask if the user would like email from us. The following is the code for our check box:

```
<INPUT TYPE='checkbox' NAME='send_promo'>
```

CHECKED (Optional)

Specifying this attribute simply marks the check box with a check when the page is first loaded. The omission of this attribute will leave the check box empty as its initial state.

VALUE (Required)

If you do not provide a value to the check box, it will be processed as "null" or "on" (checked). Unchecked check boxes are simply ignored. When there are many check box options, trying to match up which one was "on" is more error prone than reading a set of named values, such as question1=1A,& question1=1C.

Be careful not to assume that the value you supply will show up to the user in the HTML form. Although text and button form controls will display the VALUE attribute to the user upon viewing the form, other controls, such as check boxes, radio buttons, and drop-down menus, will not. To present a description associated with the check box, you will need to furnish additional text that will go alongside the <INPUT> tag.

File

This control will render a text field beside a Browse button. You can enter the path and file-name directly into the text field or use the interactive file chooser by clicking the button. To properly send the file and not just the filename to the server, you will need to set the form's ENCTYPE attribute to mutltipart/form-data as discussed in the <FORM> tag section.

The following are some common uses for this control:

- Uploading attachments in a Web-based email system.
- Uploading images and other browser-friendly files for administering Web pages. Web-based source control could fall into this category as well.
- A student uploading homework to his account to be reviewed by a professor.

VALUE (Ignored)

While most other controls allow you to specify the default value, the browser will simply ignore the VALUE attribute for security reasons. This was done to prevent malicious sites from attempting to upload files with sensitive information from an unsuspecting user. Only the user can identify which file to upload to the server.

hidden Fields

As the label implies, the name and value of this field is hidden from the user's view. However, if the user performs a View Source on the page, he can still see the tag and its attributes. This is an excellent way to pass information from one page to the next without the user knowing and without the risk of the user modifying the value. Typical uses for hidden fields include the following:

- Serving as an alternative to passing form information via the FORM tag's ACTION attribute by appending name/value pairs as a query string. Instead of

  ```
  <FORM ACTION="/cart.jsp?function=add&x=val2">
  ```

  you might want to use

  ```
  <FORM ACTION="/cart.jsp">
  <INPUT TYPE='hidden' NAME='function' VALUE='add'>
  <INPUT TYPE='hidden' NAME='x' VALUE='val2'>
  ```

7

WORKING WITH FORMS

- Including information acquired by a previous form when a very long form is broken down into several smaller forms. Due to HTTP's stateless nature, the current form will not be able to submit the data from the previous form along with the current one unless they are all passed in the same form. The only way to do this without asking the same questions all over again is to subtly include them as hidden fields. The current form might look something like the following:

```
<%String fullName = request.getParameter("fullName");
String zipCode = request.getParameter("zipCode"); %>

<FORM ACTION='IQtest3.jsp' METHOD='post'>
<INPUT TYPE='hidden' NAME='fullName' VALUE='<%=fullName%>'>
<INPUT TYPE='hidden' NAME='zipCode' VALUE='<%=zipCode%>'>

<H3>Part 2 of IQ test</H3>
What color is an orange?
<INPUT TYPE='text' NAME='question1'>
<P>
A garage is to a car as a house is to what?
<INPUT TYPE='text' NAME='question2'>
</FORM>
```

- Generating the state of the form. In addition to the previous use, it is common to pass the current state of the form, such as whether or not it has already been submitted.

The syntax of the hidden field is as follows:

```
<INPUT TYPE='hidden' NAME='someName' VALUE='someValue'>
```

In car_drawing.jsp, we use the following hidden field:

```
<INPUT TYPE='hidden' NAME='form_version' VALUE='1.0.a'>
```

VALUE (Required)
You will need to incorporate the VALUE attribute when using the hidden type or there really is no reason to use the hidden type. The value itself may be blank, however.

Image Type
There are essentially three form controls that allow you to submit the form. TYPE='button' (through JavaScript) and TYPE='submit' are basically buttons with a text label. They are covered in their respective sections. If having a plain button does not suit your site design, you have the option to incorporate an image as the submit trigger.

The NAME of the image by itself will not be submitted in the form data. Instead, the cursor position where the user clicked the image will be submitted in the format of the NAME.x and NAME.y. These positions are relative to the upper-left (0,0) position of the image.

The car drawing form uses an image to submit the form. To use the image that says Let Me Win!, we used the following code:

```
<INPUT TYPE='image' SRC='images/let_me_win.jpg' BORDER=0>
```

ALIGN

This attribute sets the alignment of text near the image. It is used essentially in the same way as the ALIGN attribute is used with an <IMAGE> tag. Possible values are TOP, MIDDLE, ABSMIDDLE, BOTTOM, ABSBOTTOM, LEFT, and RIGHT, with BOTTOM being the default value.

SRC (Required)

SRC points to the URL of the image you want to display.

VALUE (Ignored)

The VALUE attribute is simply ignored, because only the x and y coordinates where the image was clicked will be submitted to the server.

Password Fields

If you have ever used an Automated Teller Machine (ATM) at the bank, you were probably prompted for a Personal Identification Number (PIN). As you keyed in the numbers, only asterisks (*) were echoed to the screen. This was done to protect you from people nearby who might attempt to write down your PIN to gain access to your account. HTML has provided a similar security precaution. Through the use of the password type, you can create forms that will mask the user's secret PIN or password by having a special character, such as an asterisk, appear onscreen instead of the actual text being entered. Figure 7.2 shows how the password fields echo asterisks.

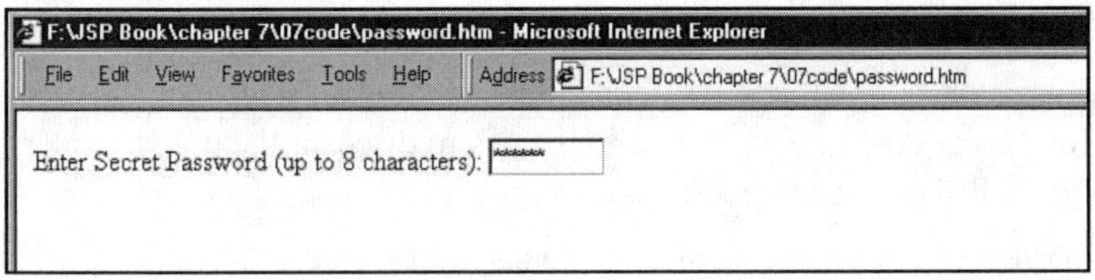

Figure 7.2

The Password field masked my abc123 *entry as* ******.

The following code produced the password field:

```
Enter Secret Password (up to 8 characters):
<INPUT TYPE='password' NAME='pass' SIZE=8 MAXLENGTH=8>
```

MAXLENGTH (Optional)

This attribute sets the maximum number of characters the browser will accept for the input field. There is no default size.

SIZE (Optional)

This sets the width of the field in characters. The default size is around 20 characters for Internet Explorer and Netscape.

VALUE (Optional, Not Advised)

It is not advised to provide this attribute when using password fields. Although the value will still be masked onscreen, a person viewing the HTML source will see the value in plain text. This opportunity will arise when the intended user steps away from the computer while some unauthorized person operates it.

> **NOTE**
>
> Special attention needs to be paid when using password fields. You should use POST as the METHOD of form submission so that the password does not appear in the URL after submission as a GET method would. Otherwise, you would be defeating the purpose of masking the entry in the first place.

Radio Buttons

You were introduced to check boxes earlier in the chapter. They allowed multiple values to be associated with one name. Radio buttons, on the other hand, allow association with only one value to a name at most. You can provide many choices to the user, but he can only check one, if any. To enforce this mutual exclusivity, checking one radio button will uncheck any previously checked button of the same name. Only the value of the one selected will be sent when the form is submitted.

Conventional uses for radio buttons are online polls, credit card selection, and color selection. In our form for the car drawing, we use radio buttons to discover the user's gender. The following code generated our gender radio buttons:

```
<TD><INPUT TYPE='radio' NAME='gender' VALUE='male'>male  
<INPUT TYPE='radio' NAME='gender' VALUE='female'>female</TD>
```

VALUE (Required)

Just like with check boxes, you will need to provide the value for your radio buttons. You will also need to provide some useful caption that will let the user know what he is selecting because the VALUE attribute is not rendered for display.

CHECKED (Optional)

If data from the radio button is required in your form, leaving it unchecked the first time around is a good idea. Reasons for doing this include the following:

- Users might be biased toward the prechecked radio button versus the other unchecked ones, thinking that it is the correct or preferred selection.

- The user might not have even seen the question and might have blindly submitted the form without knowing. This might throw off your statistical processing because the default selected value might have a higher percentage than it really should.

- After you check a radio button, you cannot uncheck it without checking another one. This forces the user to provide an answer even if he didn't intend to do so.

NOTE

You may have wondered why a form control would be called a *radio button*. If you have ever sat in a pre-1980 car, you might have seen the old-style radios on which you had to push in one of the preset buttons to select a station. Pressing another button will pop out the first one you pushed, and so on. The same concept was carried over to form controls, with the understanding that only one item can be checked at any given time.

7

WORKING WITH FORMS

Reset Button

The sole purpose of this control is to reset the form values to their original page load state upon clicking. The Reset button is never submitted to the server, so providing a NAME attribute is not necessary.

VALUE (Optional)

This attribute is for specifying the caption on the Reset button. The default is Reset.

Submit Button

As the name implies, this is the button that actually performs the submission of the form to the server. You can have more than one submit button per form. You might have seen some forms that do not provide a submit area, such as a button or image. This is because some browsers automatically identify the Enter key as a form submission. It is up to the developer to decide whether or not to provide a Submit button.

VALUE (Optional)

Just like the other buttons encountered in this chapter so far, the VALUE attribute will define the label displayed on the button. However, you can also use this value to distinguish which submit button was actually clicked when you have more than one submit button with the same NAME. This usually occurs when dealing with shopping cart items because you can provide functionality to either update the quantity of the item or simply delete it.

The default caption for the submit button is Submit Query.

Text Fields

Text fields may be the most commonly used form control of all. They are the default TYPE for the INPUT control. They serve as a simple mechanism for entering one-line, short answers. Common uses for text fields are to gather information such as the user's name, email address, phone number, and so on. Once again, we can turn to car_drawing.jsp to see an example of what we are talking about. We use text fields for first name, last name, and email address. The code for the text field for the first name is as follows:

```
<INPUT TYPE='text' NAME='first_name' VALUE=''>
```

Text fields are great when you need only a single word or line of text. For the more elaborate inputs, such as comments and instructions containing multiple lines, use the <TEXTAREA> tag, covered in a later section.

MAXLENGTH (Optional)

This attribute sets the maximum number of characters the browser will accept for the input field. There is no default size.

SIZE (Optional)

This sets the width of the field in characters. The default size is around 20 characters for Internet Explorer and Netscape.

VALUE (Optional)

This attribute sets the default value that you want to fill or refill the form when the page loads.

<TEXTAREA> Tag

As mentioned the earlier, <TEXTAREA> creates a text input area for entering and editing multiple lines of text. A <TEXTAREA> is often used for gathering user comments or for long answers because it offers an open area for typing or viewing text. This open area invites users to enter as much information as they desire.

A <TEXTAREA> must have a closing </TEXTAREA> tag. Any text typed between the two tags will be the default text to appear in the <TEXTAREA>. The syntax is as follows:

```
<TEXTAREA NAME="someName">Default text</TEXTAREA>
```

Before we give away our car, we want to find out what the winner is going to do with it. We use a text area to get the answer.

```
<TEXTAREA NAME='quote' COLS=30 ROWS=5></TEXTAREA>
```

A <TEXTAREA> is also used for displaying lengthy text in a scroll box. Disclaimers or contract terms are often displayed in a <TEXTAREA>. The READONLY attribute of the <TEXTAREA> causes the area to be uneditable.

COLS (Optional)

This attribute specifies how many columns wide the text area control will be.

ROWS (Optional)

Rows represent the height of the text area. The number specified will determine the number of rows of text the text area will display at one time.

WRAP (Optional)

This attribute determines how word wrapping inside the text area will be handled. The available options are OFF, PHYSICAL, and VIRTUAL. OFF is the default and disables word wrapping. PHYSICAL displays the text word-wrapped and submits it to the server in the same format. VIRTUAL displays the text word-wrapped but submits it as it was typed.

<SELECT> Tag (Drop-Down Lists)

The <SELECT> tag creates a drop-down menu list or a scrollable list box of options from which to choose. The list of options is created from the <OPTION> tags defined between the opening and closing <SELECT> tags. Declaring a SIZE attribute in the <SELECT> tag will create a list box instead of a drop-down menu. The SIZE attribute determines how many of the options will be visible at one time.

To give away a car, we must know the continent to which to ship it. We use a drop-down menu list to allow the entrant to select his home continent. Our select box is created as follows:

```
<SELECT NAME='continent'>
     <OPTION>Please select a continent  
     <OPTION VALUE='Antarctica'>Antarctica
     <OPTION VALUE='Africa'>Africa
     <OPTION VALUE='Asia'>Asia
     <OPTION VALUE='Europe'>Europe
     <OPTION VALUE='Australia'>Australia
     <OPTION VALUE='North America'>North America
     <OPTION VALUE='South America'>South America
     </SELECT>
```

<OPTION>

The <OPTION> tag is a child tag of the <SELECT> tag. Each <OPTION> denotes one item of the selectable list and declares the attributes of that selection.

VALUE (Required)

If you don't specify a value, some browsers will take the text next to the first <OPTION> tag and submit it as the value. This can be confusing at times when you are trying to validate the field and think that nothing was passed because no VALUE was specified. Instead, something along the lines of `Please select a...` is actually passed. The best thing to do is to continue checking against an empty string, but to specify an empty value as follows:

```
<OPTION VALUE=''>Please select one of the following real values</OPTION>
```

MULTIPLE

This attribute allows the control to accept multiple values through the same `<SELECT>` `<NAME>`. Users will be able to choose a list of options by holding down the Shift key or select individual options by holding the Ctrl key.

> **NOTE**
>
> `car_drawing.jsp` uses the JavaScript between the `<SCRIPT>` tags to serve as a user interface enhancement. When someone arrives at a form, his goal is probably to provide input. Why not make it easier by setting the keyboard focus to the first text field on the form? That way, the user doesn't have to find the location of the mouse to click the text field.

Processing Form Values

The file upload control is incredibly useful but, unfortunately, is hard to process. Whereas most form control values can be extracted via `request.getParameter("name")` and `request.getParameterValues("name")` (to be discussed further later in this chapter), reading in the actual file during upload will require writing a servlet or CGI program to scan the form data byte-by-byte and look for boundaries. This procedure goes well beyond the scope of this book. However, we have provided the following link for a file upload servlet:

```
http://home1.swipnet.se/~w-50670/yafus.html
```

> **CAUTION**
>
> Most file upload servlets are ideally used for files smaller than 10MB. Only really well-written ones support larger uploads without running out of memory.

If you have not familiarized yourself with the `getParameter(name)` and `getParamterValues(name)` of the `request` object already, you may want to do so before beginning this section.

As you might recall, `request.getParameter(name)` works wonders for items with a single value. This is great for text fields, password fields, textareas, radio buttons, single-value check boxes, single-value drop-down menus, and submit buttons. The only concern would be to check for a `null` value. Trouble appears, however, when applying the same method to a form that has multiple values associated with a check box or drop-down menu, because only the first value is recognized. Enter `request.getParameterValues(name)`. This can house multiple values of the same name into a `String` array. We can then loop through the array to retrieve the individual value to handle it. The following snippet of code might jog your memory:

```
<%
String[] fruits = request.getParameterValues("fruit");
if( fruits == null ) { fruits = new String[0]; }
for( int i=0; i<fruits.length; i++ ) { %>
        <LI><%=fruits[i] %>
<% } %>
```

But what if we had 10, 15, or even hundreds of these multiple-valued form controls, as you might find in a technical online test? It wouldn't make sense to have 100 sets of the previous code for `request.getParameterValues("Ques1");`, `request.getParameterValues("Ques2");`, and so on. Perhaps we can streamline it by writing it once as a method onto the page as a JSP declaration. Simply append the following lines of code to the end of `car_drawing.jsp` and save it as `car_drawing2.jsp`.

```
<%!
public String getValues( HttpServletRequest request, String name ) {
    String retVal = "";

    String values[] = request.getParameterValues( name );
    // No value was supplied
    if( values == null ) {
       // Do nothing, take retVal's default value;
    // Only one value supplied
    } else if( values.length == 1) {
       retVal = values[0];
    // Multiple values supplied return them all with a comma delimeter
    } else {
       for( int i=0; i<values.length; i++ ) {
          retVal += values[i] + ", ";
       }
    }

    return retVal;
}
%>
```

This method requires that you pass in the `request` object and the name of the parameter that you want to retrieve values from in exchange for a `String`. For instance, if you wanted to output the list of what interests the drawing entrant submitted, you would write the following:

```
<%=getValues( request, "interests" ) %>
```

In the first line of the method, we initialize a `String` named `retVal` as an empty string. This string will serve as a temporary placeholder for the final value that gets returned. We then initialize a `String` array called `values` to store the values of the targeted parameter. Any time you attempt to retrieve a parameter, the value can result in `null` if the user decides not to answer the question. Thus, the first possibility for `values` is `null`. If `values` is `null`, `retVal` is returned as an empty string, which indicates that no answer was given. Next we check for a single value answer. This will be the result for the majority of the input fields. For example, a text field that has been answered will return a single value. For single return values, our `retVal` is the first element of our `values` array. The last option is that `values` contains multiple answers. To deal with the answers as one element, we iterate through the array, pulling out each value and separating them with a comma. This gives us multiple answers in one return value.

There are different approaches to displaying the results. The path we will take here is the one that uses the same JSP to present the form and the results. You will see the importance of this approach in the next section when we are required to validate and dynamically populate the form.

Listing 7.1 is what `car_drawing2.jsp` looks like.

LISTING 7.1   Parts of `car_drawing2.jsp` That Differ from `car_drawing.jsp`

```
<%
String thisPage = request.getRequestURI();String displayData = "";
boolean bSuccess = false; // Flag for successful form submission

// Process the values if user submitted the form
if( "POST".equals(request.getMethod()) ) {
   bSuccess = true;

   // Set all display text to 'displayData' here, It can optionally be set
   // in the HTML area towards the bottom, but I like to set it here
   // because sometimes you are using variables that are defined in the
   // POST's if block and they cannot be accessed outside the if scope
   displayData = "<BR><B>referrer(hidden):</B> " + getValues( request,
➥"referrer" ) +
      "<BR><B>First Name:</B> " + getValues( request, "first_name" ) +
      "<BR><B>Last Name:</B> " + getValues( request, "last_name" ) +
      "<BR><B>Location to ship new car:</B> " + getValues( request,
➥"continent" ) +
      "<BR><B>Gender:</B> " + getValues( request, "gender" ) +
      "<BR><B>Email:</B> " + getValues( request, "email" ) +
      "<BR><B>Password:</B> (we can't reveal the password entered for security
➥ purposes, but it rhymes with <I>blah</I>" + getValues( request,
➥"secret_word" ) + ")" +
      "<BR><B>Interests:</B> " + getValues( request, "interests" ) +
      "<BR><B>What you would do with the car:</B> " + getValues( request,
➥"quote" ) +
      "<BR><B>Send you promotional email:</B> " + getValues( request,
```

7

LISTING 7.1   Continued

```
➥"send_promo" );

} // if POST
%>


...
<%// Keep showing the form until bSuccess is true
if( !bSuccess ) { %>

<FORM NAME='form1' ACTION='<%=thisPage %>' METHOD='post'>
...
<%// Else show the results because 'bSuccess' is true
} else { %>

<H3>Thanks for taking the time to fork up information about yourself! You are
now entered in our drawing to win an unspecified car in the year 2025. Below
is the data you submitted to us.</H3>
<%=displayData %>

<P></P>
Let someone else <A HREF='<%=thisPage %>'>enter</A> his or her information!

<% } // if !bSuccess%>

...

<%!
public String getValues( HttpServletRequest request, String name ) {
   String retVal = "";

   String values[] = request.getParameterValues( name );
   // No value was supplied
   if( values == null ) {
      // Do nothing, take retVal's default value;
   // Only one value supplied
   } else if( values.length == 1) {
      retVal = values[0].trim();
   // Multiple values supplied return them all with a comma delimeter
   } else {
      for( int i=0; i<values.length; i++ ) {
         retVal += values[i].trim() + ", ";
      }
   }

   return retVal;
}
%>
```

The form itself looks the same, but providing some values and submitting the form now will display results, as shown in Figure 7.3.

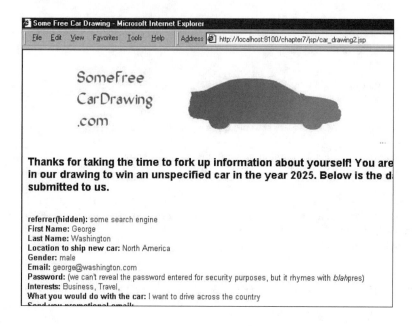

FIGURE 7.3

car_drawing2.jsp *displaying the results of a submission.*

The other option is to display the results on another page altogether. However, because we have established that required fields need to be completely filled out before a proper submission can be made, we need to redisplay the form with the user-supplied values, along with informative messages that help the user correct errors in the form.

Some browsers allow the user to simply click the Back button to correct the error, because the form still contains the values the user last entered. Unfortunately, there are two things wrong with this scenario. One, not all browsers cache form information so that it is still there when traversing back one or two pages. Second, the error message(s) is not in front of the user when he is attempting to correct the errors.

However, if you find that this approach is unfeasible or undesirable in your environment, you can take the code from the "Considering Frames" section, later in this chapter, and set the TARGET of drawing_form.jsp to _self, which will point the results page to itself.

Before we start processing the form and display the results, we need to know if the form was submitted in the first place. This is to prevent accidentally displaying the error message area when the user hasn't actually submitted yet. We shouldn't be yelling at the user when he has not done anything wrong...yet. It's more work for us, but it provides a better user experience.

Validating the Form and Populating It Dynamically

Now that you are able to display and retrieve values from a form, let's look at how to make the form more reliable and user-friendly in the process. Assume for the moment that the storage mechanism for the form data is a database. Chapter 8, "Interacting with Databases," should get you up and running soon enough if you have not dealt with JSP and databases before. One day, Webmaster John notifies salesperson Billy that the one millionth entry has been submitted. Billy anxiously starts looking through the data and notices that 90% of the forms are incompletely filled out. Some have first names but no email, while others do not have the necessary shipping location data. Essentially, 90% of the data is useless. This scenario can occur because with the current implementation of the form, we did not force the user to completely fill out all the necessary information, such as first name, last name, shipping location, and so on. Providing a good validation system will help filter out bad data before it arrives at its final destination. There is the option to supplement your server-side validation with client-side JavaScript, but don't rely completely on client-side validation because you never know if the client-side tool will support JavaScript.

In car_drawing3.jsp, we add code to validate our information and to fill in the form dynamically. To fill in the form, we use the getValue() method to return the values submitted. For example, to display the first name entered, we define a String variable called first_name and call getValue() for the first_name from the request object. We then set the variable first_name as the value for the first name text field. The following code snippets from car_drawing3.jsp show how the first name text field is populated:

```
String first_name = getValues( request, "first_name" );
<INPUT TYPE='text' NAME='first_name' VALUE='<%=first_name %>'>
```

We have also added a method called getState() to the selected item in the drop-down menus, check boxes, and radio buttons. Listing 7.2 shows the code for getState(). The getState() function is used in the form as follows:

```
<OPTION VALUE='Asia' <%=getState( request, "continent" , "Asia", "SELECTED")
%>>Asia
```

LISTING 7.2   The getState() Method, New to car_drawing3.jsp

```
public String getState( HttpServletRequest request, String name,
➥String matchVal, String state ) {
// Returns the submitted state of check boxes(CHECKED), radio buttons(CHECKED),
➥ and drop-down menu options(SELECTED)
  String retVal = "";
  String values[] = request.getParameterValues( name );
  if( values == null ) { // Quickly exit if no value was passed
    return retVal;
  } else {
    boolean bLoopDone = false;
   int i = 0;
```

LISTING 7.2 Continued

```
    while( !bLoopDone && i<values.length ) {
      if( matchVal.equals(values[i]) ) {
        retVal = " " + state; // An extra space cushion for the attribute
        bLoopDone = true; // Stop looping on any match
        }
   i++;
   }
   return retVal;
   } // if values==null

} // getState()
```

Listing 7.3 is the code used to validate the information submitted in the form. The resulting error message is then displayed on the page.

LISTING 7.3 car_drawing3.jsp—Code for Verifying That the Form Has Been Filled in Completely

```
String errorMsg = "";

boolean bSuccess = false; // Flag for successful form submission

// Assign values to all the form controls coming in. These values will also
// be used to dynamically repopulate the form for re-submission should an error
// occur.
// If entering the form for the first time, they should all be blank with the
// exception of 'referrer' which could have been passed from another form or
// via query string.
String referrer = getValues( request, "referrer" );
String first_name = getValues( request, "first_name" );
String last_name = getValues( request, "last_name" );
String continent = getValues( request, "continent" );
String gender = getValues( request, "gender" );
String email = getValues( request, "email" );
String secret_word = getValues( request, "secret_word" );
String secret_word_confirm = getValues( request, "secret_word_confirm" );
String interests = getValues( request, "interests" );
String quote = getValues( request, "quote", "Let us know here." );
String send_promo = getValues( request, "send_promo" );


// Process the values if user submitted the form
if( "POST".equals(request.getMethod()) ) {
```

LISTING 7.3   Continued

```
// Perform validation for required items
if( first_name.equals("") ) {
   errorMsg += "<LI>You must supply your first name.";
}
if( last_name.equals("") ) {
   errorMsg += "<LI>You must supply your last name.";
}
if( continent.equals("") ) {
   errorMsg += "<LI>You must indicate a continent to ship the car...in case
➥ you win.";
}
if( gender.equals("") ) {
   errorMsg += "<LI>You must supply your gender.";
}
if( email.equals("") ) {
   errorMsg += "<LI>You must supply your email.";
// email present, but need to do a loose check for @. format
} else {
   int atPos = email.indexOf('@');
// Bad format if no '@' sign or no character + '.' after the '@' sign
if( atPos == -1 || email.indexOf('.',atPos+2) == -1 ) {
      errorMsg += "<LI>Please provide a valid email address.";
}
}
if( secret_word.equals("") ) {
   errorMsg += "<LI>You must supply a password.";
}
if( secret_word_confirm.equals("") ) {
   errorMsg += "<LI>You must supply a confirmation password.";
}
if( !secret_word.equals(secret_word_confirm) ) {
   errorMsg += "<LI>You password and confirmation password MUST match each
➥ other.";
}
if( quote.startsWith("Let us know here.") ) {
   errorMsg += "<LI>Come on, tell us what YOU want to do with the car.
➥Erase that 'Let us know here.' stuff!";
}

// Non-required items, but can optionally perform formatting
if( interests.equals("") ) {
   interests = "none"; the information submitted in the form. The resulting
}
if( send_promo.equals("") ) {
   send_promo = "no";
}
```

LISTING 7.3   Continued

```
    // There are 1 or more error messages, append the header for display
    if( !errorMsg.equals("") ) {
        errorMsg = "<P>Please correct the following error(s) in order to properly
➡ submit the form</P>" + errorMsg;
    } else {
        // No errors, set the flag to display the results
        bSuccess=true; the information submitted in the form. The resulting
...
```

Figure 7.4 shows `car_drawing3.jsp` redisplaying the form with error messages and maintained state for text, select, and radio button controls. The complete code listing for `car_drawing3.jsp` is available on the accompanying CD-ROM.

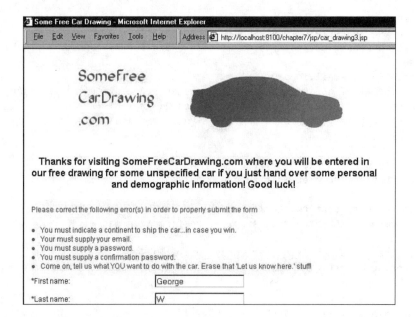

FIGURE 7.4

`car drawing3.jsp` *redisplaying the form.*

Considering Frames

Perhaps all this trouble to maintain the state of the form after submission is a bit too much. In certain cases where the form is extraordinarily long and complex, this will be true. To keep checked all the check boxes and radio buttons, to select all the options of a drop-down list selected, to fill back in all the text fields and textareas—what a headache! Well, there is an alternative to all this mess.

We can use HTML frames to separate the form itself and the results. Having the form submit its action to another page means that the form with all its user-supplied values will be unchanged when the user submits. The processing of the form and the presentation of its results/errors will be done on a completely different JSP. This separation means that you are responsible for creating the form only once—not over and over again if there are errors in the user's input.

When to Use Frames

With the previous drawing example, you might consider using frames by setting the form as the top frame and targeting the action of the form to a bottom result frame. This is ideal when you have a lot of data to enter using the same form and don't want to interrupt momentum by refreshing the form. Assume that this drawing isn't publicly available and entrants can only submit 3×5 cards with all of the required information. The person entering the information can simply focus on the top portion of the screen and quickly glance at the bottom frame for red error messages.

Figure 7.5 is comprised of three JSP pages. The URL to request will be `drawing_frames.jsp`, which contains HTML `<FRAMESET>` and `<FRAME>` tags necessary to define how the form and result frames are displayed.

FIGURE 7.5

Drawing example using frames.

Basically, `drawing_form.jsp` looks exactly like the original `car_drawing.jsp` except for the following details:

- `drawing_form.jsp`'s form ACTION points to `drawing_results.jsp`.
- `drawing_form.jsp`'s form TARGET points to the results frame.
- `drawing_form.jsp` has requirements marked by asterisks for properly submitting the form.
- The window target for the Cancel Entry button points to the top window versus `self`.

On the other hand, `drawing_results.jsp` is essentially the processing portions of `car_drawing3.jsp`. Because we have already stepped through the code for the form and to process the results, we will not do so again. For the complete code, the JSPs are available on the CD-ROM. Let's just emphasize that we are moving the form processing code to `drawing_results.jsp`, and we no longer need to dynamically fill in the form because it will only be rendered once.

Another important use for frames is when there is a significant number of form controls that require you to keep state. A case in point would be a query for reporting purposes. These can be extremely detailed with "from" and "to" dates using drop-down menus for the month, day, and year. There are many occasions when you need to keep track of multiple check boxes and radio buttons. Using the frames approach, you can save yourself a lot of development time by simply targeting the form action to a results frame, because the top frame stays there with the state of the controls unchanged when the user clicks the Submit button. Figure 7.6 is an example of a complex form that is best handled with frames for keeping state.

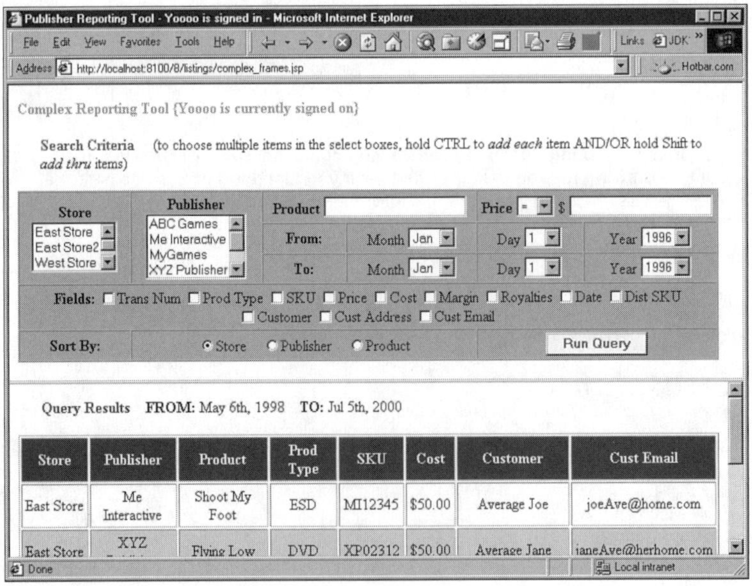

FIGURE 7.6

Use frames to save form control state for complex forms.

Issues with Frames

There are shortcomings to using frames. Using frames for forms lends itself to these shortcomings.

- While the use is rare, you might have to consider older browsers that cannot support frames. In this case, you may have to use the <NOFRAMES> to provide an alternative means to using the form or a suggestion to upgrade to a browser that will support frames.

- Using frames is not allowed with the user interface design.

- Clicking the Back button of a browser goes back one page from the last focused frame, which doesn't always mean the top-level frame.

- Bookmarking might be another issue because most browsers will only save what's in the Address Bar. This problem mainly presents itself when you have hyperlinks in the results frame that doesn't target a new window, a dedicated window, or the top window.

- Some versions of Netscape will reload each frame by making a new HTTP request. This will cause the entire frameset to reload with every request, thus losing your form data and current state.

As with any design choice, you must weigh the pros and cons to determine which option best fills your needs. Frames can add power and ease to your application, but they do have their shortcomings.

Summary

In this chapter we have discussed the following:

- Using form controls on a Web page
- Processing form values with standard HTML as well as JSP
- Populating forms dynamically using JSP
- Using frames with your forms

In many ways, forms have become the bread and butter of displaying, collecting, and passing information from the Web server to the user's browser and then back to the Web server. With JSP, we have discovered ways to interact with the user dynamically, allowing us to give the user a much more exciting experience and ourselves more usable data.

It would be impossible to cover in one chapter all the possibilities of using JSP with forms. Entire books have been written on developing static HTML forms. The purpose of this chapter was to whet your appetite and to let your imagination consider what this combination can offer.

Interacting with Databases

IN THIS CHAPTER

One of the main reasons for inventing many Internet technologies such as Servlets and JSP was to add greater interactivity to what would otherwise be static HTML pages. Realistically speaking, it is difficult to add serious interactivity without integrating with a database. Nearly every popular Internet destination relies heavily on back-end databases to provide information on demand. Some examples of typical database-intensive applications include Internet messageboards, shopping sites, and stock-charting applications, just to name a few. Thankfully, we can rely on the Java Database Connectivity (JDBC) API to easily add a high degree of database interactivity to your application.

JDBC is a Java API for accessing any kind of tabular data. It consists of a set of classes and interfaces that provide a standard way for Java programmers to access relational databases via ANSI SQL-92. The value of JDBC is that an application can access virtually any datasource independently of the underlying database, provided that there are JDBC drivers available. This is an important feature that is required to achieve true application portability. JDBC has enjoyed widespread industry adoption and has been a major contributing factor to Java's success on the server side.

Free Databases

Choosing a database can be a big task, because there are many options to choose from. Typically, a business manager will favor Oracle and Microsoft databases regardless of whether he has used either product, because those are the industry leaders in terms of market share. However, an investment in an Oracle or Microsoft database system isn't a trivial matter. It costs a lot of money up front, costs still more to support, and is often overkill for simple applications. There are numerous databases that cater to the open source and free software communities, having moved to the GNU General Public License (GPL). These include MySQL (www.mysql.com) and PostgreSQL (www.postgresql.org), both of which are excellent products and can help keep your database development simple and cost effective.

JDBC Data Access Models

JDBC relies on drivers that are written by independent software companies and database vendors. JDBC drivers are specific to a particular database and data-access model and are available for virtually all of the major databases, including Microsoft, Oracle, Informix, Sybase, Postgress, MySQL, and many more. A complete listing of available JDBC drivers is at http://industry.java.sun.com/products/jdbc/drivers.

In general, a JDBC driver is responsible for establishing a connection to a database, sending SQL queries and update statements to the datasource, and result processing—all of which will be covered in detail. These tasks are easy as a result of Java's built-in networking capabilities.

JDBC provides support for both two- and three-tier database access models. In a two-tier model, the JDBC driver communicates directly with the database. This is in contrast to a three-tier model, in which the JDBC driver sends commands to a middle tier, which in turn communicates with the database. Sun Microsystems has defined four database driver types, each with different data access models.

Type 1: JDBC-ODBC Bridge and ODBC Driver

The JDBC-ODBC bridge driver (see Figure 8.1) is included with the Java Development Kit (JDK). The bridge provides JDBC access to databases through Object Database Connectivity (ODBC) drivers, Microsoft's database-access model. The bridge was provided by Sun because initially there were no JDBC drivers for any databases, but every database had an ODBC driver. The bridge is excellent for prototyping and development, but the three-tier approach is less optimized for performance and thus is not recommended for use on production servers. In this chapter we will be using the bridge driver.

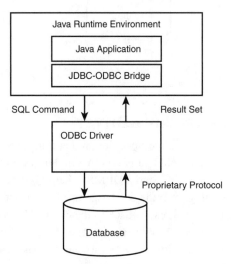

FIGURE 8.1
Data access model for a JDBC type 1 driver.

Type 2: Native-API Partly Java Driver

The Native-API Partly Java driver converts JDBC commands to DBMS-specific native calls, which communicate directly to the database. This two-tier model (see Figure 8.2) is faster than

8

INTERACTING WITH
DATABASES

the type 1 bridge driver, but every client requires specific files loaded on its machine, just like a type 1 driver.

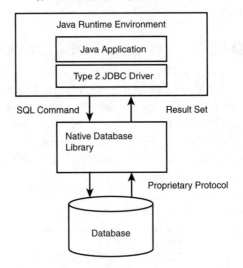

FIGURE 8.2
Data access model for a JDBC type 2 driver.

Type 3: JDBC-Net Pure Java Driver

The JDBC-Net Pure Java driver is a three-tier solution that translates JDBC calls into a database-independent network protocol that is sent to a middleware server. This server translates the database-independent protocol into a DBMS-specific protocol, which is sent to a particular database. Results returning from the database must be translated via this middleware server, which forwards the translated results back to the client. The type 3 driver (see Figure 8.3) allows a developer to implement a pure Java client and allows for swapping databases without modifying any client code. This is a very flexible database access model.

Type 4: Native Protocol Pure Java Driver

A type 4 driver is written in Java and communicates directly with the database. It converts JDBC commands directly on-the-wire into the database's native protocol. The absence of a middle tier results in considerable performance improvement.

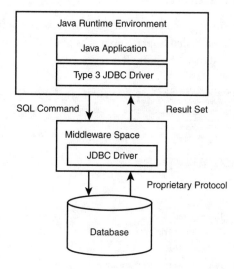

FIGURE 8.3

Data access model for a JDBC type 3 driver.

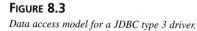

FIGURE 8.4

Data access model for a JDBC type 4 driver.

SuperBookmarks.com

Throughout the remainder of this chapter we'll be working towards building an interactive database-driven Web application called SuperBookmarks.com. The concept behind this futuristic killer Web application is shown in Figure 8.5.

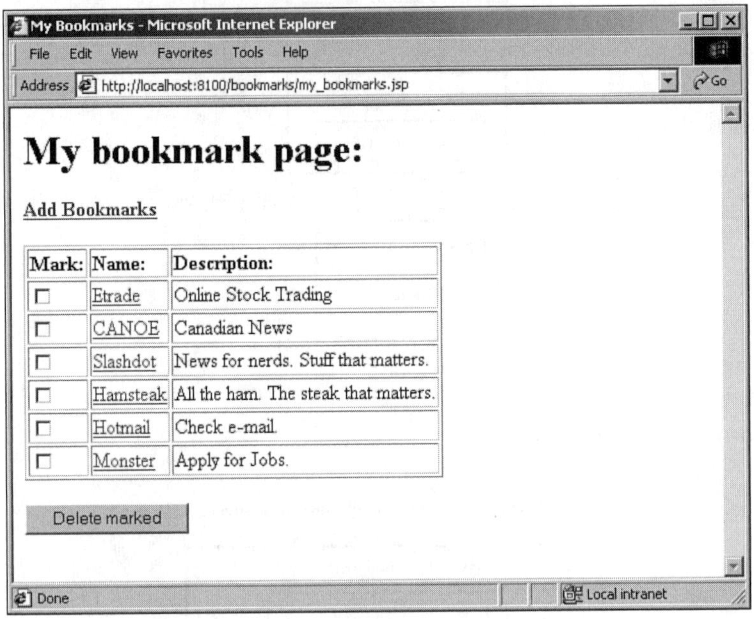

FIGURE 8.5
Access your Internet bookmarks from any Web browser using SuperBookmarks.com.

Instead of storing Internet bookmarks (also known as *favorites*) on a browser, we will store them in a relational database and provide a JSP Web interface to retrieve and update them. By storing your bookmarks in this manner, you will be able to access them from any Web browser.

The JSP page for adding a new bookmark is shown in Figure 8.6.

Creating Your Database

The first thing to do is to install a database software package and create a new database. In this chapter we'll be using the Windows 2000 operating system and Microsoft Access 2000 as the underlying database. The connection between our Java program and the database will be handled by the JDBC:ODBC bridge, which ships with the standard JDK. Note that the concepts are essentially the same regardless of what database or operating system you are using, which was the line of reasoning behind using JDBC in the first place. Launch Microsoft Access, create a new database, and save it anywhere under the name SuperBookmarks.mdb. If all goes well, the new database will be created automatically in the directory that you specified, and the screen will show an empty database, as seen in Figure 8.7.

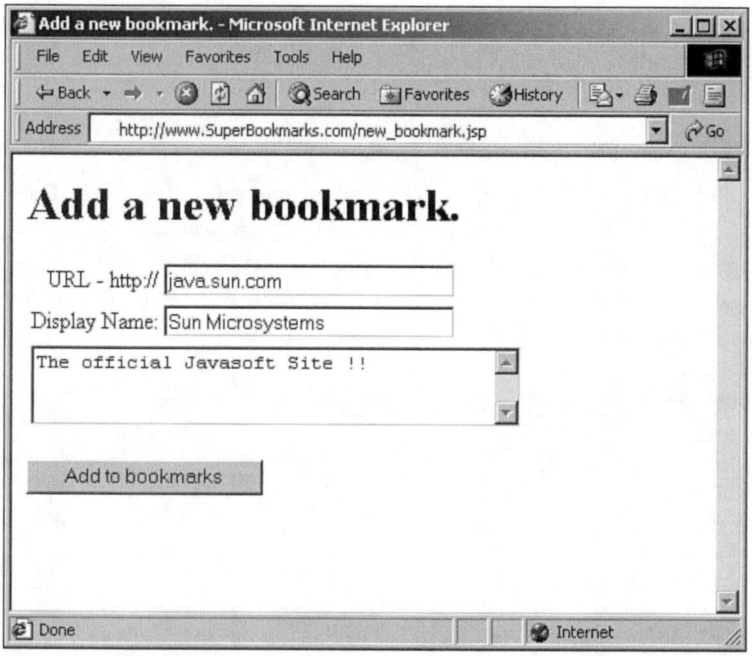

FIGURE 8.6

Inserting a new bookmark to be saved in a database table.

FIGURE 8.7

Creating an empty database.

Figure 8.7 shows the SuperBookmarks database in Microsoft Access 2000, which consists of a collection of tables, queries, and other related objects. In order to build the SuperBookmarks Web application, we need to think about the data to be modeled. A bookmark typically consists of a URL (an address), a display name, and description of the Web page. These properties are represented as strings that need to be stored in a database. To do this, double-click on Create Table in Design View.

Figure 8.8 shows where we model the data in our database.

Create three fields called URL, Name, and Description, and select Text as the Data Type. Right-click on the URL field name and select Primary Key. A *primary key* refers to one or more table columns (also called attributes) that uniquely identify a record (also called a row or tuple) in a database table. Since a URL uniquely identifies a Web page (no two Web pages can have the same URL), we will make URL the primary key.

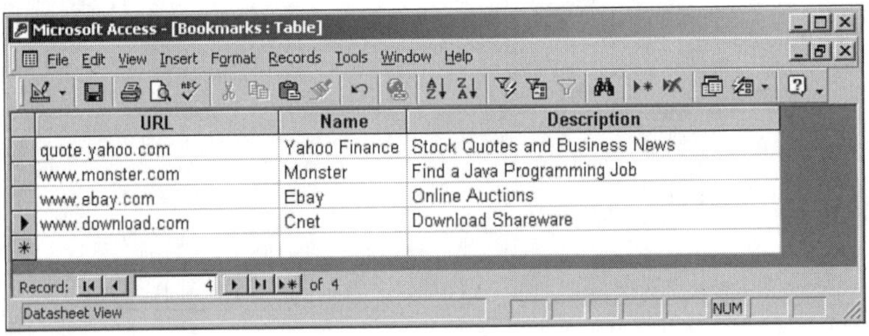

FIGURE 8.8
Creating a new table definition in Microsoft Access 2000.

Close the table and you will be prompted to save it. Since this table represents bookmark properties, use the name Bookmarks and click Save. You will be returned to the main page, but now the database will consist of the Bookmarks table that we just created. We will now manually enter some sample data into the new table to help become familiar with the database. Double-click on the Bookmarks table that you just created and type in some of your favorite bookmarks, as shown in Figure 8.9.

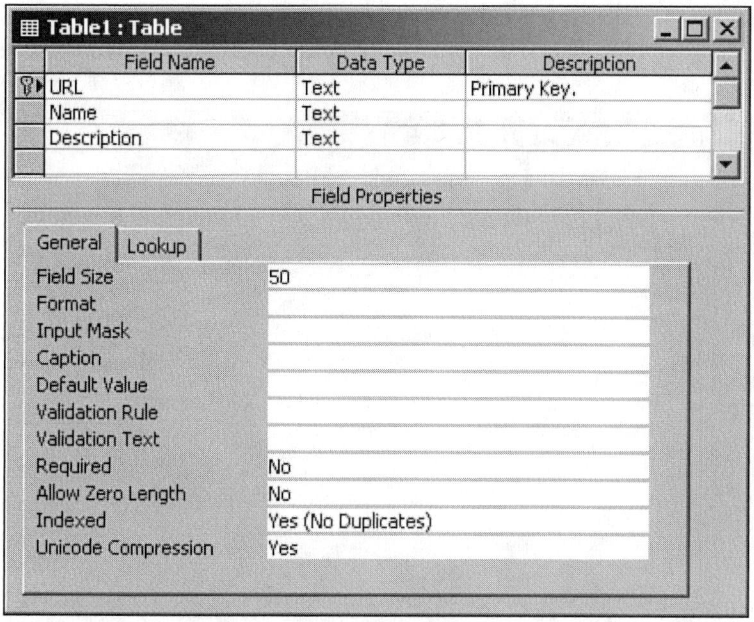

FIGURE 8.9

Manually inserting data into a database table.

For this application, when entering bookmarks, do not enter the http:// prefix. Since this is common across all Web pages (viewed using HTTP protocol), we'll have our JSP pages auto-append the prefix later. Close the table in Figure 8.9; you have successfully created a database consisting of a table and some sample data. Later in this chapter we will show how to create tables and populate them with data by executing SQL statements directly from Java code, rather than with this graphical user interface. We now turn our attention to creating an ODBC data-source with which the JDBC bridge driver will communicate. If you are using Windows 2000

1. Click Start

2. Click Programs

3. Click Administrative Tools

4. Click Data Sources (ODBC)

If you are using Windows 98

1. Click Start

2. Click Control Panel

3. Click ODBC Data Sources

Figure 8.10 shows the Microsoft Windows 2000 ODBC Administrator Panel, which is used to register and manage ODBC data sources. The concepts are identical for Windows 98.

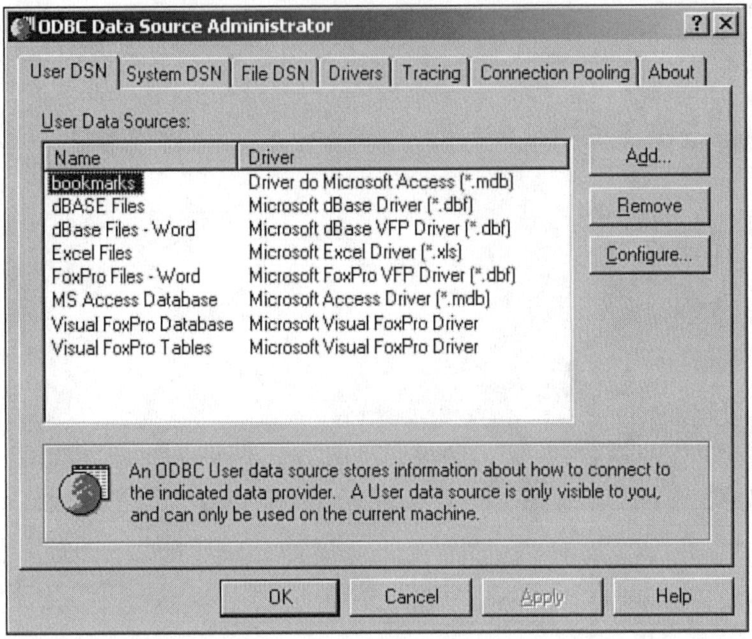

FIGURE 8.10
The Microsoft Windows ODBC Administrator Panel.

4. From the ODBC Administrator Panel, click Add to create a new datasource. You will see the Create New Data Source panel seen in Figure 8.11.

5. On the panel, specify that you will be using a Microsoft Access database driver. Click Finish.

6. Finally, you will be prompted to name the datasource and specify the path to the data-source. In the Data Source Name field, enter **bookmarks** (all lowercase). We will refer to this name from our Java files. You may enter an optional description of the datasource. Press the Select button in the Database box and pick the Microsoft Access `SuperBookmarks.mdb` database file that we created earlier. This is shown in Figure 8.12.

We are now finished configuring the datasource and can start writing our Java programs.

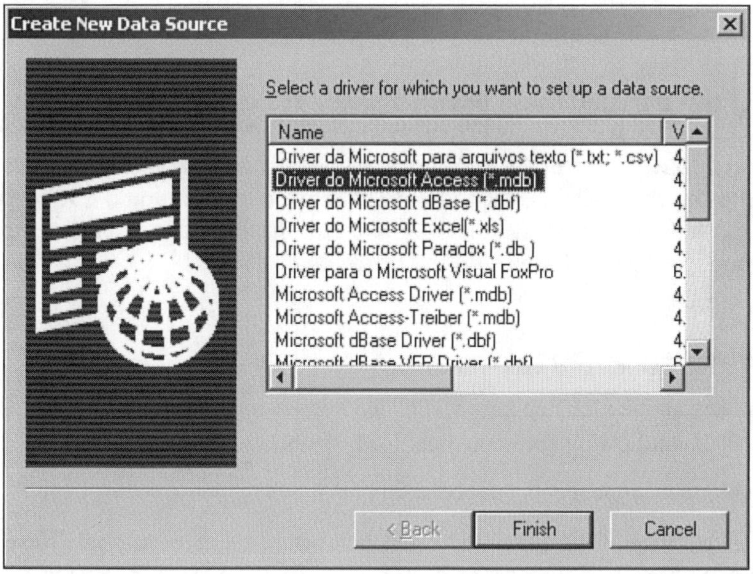

FIGURE 8.11

Selecting the proper ODBC driver for an ODBC datasource.

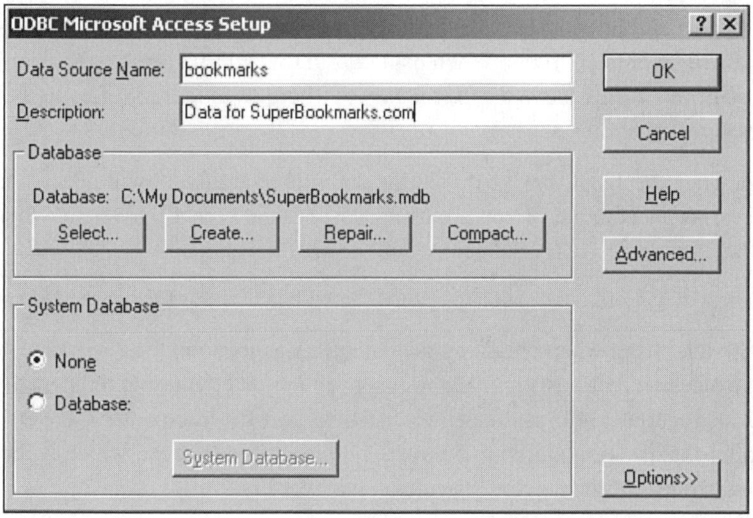

FIGURE 8.12

Naming an ODBC datasource and specifying the location of the database file.

8

INTERACTING WITH DATABASES

> **NOTE**
>
> Remember that the JDBC type 1 bridge driver delegates the database access tasks to the native ODBC driver, which is why we must create the ODBC data source. If you were using a JDBC type 4 driver, which communicates directly with a database, this process of using the Microsoft Windows ODBC Driver Wizard would not be necessary. Your database driver vendor will have vendor-specific instructions and examples of how to connect to a database using their drivers.

Connecting to a Database

When writing any application that uses JDBC, we start by loading a JDBC driver and making the connection. The following code fragment loads the bridge driver.

```
Class.forName("sun.jdbc.odbc.JdbcOdbcDriver");
```

This creates an instance of the driver and registers it with the `DriverManager`. Next we will connect to the database by calling `DriverManager.getConnection()`, a static method that returns a `java.sql.Connection` object, as shown here:

```
Connection con = DriverManager.getConnection("jdbc:odbc:bookmarks", "", "");
```

In this case, the arguments for the `getConnection()` method are the datasource, username, and password. Since we did not configure any security settings on our datasource, the username and password will be empty strings. When using the JDBC:ODBC bridge, the datasource name will always be of the form `jdbc:odbc:DataSource`, where `DataSource` refers to the name of the datasource created earlier.

If you are not using the JDBC bridge driver, the datasource argument will instead be the URL to the database. As an example, if you are using a WebLogic type 4 jDriver for Microsoft SQL Server 7.0, the datasource URL argument would be as follows:

```
String url = "jdbc:weblogic:mssqlserver4:db@myhost:myport?user=sa&password=";
```

You would use this string when obtaining the database connection where `myhost` is the IP address of the machine that hosts the database application and `myport` is the port the database listens to for instructions (1433 is the default listening port for Microsoft SQL Server). The parameters after the question mark are optional, in this case we use `sa`, which is the default System Administrator username, and provide no password.

After obtaining a connection, you use it to create and execute SQL statements against the database. Listing 8.1 shows how you would do this in an actual Java application.

LISTING 8.1   TestDataSource.java—A First JDBC Application: Connecting to and
Releasing a JDBC Datasource

```java
import java.sql.*;

// This program loads a JDBC Driver and attempts to connect a datasource.
// After establishing the connection it simply releases it.

public class TestDataSource
{

    public TestDataSource()    { }

    public void connectAndDisconnect()
    {

    try
    {
        System.out.println("Attempting to load the JDBC Driver...");
        Class.forName("sun.jdbc.odbc.JdbcOdbcDriver");
        System.out.println("JDBC driver loaded.");

        System.out.println("Connecting to database...");
        Connection con;
        con = DriverManager.getConnection("jdbc:odbc:bookmarks","", "");
        System.out.println("Database connection established.");

        // here you would do database queries, updates, etc.

        System.out.println("Attempting to close database connection...");
        if ( con != null )
        {
            // Close the connection
            con.close();
        }
        System.out.println("Database connection closed. ");
    }
    catch (ClassNotFoundException cnfe)
    {
        System.out.println("ClassNotFoundException: Could not locate DB driver");
    }
    catch (SQLException cnfe)
    {
        System.out.println("SQLException: Database reports an error.");
    }
    catch (Exception e)
```

LISTING 8.1   Continued

```
    {
        System.out.println("An unknown error occurred while connecting to DB.");
    }
    } // end of connectAndDisconnect()

    public static void main(String args[])
    {
        TestDataSource test = new TestDataSource();
        test.connectAndDisconnect();
    }
} // eof
```

We have inserted a few simple `System.out.println("")`; calls to help convince you that the application has actually run. Providing that the system's Java and database settings are correct, the output of this program should look like this:

```
Attempting to load the JDBC Driver...
JDBC driver loaded.
Connecting to database...
Database connection established.
Attempting to close database connection...
Database connection closed.
```

Troubleshooting Tips

A `ClassNotFoundException` occurs if the class loader is unable to locate a class file, such as the JDBC bridge driver class files. To resolve this problem, ensure that your classpath contains all of the standard JDK class libraries or, if you are using a different JDBC driver, ensure that they are included in your classpath settings.

An `SQLException` occurs if problems arise when communicating to the datasource. This could be many things, such as invalid SQL statements, invalid username / passwords, and other database errors. In this simple application, first ensure that the datasource was properly created. Also, check the spelling of your datasource in both your Java program and the Windows ODBC Data Sources panel to ensure that they match.

Executing SQL Statements

Structured Query Language (SQL) is a standard language for interacting with databases. This includes creating and deleting tables, performing queries, updating tables, and other functionality.

SQL statements are executed in Java by creating a `java.sql.Statement` object using the connection's `CreateStatement()` method. The method signature is shown here:

```
public Statement createStatement() throws SQLException
```

This method returns a `Statement` object, which is commonly used for executing basic SQL statements against the database. In general, an SQL statement can be classified as one of two types:

1. Those that query a database and return a `ResultSet` object corresponding to the result of a database query. These statements are executed using the `executeQuery()` method.

2. Those that create, modify, or drop tables and insert or delete data. This type uses the `executeUpdate()` method.

The respective method signatures are as follows:

```
ResultSet executeQuery(String sql) throws SQLException
int executeUpdate(String sql) throws SQLException
```

Notice that, as expected, the `executeQuery()` method returns a `ResultSet` object corresponding to the results of a database query. The `executeUpdate()` method does not return a `ResultSet`, because it is not a query. However, it does return either an integer corresponding to the row count for an `insert`, `update`, or `delete` statement or `0` for an SQL statement that returns nothing.

Listing 8.2 demonstrates the use of a `Statement` object that executes an SQL statement. In this example, the SQL statement is simply to create two sample tables within our `Bookmarks` database. It uses the `executeUpdate()` method because creating tables is not a query and as such does not return a `ResultSet` object.

8

INTERACTING WITH
DATABASES

LISTING 8.2   `CreateTables.java` — Creating Database Tables Using JDBC `Statement` Objects

```
import java.sql.*;

// Create two Database Tables using the SQL statements

public class CreateTablesApp
{

   public CreateTablesApp()    { }

   public void createTables()
   {
      Connection con = null;
      try
      {
         // Connect to database.
         Class.forName("sun.jdbc.odbc.JdbcOdbcDriver");
         con = DriverManager.getConnection("jdbc:odbc:bookmarks","", "");
```

LISTING 8.2   Continued

```
            // create some tables
            Statement stmt = con.createStatement();
            String update = "CREATE TABLE User(Name VARCHAR(15) primary key,
                                    Rank VARCHAR(15), Password VARCHAR(15));";
            stmt.executeUpdate(update);
            update = "CREATE TABLE Credits(Name VARCHAR(15), Credits INTEGER);";
            stmt.executeUpdate(update);
        }
        catch (ClassNotFoundException cnfe)
        {
            System.out.println("ClassNotFoundException:
                                        Could not locate DB driver");
        }
        catch (SQLException cnfe)
        {
            System.out.println("SQLException: Could not connect to DB.");
        }
        catch (Exception e)
        {
            System.out.println("An unknown error occurred.");
         }
        finally
        {
            try
            {
                if ( con != null )
                {
                    // Close the connection no matter what.
                    con.close();
                }
            }
            catch(SQLException sqle)
            {
                System.out.println("Unable to close database connection.");
            }
        }
    } // end of createTables()

    public static void main(String args[])
    {
        CreateTablesApp cta = new CreateTablesApp();
        cta.createTables();
    }

} // eof
```

Compile and execute the code in Listing 8.2 only once. Now switch to your Microsoft Access application and notice that two new tables, User and Credits, have appeared in your database. (You may need to refresh the screen.) These tables are hypothetical tables that could represent data about users or credit information. But how did this happen? We first created a Statement object, which can be used for executing nearly any SQL command. We then made an SQL command: CREATE TABLE User(Name VARCHAR(15) primary key, Rank VARCHAR(15), Password VARCHAR(15));"; This says to create a Table called User consisting of three columns, Name (the primary key), Rank and Password. All columns store *variable* length *character* strings (hence the meaning of the word VARCHAR) of maximum length 15 characters. The SQL command is passed as an argument to the statement object's executeUpdate() method which results in the creation of the User table as specified in the SQL command.

Note that if you try to execute the application a second time, you will receive an SQLException and the application will terminate abnormally. This is because you are trying to create tables that have already been created once; to have two tables with the same name is a violation of a fundamental data integrity constraint.

Although we already created the Bookmarks table manually at the beginning of this chapter, we could just as easily have written a Java application to create them. Turning our attention away from these hypothetical sample tables, we will now populate the Bookmarks table with more hyperlinks from within a Java application. This time we will use a PreparedStatement object, which differs from a Statement object in that it is precompiled, and the statement can be parameterized at runtime. The advantages of using a parameterized PreparedStatement can be best explained in an example, seen in Listing 8.3.

8

INTERACTING WITH DATABASES

LISTING 8.3   PopulateTablesApp.java—Inserting Data into a Table Using a Parameterized PreparedStatement

```java
import java.sql.*;

public class PopulateTablesApp
{

    public PopulateTablesApp()    { }

    public void insertData()
    {
        Connection con = null;
        try
        {
            // connect to database.
            Class.forName("sun.jdbc.odbc.JdbcOdbcDriver");
            con = DriverManager.getConnection("jdbc:odbc:bookmarks","", "");
```

LISTING 8.3   Continued

```
        // create some sample data.
        String URLs[] = {"www.javaworld.com", "www.jguru.com",
                                            "www.sys-con.com/java"};
        String Names[] = {"Javaworld", "JGuru", "Java Developers Journal"};
        String Descriptions[] = {"Java Resource",
                                    "Java FAQ", "A Cool Java Magazine"};

        // Create a customizable PreparedStatement
        String update = "INSERT INTO Bookmarks VALUES(?,?,?);";
        PreparedStatement ps = con.prepareStatement(update);

        for (int i=0; i < URLs.length; i++)
        {
            ps.setString(1, URLs[i]);
            ps.setString(2, Names[i]);
            ps.setString(3, Descriptions[i]);
            ps.executeUpdate();
        }
    }
    catch (ClassNotFoundException cnfe)
    {
        System.out.println("ClassNotFoundException:
                                        Could not locate DB driver");
    }
    catch (SQLException cnfe)
    {
        System.out.println("SQLException: Problem Reported by DB.");
    }
        catch (Exception e)
    {
        System.out.println("An unknown error occurred.");
    }
    finally
    {
        System.out.println("Attempting to close database connection...");
        try
        {
            if ( con != null )
            {
                // Close the connection no matter what.
                con.close();
            }
        }
        catch(SQLException sqle)
        {
```

LISTING 8.3   Continued

```
            System.out.println("Unable to close database connection.");
        }
    }
} // end of insertData()

public static void main(String args[])
{
    PopulateTablesApp pta = new PopulateTablesApp();
    pta.insertData();
}

} // eof
```

We see in this example that a PreparedStatement object has considerable performance advantages over a Statement object in that it can be parameterized and quickly iterated over. This is ideal if similar SQL statements need to be executed multiple times, as is the case in this example, which inserts three bookmarks into a table. Rather than creating three separate update statements, we create one string corresponding to the general form of the SQL statement. Notice that it contains several question marks, which are placeholders for dynamic data. Because this update statement is inserting string data into the Bookmarks table, the question marks are substituted for strings by using the setString() method. This method takes as parameters an integer corresponding to the question mark being set and a string corresponding to the value being inserted. If we were inserting a different data type into the table, we would use the appropriate set method instead, such as setInt(). The PreparedStatement is precompiled once into memory and subsequently recycled three times (once for each bookmark being inserted), avoiding the cycle-expensive task of unnecessary object instantiation. If we were inserting a large number of bookmarks, the performance benefits would be tremendous.

8

INTERACTING WITH
DATABASES

NOTE

Remember to compile and execute this application only once. Executing the application a second time will result in an SQLException being thrown and the application exiting abnormally. This is because we set the URL column of the Bookmarks table as a primary key, which disallows duplicate data. Running the application a second time without either changing the bookmarks being inserted or deleting the data that was inserted previously will result in a violation of the uniqueness integrity constraint.

Finally, we investigate querying the database using JDBC. This is done by creating either a `Statement` or `PreparedStatement` object and calling its `executeQuery()` method. A `ResultSet` object containing the results of the query is returned. This is best illustrated in a simple example (see Listing 8.4).

LISTING 8.4   `SimpleQueryApp.java`—Execute a Query Against the Database and Iterate Over the `ResultSet`

```java
import java.sql.*;

public class SimpleQueryApp
{
    public SimpleQueryApp()    { }


    public void queryDatabase()
    {
        Connection con = null;
        ResultSet rs = null;
        try
        {
            // Connect to database.
            Class.forName("sun.jdbc.odbc.JdbcOdbcDriver");
            con = DriverManager.getConnection("jdbc:odbc:bookmarks","", "");

            // A simple SQL query.
            String queryString = "SELECT * FROM Bookmarks;";
            Statement stmt = con.createStatement();
            rs = stmt.executeQuery(queryString);
            while (rs.next())
            {
                System.out.println(rs.getString("URL"));
                System.out.println(rs.getString("Name"));
                System.out.println(rs.getString("Description"));
                System.out.println("\n");
            }
        }
        catch (ClassNotFoundException cnfe)
        {
        System.out.println("ClassNotFoundException: Could not locate DB driver");
        }
        catch (SQLException cnfe)
        {
            System.out.println("SQLException: Problem reported by DB.");
        }
        catch (Exception e)
        {
```

LISTING 8.4   Continued

```
        System.out.println("An unknown error occurred while connecting to DB.");
        }
        finally
        {
          try
          {
            if (rs != null)
            {
              // close the ResultSet
              rs.close();
            }
            if ( con != null )
            {
              // Close the connection no matter what.
              con.close();
            }
          }
          catch(SQLException sqle)
          {
            System.out.println("Unable to close database connection.");
          }
        }
      } // end of queryDatabase()

      public static void main(String args[])
      {
        SimpleQueryApp sqa = new SimpleQueryApp();
        sqa.queryDatabase();
      }

} // eof
```

As previously stated, the executeQuery() method returns a ResultSet object, which is worthy of some discussion. A ResultSet is a collection of data representing the results of querying a database. A ResultSet object maintains a cursor (also called an iterator) that points to the current row of data. The cursor initially is positioned just before the first row. The next() method advances the cursor to the next row and returns true if there are still more rows left or returns false when you have run off the last row in the ResultSet object; thus, it is commonly used in a while loop to iterate through the ResultSet.

The ResultSet interface is very large and contains hundreds of methods for getting database results in the correct data type. Depending on the data that you entered into your Bookmarks table, a sample output for this program might look like the following:

```
www.slashdot.com
Slashdot
```

```
News for nerds.

www.javaworld.com
Javaworld
Java Resource

www.jguru.com
JGuru
Java FAQ

www.sys-con.com/java
Java Developers Journal
A Cool Java Magazine
```

Now that we have covered creating tables, inserting data, and querying the database, we can finish the SuperBookmarks.com application. The SuperBookmarks.com site employs a JSP-bean design idiom. All of the interactive database functionality required by the page is encapsulated into a single JavaBean named BookmarkBean, as shown in Listing 8.5. This removes virtually all of the application code from the JSP. BookmarkBean defines methods for connecting and disconnecting the datasource, as well as methods for viewing, adding, or deleting your current bookmarks. Exceptions are caught and rethrown into the context of the JSP page, to be caught again by a standard error page named error.jsp. The code is mostly self-explanatory and is presented in Listing 8.5.

LISTING 8.5   BookmarkBean.java—A JavaBean That Encapsulates All of the JDBC Functionality Required for the SuperBookmarks.com Application

```java
import java.sql.*;
import java.util.*;

// A bean used for retrieving & updating your saved bookmarks.
// by: L. Kim

public class BookmarkBean
{

    String error;  // used for storing an error message.
    Connection con;

    public BookmarkBean()    { }

    public void connect() throws ClassNotFoundException, SQLException, Exception
    {
        try
        {
            // Load the Driver class file
            Class.forName("sun.jdbc.odbc.JdbcOdbcDriver");
            // Make a connection to the ODBC datasource "store",
```

LISTING 8.5 Continued

```
         // no username or password.
         con = DriverManager.getConnection("jdbc:odbc:bookmarks","", "");
      }
      catch (ClassNotFoundException cnfe)
      {
         error = "ClassNotFoundException: Could not locate DB driver.";
         throw new ClassNotFoundException(error);
      }
      catch (SQLException cnfe)
      {
         error = "SQLException: Could not connect to DB.";
         throw new SQLException(error);
      }
      catch (Exception e)
      {
         error = "Exception: An unknown error while connecting to DB.";
         throw new Exception(error);
      }
} // end of connect()

public void disconnect() throws SQLException
{
   try
   {
      if ( con != null )
      {
         // Close the connection
         con.close();
      }
   }
   catch (SQLException sqle)
   {
      error = ("SQLException: Unable to close the DB connection.");
      throw new SQLException(error);
   }
} // end of disconnect()


public ResultSet viewBookmarks() throws SQLException, Exception
{
   ResultSet rs = null;
   try
   {
      // Execute query
      String queryString = ("SELECT * FROM Bookmarks;");
      Statement stmt = con.createStatement(); //
      rs = stmt.executeQuery(queryString); //sql exception
```

LISTING 8.5   Continued

```
        }
        catch (SQLException sqle)
        {
            error = "SQLException: Could not execute the query.";
            throw new SQLException(error);
        }
        catch (Exception e)
        {
            error = "An exception occured while retrieving bookmarks.";
            throw new Exception(error);
        }
        return rs;
    } // end of viewBookmarks()

    public void addBookmark(String url, String name, String description)
    throws SQLException, Exception
    {
        if (con != null)
        {
            try
            {
                // create a prepared SQL statement
                PreparedStatement updatecustomers;
                String s = new String("insert into Bookmarks values(?, ?, ?);");
                updatecustomers = con.prepareStatement(s);
                updatecustomers.setString(1, url);
                updatecustomers.setString(2, name);
                updatecustomers.setString(3, description);
                updatecustomers.execute();
            }
            catch (SQLException sqle)
            {
                error = "SQLException: update failed, possible duplicate entry";
                throw new SQLException(error);
            }
        }
        else
        {
            error = "Exception: Connection to database was lost.";
            throw new Exception(error);
        }
    } // end of addBookmark()


    public void removeBookmarks(String[] primaryKeys)
    throws SQLException, Exception
```

LISTING 8.5   Continued

```
    {
        if (con != null)
        {
            try
            {
                // create a prepared SQL statement
                PreparedStatement delete;
                delete = con.prepareStatement("DELETE FROM Bookmarks WHERE url=?;");
                for (int i = 0; i < primaryKeys.length; i++)
                {
                    delete.setString(1, primaryKeys[i]);
                    delete.execute();
                }
            }
            catch (SQLException sqle)
            {
                error = "SQLException: update failed, possible duplicate entry";
                throw new SQLException(error);
            }
            catch (Exception e)
            {
                error = "An exception occured while deleting bookmarks.";
                throw new Exception(error);
            }
        }
        else
        {
            error = "Exception: Connection to database was lost.";
            throw new Exception(error);
        }
    } // end of removeBookmarks()

} // eof
```

We see that the connect() method takes care of connecting to the datasource, and the disconnect() method disconnects from the datasource—no surprises there. The viewBookmarks() method performs a simple query and returns a ResultSet object to the caller, in this case the JSP, which will handle the formatting of the results; this is generally good practice since it de-couples business and presentation logic. The addBookmark() method takes as parameters url, name, and description strings (supplied by the user through interaction with a JSP) that are used to populate a PreparedStatement object corresponding to an SQL insert statement.

Finally, the removeBookmarks() method is worthy of additional mention. Since the user is able to delete multiple bookmarks simultaneously, we should be automatically thinking that this is a good opportunity to use a PreparedStatement object. The removeBookmarks() method takes an array of strings as arguments, corresponding to the primary keys of the records to be deleted. We create a parameterized PreparedStatement object corresponding to the SQL delete statement and execute the delete statement for every entry in the array of strings. As stated previously, because the PreparedStatement object is precompiled and recycled (depends on the driver), it can be used to efficiently execute this statement multiple times.

We now turn our attention to the presentation logic of the SuperBookmarks.com application. Listing 8.6 shows the JSP code for the main page, which was shown earlier in this chapter in Figure 8.5. The JSP instantiates the BookmarkBean with session scope and then invokes the bean's connect() and viewBookmarks() methods. The ResultSet returned by the viewBookmarks() method is iterated over and placed into a nice table layout. Note that if you click on the display name of a particular bookmark, the contents of the corresponding URL will be opened in a new browser window, due to the HTML target attribute. Finally, we will close the datasource connection to free up memory.

LISTING 8.6   my_bookmarks.jsp—A Main Page for the SuperBookmarks.com Web Application

```
<%-- my_bookmarks.jsp --%>
<%@ page language="java" import="java.sql.*" errorPage="error.jsp" %>
<jsp:useBean id="bb" scope="session" class="BookmarkBean"/>

<html>
<head>
    <title>My Bookmarks</title>
</head>


<body>
<h1> My bookmark page:</h1>
<a href="new_bookmark.jsp"><b>Add Bookmarks</b></a>

<form action="delete.jsp" method="post">
<table border="1">
<tr>
<td><b>Mark:</b></td>
<td><b>Name:</b></td>
<td><b>Description:</b></td>
</tr>


<% bb.connect();
   ResultSet rs = bb.viewBookmarks();
   while (rs.next())  {
```

LISTING 8.6   Continued

```
    String url = rs.getString("URL");
%>
<tr>
<td><input type="checkbox" name="primarykey" value="<%= url %>" /></td>
<td>
<a href="http://<%= url %>" target="NewBrowser"><%= rs.getString("Name") %></a>
</td>
<td><%= rs.getString("Description") %></td>
</tr>

<%    }
%>
</table><br/>
<input type="submit" value="Delete marked">
</form>

<%    bb.disconnect(); %>

</body>
</html>
```

Clicking the Add Bookmarks hyperlink from the main page will bring up a form to enter new bookmarks, as shown in Figure 8.6, earlier in this chapter. Listing 8.7 is a regular HTML form page that points to the add.jsp file when submitted.

LISTING 8.7   new_bookmark.jsp—A Simple Form That Collects Data for a New Bookmark to Be Inserted into a Database Table

```
<%-- new_bookmark.jsp --%>
<html>
<head>
    <title>Add a new bookmark.</title>
</head>

<body>

<h1> Add a new bookmark.</h1>

<form action="add.jsp" method="post">
<table>
<tr>
    <td align="right">URL - http://</td>
    <td><input type="text" name="url" size="30"></td>
</tr>
```

LISTING 8.7   Continued

```
<tr>
    <td>Display Name:</td>
    <td> <input type="text" name="name" size="30" /></td>
</tr>

<tr>
<td colspan="2"><textarea name="description" cols="40" rows="3">
Enter a short description here:</textarea></td>
</tr>
</table><br/>
<input type="submit" value="Add to bookmarks" />

</form>

</body>
</html>
```

The add.jsp file (see Listing 8.8) determines the request parameters and invokes BookmarkBean's addBookmark() method, which takes care of inserting the data into the database.

LISTING 8.8   add.jsp—A JSP That Processes the Request *to* Insert a New Bookmark

```
<%-- add.jsp --%>
<%@ page language="java" import="java.sql.*" errorPage="error.jsp" %>
<jsp:useBean id="bb" scope="session" class="BookmarkBean"/>

<html>
<head>
    <title>Bookmarks have been added.</title>
</head>

<body>

<%    String url = request.getParameter("url");
      String name =  request.getParameter("name");
      String description =  request.getParameter("description");

      bb.connect();
      bb.addBookmark(url, name, description);
      bb.disconnect();
%>
```

LISTING 8.8   Continued

```
The requested bookmark has been added. <br/>
Click <a href="my_bookmarks.jsp">here</a> to re-load your bookmarks.

</body>
</html>
```

In order to determine which bookmarks are to be deleted, delete.jsp (see Figure 8.9) parses out the HTTP request parameters using the getParameterValues() method, which returns an array of strings. This array of strings corresponds to the URLs (primary keys) of the entries in the Bookmarks table, which are to be deleted. The array of primary keys is then used as a parameter for the RemoveBookmarks() method, which performs the necessary deletions.

LISTING 8.9   delete.jsp—A JSP That Deletes Specified Bookmarks from the Bookmark Table

```
<%-- delete.jsp --%>
<%@ page language="java" import="java.sql.*" errorPage="error.jsp" %>
<jsp:useBean id="bb" scope="session" class="BookmarkBean"/>


<html>
<head>
    <title>Bookmarks have been deleted.</title>
</head>

<body>

<%    String[] s = request.getParameterValues("primarykey");
      bb.connect();
      bb.removeBookmarks(s);
      bb.disconnect();
%>


The requested bookmarks have been deleted. <br/>
Click <a href="my_bookmarks.jsp">here</a> to re-load your bookmarks.

</body>
</html>
```

And finally, the error page that catches and reports any unexpected exceptions.

LISTING 8.10   error.jsp—A Standard JSP Error Page

```
<%-- error.jsp --%>
<%@ page language="java" isErrorPage="true"%>
<html>
<head>
    <title>Untitled</title>
</head>

<body>

<h2>We regret to report that an error has occurred.</h2>
<h4>Error:</h4>
<%= exception.toString() %><BR>

Please contact the webmaster if this problem persists.
</body>
</html>
```

Summary

By now you should have an understanding of the different database access models available to Java programmers and the concepts of JDBC database drivers. We also covered creating ODBC datasources in Microsoft Windows and accessing the datasources from Java applications.

We covered most commonly used methods in the JDBC API, including those for creating tables, inserting data, and querying tables. Our final sample application investigates integrating JDBC with JSP to provide dynamic content for the Web. This application could use additional security measures such as verifying a username and password against values stored in a database table, error checking, and database connection pooling (although many JSP servers implement automatic database pooling these days), all of which is left as an exercise for the user.

Securing Your Applications

IN THIS CHAPTER

Security is such a broad topic that many developers neglect it until the last minute of a project, then try to implement some bandaids to make the application secure. As you would expect, this doesn't work. If you're reading this now, congratulations!

Security isn't as bad as you think. We'll walk through the various concerns, specifically what areas to focus on, what options you have for implementing security, a quick review of directory services, and finally some implementation examples.

A lot of the material in this chapter is introductory in nature, so if you're already a security guru, please feel free to dig right into the example code. Otherwise, we hope this extra material will help you understand what parts of the security "problem" we can solve within a typical JSP application.

Understanding Security Concerns

So you want to secure your application. This could mean you have some information or functionality that you want to protect. You also may want to focus on protecting your users from external attacks while they use your application. Or perhaps you simply want to protect the machine that runs your application but leave your application and its users free to have some fun!

Implementing security involves encryption, authentication, access control lists, and sometimes certificates. Each has a specific purpose, to guard against a specific kind of attack, and they come together to provide a complete solution.

So much technology can be daunting, which brings us to the main point: Know what you are trying to protect. Is it the application, the user, your data, your server, some combination of these things, or something altogether different? Once you know what you are trying to protect, you can effectively pick the pieces you need and implement a clean solution.

Next we'll walk through each of those areas that you can protect and describe what can be done to secure them. We'll end with application security. By going from least relevant to most relevant, we hope to provide the background that helps you see what areas you can focus on and what assumptions you can make along the way.

Protecting Your Server

Obviously, your server machine is vital to the functioning of your application. It may also be vital to the functioning of hundreds of other applications, as is the case for Web hosting companies, Internet service providers, and even corporate IT departments. We aren't here to convince you how important the server is, but rather to outline what is already in place to protect it.

Any serious network center has physical security. This means locked rooms, security guards, and alarms. Often, it also means power conditioning, backup power (generators or batteries), and automatic fire extinguishers. All this is very important and, luckily, it is someone else's problem!

Next, we move to the network. Unplugging it would guarantee security but, not surprisingly, this method has not caught on. Rather, networks are routed through special computers called *firewalls* that analyze the traffic and allow only some data to flow through.

Firewalls come in all shapes and sizes but generally are designed to limit the flow of data to only what is considered safe and do so transparently. For many Web servers, this often means allowing only HTTP and HTTPS protocols to come through. All other protocols are blocked. Since all data flows through the firewall, this gives a great degree of control over security.

Sooner or later we get into the server itself, and processing takes place within various processes on the computer. Often, the Web server and application server(s) are separate processes and thus give one more opportunity to apply security. If any one process goes haywire or gets hacked into, the operating system can limit the damage to other processes (and their data) through operating system–level security. Again, this is someone else's problem.

Additional safeguards may be imposed by the operating system to protect access to other resources such as memory, disk space, IO ports, or even CPU cycles. The application server and Web server run as processes and therefore can't do anything about this security. If everything is configured properly, it is transparent anyway.

By now you should be convinced that the server running your application is secure, or at least that it can be secured by other means that don't directly affect your application. This should reduce the scope of your concerns over security by pointing out other areas to investigate. More importantly, it points out areas you don't need to worry about for application security.

Protecting Your Data

Let's assume for now that your data is stored in a database. Security for the database server is generally similar to security for your application server, even if they are on different machines. From the database server's point of view, your application is a database client and therefore must also have a username and password to connect to the database.

As the application designer, you have the choice to use your user's credentials to connect to the database or use a standard "system" user account instead. Most Web applications take the latter approach. Furthermore, most database connection pool implementations accept only one username and password entry for all connections.

Once you have locked down the database, are you done? Probably not. Your data is exposed as it streams across the Internet, and you have to decide whether this is OK. If not, SSL (Secure Sockets Layer) is the answer. With SSL, the link between the Web server and the browser is encrypted, preventing anyone from deciphering the data as it streams across the Net.

> **NOTE**
>
> Secure Sockets Layer (SSL) uses a combination of a public key and shared key encryption to protect the data flowing on a socket. When used with the HTTP protocol, the combination is commonly referred to as HTTPS, and you can see this in the URL when you are using a secure connection to a Web server.

When your browser first makes a secure connection to the server, the server supplies the client with a public key that the client uses to encrypt everything it sends to the server. Because of how public/private keys work, only the server can decrypt this data. The client then creates a random shared key, encrypts it with the server's public key, and sends it to the server.

Once the server has the shared key, the two can send data back and forth securely. Security comes from the assumption that nobody can guess the shared key (because it is very long and random) and that nobody can guess the server's private key (because it is even longer and more random).

Protecting Your Users

Protecting your users' data is just as important as protecting your own data, if not more so. Once again, we can use SSL to encrypt any data users send, including posted form information, what links they are clicking on and, most importantly, usernames and passwords.

Users are often concerned with giving sensitive information to an untrusted server. This is the security problem in reverse, but what can the application writer do about it? A key area of SSL is the use of digital certificates to prove authenticity.

In a nutshell, a digital certificate is a very long string of bits that indicates that the server is who it says it is. The bits are created by an independent authority that you trust, such as Verisign, Inc. The method by which the certificate is produced is cryptographically secure; the certificate can't be forged by any known means, aside from a brute force attack.

By providing a certificate for your site, you enable the user to trust the site and all the applications that run on it. Luckily, the administration of certificates is a Web server administration function that application developers can usually ignore.

As the application writer, your job is to make sure that the users' sensitive information (passwords, account numbers, credit card numbers, and the like) is passed to the server in a secure way. Likewise, any of the users' information that you send back should be sent securely. Most often this means using SSL.

You can check to see whether the HTTP link is secure by calling the `request.isSecure()` method in your pages. By using this method, you won't create any dependencies on the particular encryption scheme being used or even require that encryption be used at all.

Protecting Your Application

Finally, we can talk about the application itself! To give some scope to the discussion, we'll create the login mechanism for a simple online message forum. Anyone can view the messages, but we will use simple authentication before we allow anyone to post messages.

This requires us to protect part of the application with differing levels of security. Following our example, we want valid users to be allowed to post messages, but only moderators to be able to edit and delete messages. Just to make it interesting, we don't necessarily assume that moderators can post.

Authentication Options

Now we have a more focused picture of what we want to do: protect the application. This means we have to know who the user is. If we know that, we can programmatically decide what he can and cannot do. Knowing who the user is also helps in other ways; for example, we can display his given name, automatically email him when someone replies to his message, and so on. Personalization, content management, and even games all need to know the identity of the user and various things about him.

So how do we know who the user is? Either the user has to tell us or we can find out from some other program to which the user identified himself. Remember that, since we're talking about securing the application against users, we don't trust the user. They have to tell us who they are and prove it.

Proving it is where all these great security technologies come in. Hundreds of years ago, if you wanted to prove who you were to get into a secret club, you had to know the secret password at the door. Only then would they let you in. It worked pretty well back then, and this simple approach has survived until today: the password. The user tells you his password and, if he gets it right, you assume he is who he says he is.

If anyone is listening when the user gives his password, both the user and the application are at risk. SSL encryption can protect against this. As we have seen, encryption is only as strong as its keys. Luckily, technology comes to the rescue.

NOTE

What if we do not have a secure link, but we still want secure authentication? The science of *zero-knowledge proofs* has given us a solution.

With this approach, the user never discloses his password, but instead engages in a conversation that convinces both participants that the other can be trusted. This sounds weird, and it is.

A simple way to understand how it works is to imagine that the "secret" is a random number generator seed. The user tells the server what the next number is in a sequence. Then the server responds with the next number. After a few exchanges, the odds are exceedingly small that the other side could have guessed the numbers correctly, so each can assume the other has the correct seed and therefore can be trusted. Of course, all of this is automated.

> The details of zero-knowledge proofs are far beyond the scope of this book. It is only important to note that this is a super–high-tech way for two parties (the user and the application) to prove their identities to each other without giving away any secrets.

We will stick with passwords for this chapter, since passwords are the time-honored, most widespread, and simplest approach. The task at hand now is simply to obtain the username and password from the user, then check to see if it is correct. We'll see that the application server can do most of this work for us.

Rolling Your Own Authentication

The first approach to security (it used to be the only approach) is simply to roll your own. This example will demonstrate the basic steps to doing your own authentication. After that, we will show how the same authentication can be described in a Web application deployment descriptor (web.xml) using the standard Servlet 2.2 security model.

Our main login page will simply display a notification message that we don't have any messages yet and provide a place for the user to post one. Since this is just to demonstrate security, the actual posting logic is not implemented.

We will also gloss over the logic of how the user is actually authenticated once we have his username and password. For now, the task is to obtain this information and implement the flow through the application to a secure page. After that, we will double back and see how we actually validated the user.

Note that, for clarity, we have left out the error-checking code that would normally be in the application. Also, this page logic could be implemented quite simply using a JSP custom tag or two. We will leave this as an exercise for the reader.

Let's start with the welcome page, the code for which is shown in Listing 9.1. The main page of the application would normally display some recent messages, but we'll just display a welcome message and give the user a link to the login page. Since any user can view messages, we aren't concerned with security until the user tries to post a message.

LISTING 9.1   index.jsp—Our Simple Forum's Welcome Page

```
<html><head><title>Simple Forum Main Page</title></head><body>

<h2> Welcome to the Simple Forum</h2>

Sorry, we don't have any messages to view.  If you want
to post a message, click
```

LISTING 9.1 Continued

```
<a href='form-login.jsp'><b>Form Login</b></a>, or
<a href='http-login.jsp'><b>HTTP Login</b></a>

to try out either authentication technique.  Once you are
authenticated, you don't have to authenticate again.

</body></html>
```

The Form Login link on the index page goes to the first login page, form-login.jsp. This page first checks to see if the user has logged in. If so, it proceeds to the post page so the user can enter his message. That way he doesn't have to log in every time he wants to post a message.

In this example we use cookie-based session tracking. Once the user has been authenticated, we store his full name in the session as an indicator that he is authenticated. The cookie sent by the browser is important for this approach to work.

Form-Based Authentication

Many applications use *form-based authentication*. This approach allows full control over what the login screens look like and does not depend on the browser to gather the username and password. Once submitted, this form must supply the username and password in the username and password fields. Since we are rolling our own security, we can choose any field names; why not use straightforward ones?

In this design, the form is submitted right back to the same page that generated it, only as an HTTP post. We can then validate the information and allow the request to proceed to the message post page (post.jsp). Then the Web application tracks the user in the session. Refer to Listing 9.2 to see how it works.

LISTING 9.2   form-login.jsp—A Simple Login Page Using Form-Based Authentication

```
<%@page import='java.io.*, java.util.*,
                javax.naming.*, javax.naming.directory.*' %>
<%@include file='prop-auth.jsp' %>
<html><head><title>Form Login Page</title></head><body>

<% if (request.getMethod().equalsIgnoreCase("POST")) {
    String username = request.getParameter("username");
    String password = request.getParameter("password");
    if (userIsValid(request, application, username, password)) {
        // this is a valid login
        response.sendRedirect("post.jsp");
        return;
    } else { %>
        <h2>Invalid credentials!</h2>
```

LISTING 9.2 Continued

```
<%    }
    } else if (session.getAttribute("fullname") != null) {
        response.sendRedirect("post.jsp");
        return;
    } %>

<FORM ACTION="<%= request.getContextPath() %>/form-login.jsp" METHOD="post">
<H3>SimpleForum Login</H3>
Please enter your username and password, then press <strong>Login</strong>.<p>
<B>Username:</B> <INPUT TYPE="text" NAME="username" SIZE="20" VALUE=""><br>
<B>Password:</B> <INPUT TYPE="password" NAME="password" SIZE="20" VALUE=""><br>
<INPUT TYPE="submit" NAME="submit" VALUE="Login">
</FORM>

</body></html>
```

Once the login is known to be valid, we redirect the user to the page where he can post the message. From there, you can use your imagination as to what happens next. The user is in and we know who he is, so we're finished with the authentication. Any other page that needs to know anything about the user can simply get it from the session.

As you can see, this approach is quite simple so far. Next we will see how we can apply some of the browser's built-in GUI skills by using HTTP basic authentication.

HTTP Challenge and Response

Let us first note that HTTP basic authentication is no more secure than a form-based login. Since we are assuming that the link will be SSL encrypted, this should not be a problem. With a good SSL link and JSP, basic authentication is not as popular as it used to be.

If you remember the days of static content, however, you can appreciate how this would work with a traditional Web server. Here we use the HTTP protocol headers to pass information. If the user clicks on a page that requires a secure login, we respond with an HTTP 401 (Unauthorized Access) error, and the browser opens a username/password login window.

The user fills in the information, and the browser sends the same request to the server. This time it has the authentication information added to it in the form of the Authorization header. The Web server or application server can then validate the information and allow the request to proceed to the application.

Let's look at Listing 9.3 to see how this is implemented. You will notice that this example uses a method called decodeBase64(). In the CD-ROM supplied with this book, this function is present. It is not shown here for brevity.

LISTING 9.3   `http-login.jsp`—Login Page Using HTTP Basic Authentication

```
<%@page import='java.io.*, java.util.*,
                javax.naming.*, javax.naming.directory.*' %>
<%@include file='prop-auth.jsp' %>
<html><head><title>HTTP Login Page</title></head><body>

<%
    String auth = request.getHeader("Authorization");
    if (auth != null) {
      // trying to authenticate
         auth = decodeBase64(auth.substring(6));
         String username = auth.substring(0,auth.indexOf(':'));
         String password = auth.substring(1+auth.indexOf(':'));
      if (userIsValid(request, application, username, password)) {
         // this is a valid login
         response.sendRedirect("post.jsp");
         return;
      } else { %>
         <h2>Invalid credentials!</h2>
<%    }
    } else if (session.getAttribute("fullname") != null) {
      response.sendRedirect("post.jsp");
      return;
    } %>

<H3>SimpleForum Login</H3>
Please authenticate using your browser.

<%
    response.setStatus(response.SC_UNAUTHORIZED);
    response.setHeader("WWW-Authenticate", "Basic Realm=\"SimpleForum\"");
%>

</body></html>
```

Now that we've seen two kinds of authentication, we'll wrap up with the post page, shown in Listing 9.4. This simply presents the form for posting a message and, when a post is received, uses the authentication information that we stored in the session to display the user's name.

LISTING 9.4   `post.jsp`—Post Form That Accepts a Posted Message and Displays a Thank-You Note

```
<html><head><title>Post a message</title></head><body>

<% String name = (String) session.getAttribute("fullname");
   if (request.getMethod().equalsIgnoreCase("post")) {
       // process the posted message here
```

LISTING 9.4   Continued

```
%>
        Thanks for your post, <b> <%= name %></b> <p>
        <b>Message:</b><br>
        <%= request.getParameter("message"); %>


<% } else { %>

<FORM ACTION="<%= request.getContextPath() %>/post.jsp" METHOD="post">
<H3>SimpleForum Post</H3>
  Hi <b><%= name %></b>.
  Please enter your message below,
  then press <strong>Post</strong>.<p>
<B>Message:</B>   <br>
<textarea cols="50" rows="5" name="message"></textarea> <br>
<INPUT TYPE="submit" NAME="submit" VALUE="Post">
</FORM>


<% } %>


</body></html>
```

Directory Services

The previous authentication methods require the application to have a set of usernames and passwords already defined. This information has to be stored somewhere and, just as you would suspect, there are lots of ways to do it.

The Java Naming and Directory Interface (JNDI)

Our first examples used a simple property file to store names and passwords. Although this is simple, it is not fast, robust, secure, or shared. If we want to support more than one approach to storing this type of information (and we do), then we need an API.

Luckily, we have a Java standard for this type of thing: the Java Naming and Directory Interface (JNDI). The JNDI lets us plug in different storage implementations (directories) and use them through a common interface. If we want to, we can write a JNDI interface for our simple property file mechanism. This might not be very useful for a production server, but it certainly makes testing easier when you're offline.

The JNDI provides a standard API for organizing any kind of information into a hierarchy of names and directories (hence the name). It is intended to be the primary means for looking up users, passwords, email addresses, database connection factories, and other configuration information.

We can access the JNDI API directly from our roll-your-own solution for a vendor-neutral method of accessing user information. The standard JNDI implementation includes support for the Lightweight Directory Access Protocol (LDAP), and all other popular directory interfaces for Java (such as NetWare) provide JNDI drivers as well. There aren't many reasons to go with a proprietary API with this kind of flexibility.

Using the JNDI is fairly simple. In general, any Java object can be stored under any name in the JNDI. To use it, you initialize a `Hashtable` object with the URL and class name of a JNDI provider's `InitialContext`. The context allows us to look up objects in a namespace directory tree (hence the *directory* part of the name). The initial hashtable that you supply contains any information that you need to connect to the server using the driver specified.

The JNDI is actually used to locate many types of distributed objects, including JDBC drivers, authentication servers, EJB containers, and so on. Many JNDI providers also provide reliable data storage for application settings. If it helps, you can think of this as a very enhanced and distributed equivalent to the Windows Registry.

LDAP Integration

Even before the JNDI came about, the industry had mostly standardized on a common network protocol for accessing different directories. The Lightweight Directory Access Protocol (LDAP) serves this purpose in a machine- and vendor-independent way. LDAP is so widespread that the Java platform includes an implementation that plugs into the JNDI.

Because of the JNDI, we don't talk to an LDAP directory server directly. Instead, we just open up the initial JNDI context using the username and password provided. If it works, then we know the user is valid, and we can obtain his full name and put it into the session.

The next example shows a simple directory implementation using a property file, then a more robust example using the JNDI and LDAP together to validate against a corporate mail server.

Implementing Access Control

Armed with some background on directory services and wondering how we just did an example without using one, let's take a look at how we actually authenticated users. We have seen how to obtain their usernames and passwords and the basic mechanics of using the session to keep track of whether or not the user has been authenticated.

Using a Text File for Authentication

For the two login examples we have seen so far, we used a simple property file to authenticate users. The example property file assumes we have three users: Curly, Moe, and Larry. Let's take a look at Listing 9.5, the code fragment that actually performs the property file authentication.

LISTING 9.5   `prop-auth.jsp`—Using a Property File for Authentication

```
<%!
/** validate a user using a property file */
public boolean userIsValid(HttpServletRequest request,
                           ServletContext application,
                           String username, String password)
    throws java.io.IOException
{
    Properties users = new Properties();
    InputStream in = application.getResourceAsStream
➥("/WEB-INF/users.properties");
    try {
        users.load(in);
        String fullname = users.getProperty(username);
        if (fullname != null &&
            password.equals(users.getProperty(username+".password"))) {
            request.getSession(true).setAttribute("fullname", fullname);
            return true;
        } else {
            return false;
        }
    } finally {
        in.close();
    }
}
%>
```

As you can see, we simply load the property file and validate the user. If we find the user's full name in the file, we check the password, and if everything matches, we store the full name in the session so that other pages can skip the login code.

Of course, your application would need to maintain the list of usernames and passwords in this file. Furthermore, you might want to share this list between applications or even import the list from a central server in your company. Alternatively, you could allow users to register and choose their own passwords, which you would store in the file.

Using LDAP Authentication

Moving on with our example, we will use an existing LDAP server to perform authentication. This could be a public server such as from Yahoo! or an internal one. These examples were written using standard LDAP talking to a Microsoft Exchange mail server.

To test the previous code, edit the `include` directive at the top of either login page from before (`http-login.jsp` or `form-login.jsp`). Listing 9.6, `ldap-auth.jsp`, contains an alternate implementation of the `isUserValid()` method for our application.

LISTING 9.6   `ldap-auth.jsp`—Using JNDI to Perform LDAP Authentication

```
<%!
/** validate a user using an LDAP server */
public boolean userIsValid(HttpServletRequest request,
                           ServletContext application,
                           String username, String password)
    throws java.io.IOException
{
    // you would need to change the hostname and organization name
    // below to real servers.  Of course, the server administrator
    // can supply this information.
    String url = "ldap://ldap.simpleforum.com/cn=Recipients,ou=HQ,
➥o=SimpleForum";

    Hashtable environment = new Hashtable();
    environment.put( Context.INITIAL_CONTEXT_FACTORY,
                     "com.sun.jndi.ldap.LdapCtxFactory" );
    environment.put( Context.PROVIDER_URL, url);
    environment.put( Context.SECURITY_AUTHENTICATION, "simple" );
    environment.put( Context.SECURITY_PRINCIPAL, "cn=" + username );
    environment.put( Context.SECURITY_CREDENTIALS, password );

    try {
        DirContext dirContext = new InitialDirContext(environment);
        Attributes attributes = dirContext.getAttributes("cn=" + username);
        String fullname = (String) attributes.get("givenName").get();
        request.getSession(true).setAttribute("fullname", fullname);
        return true;
    } catch (Exception ex) {
        // could not authenticate
        return false;
    }
}
%>
```

As we outlined in the previous section, using the JNDI with LDAP means first creating a hashtable that lets us obtain the initial naming context. We add the type of authentication we want to use (simple), the user's name, and his credentials (password). This is enough information for the JNDI system to locate the server and log in.

From there, we get the initial context and request the user's givenName, or first name. If we get it back, we store it in the session so that we know the user has logged in, just as we saw earlier.

If anything goes wrong in the process, we simply return false. Of course, you would want to implement more graceful security measures in your application.

Using Servlet 2.2 Web Application Security

All of the previous material traditionally has been the problem of the application writer. Recently, the Servlet API version 2.2 added support for an optional mechanism that lets application writers defer these problems to the application server.

To do this, we have to tell the application server three important pieces of information: what application pages and HTTP methods to secure, what roles are required to access them, and what type of authentication we want to use. The rest is up to the application server.

A *role* is a simple way to describe security in terms of actions instead of people. To simplify security management, the application server allows you to define administratively what users (or user groups) take on what roles. In other words, who can do what. For our example, we have a user role and a poster role. Only the poster role can access the post.jsp page.

Since the details of configuring the application server vary so greatly from server to server, Listing 9.7 shows only a simple example of the Web.xml deployment descriptor required for this security.

LISTING 9.7   Web.xml—Simple Deployment Descriptor with Security Constraint Directives

```xml
<Web-app>
 <display-name>SimpleForum</display-name>
 <description>Application to demonstrate security</description>

 <security-constraint>
  <Web-resource-collection>
   <Web-resource-name>Post</Web-resource-name>
   <url-pattern>/post.jsp</url-pattern>
   <http-method>POST</http-method>
   <description>Only for users that can post</description>
  </Web-resource-collection>
  <auth-constraint>
   <role-name>poster</role-name>
  </auth-constraint>
 </security-constraint>

 <security-role>
  <description>Forum Reader</description>
  <role-name>user</role-name>
 </security-role>

 <security-role>
  <description>Forum Poster</description>
  <role-name>admin</role-name>
 </security-role>
```

LISTING 9.7   Continued

```
<login-config>
 <auth-method>BASIC</auth-method>
 <realm-name>SimpleForum</realm-name>
</login-config>

</Web-app>
```

For more information, please see the Servlet 2.2 specification and your application server's security documentation. Just to make things even more interesting, many servers allow you to plug in your own authentication mechanism. Since this varies from server to server, and since the JSP engine allows you to build your own authentication anyway, we don't cover the details here.

As time goes on, authentication will be easier and easier. The Servlet 2.2 authentication scheme is just the beginning. For servers running in common security environments such as a corporate intranet with LDAP, the solutions will largely be off-the-shelf.

For public applications, however, you may still need to manage your own user directory or perform additional authentication steps (more than just a password). Now that you are well informed, you can design precisely what your application needs. If you're lucky, the application server will make it all a piece of cake!

Managing Session States

IN THIS CHAPTER

Understanding Session State Management

Managing session state is a problem common to Web development rather than to any single individual environment or language. Each of the major Web application environments, such as Java, JSP, Microsoft's ASP, and Allaire's ColdFusion, face the same issue. The problem stems from the fact that the underlying protocol of the Web—Hypertext Transfer Protocol (HTTP)—is "stateless." In other words, it does not include any means for remembering a user from one moment to the next.

HTTP (and HTML) was created in the early 1990s by Tim Berners-Lee at the European Organization for Nuclear Research (CERN) as a way to help organize and make available the wide variety of documents generated and maintained by various sections of the CERN lab. The intent was to provide a fast way to link documents and information to make it available to the larger CERN community. In the beginning, it served up static pages—it was merely a way to interlink those pages. Originally, it was the links between documents that tended to be dynamic—growing as new collections of data became available or as old data became obsolete. Of less concern was allowing for dynamic interaction between a user and a particular piece of content.

To accommodate this purpose, HTTP was designed to be a simple request-response protocol—clients request information, and the HTTP server looks for and finds the requested data and returns it to the client. It was more important that it be fast and compact than that it provide a range of traditional network services. Within these goals, it succeeded fantastically—what was sacrificed were those higher-level network services, such as facilities for establishing and maintaining a "session." Given HTTP's original purpose, it made perfect sense to avoid the coding and performance overhead of trying to provide the higher-level services.

To this day, each HTTP request from a client to a server for a document is treated by the server as a completely unique occurrence. The server retains no memory of past requests, nor does it have any anticipation of possible future requests.

While this model works well for a system aimed at servicing up relatively static content, it does not work for most business type operations. In fact, a key component of business operations is the ability to know from one request to the next who is making the request. A shopping cart is a perfect example—as the user moves through the application adding items to and removing items from the shopping cart, it is imperative that the server remembers who has added which items to which cart. In other words, each user must have his *own* shopping cart with his *own* items.

If the server weren't able to maintain and track separate users, an individual might find himself requesting one book but getting another.

As HTTP began to move out of the lab and into the general world—and into commerce, in particular—the need to maintain state become more important. Several methods were used to keep track of individual users across requests, none of which involved changes to the underlying

HTTP protocol (in other words, it was never made into a "stateful" protocol). Each method built on aspects of HTML or on functions added to browsers.

Some early attempts at identifying individual users entailed using CGI variables to note the IP address of the requesting client. By tracking the requesting IP address, developers could track the path a user took through a site and provide the appearance of maintaining state. However, with the advent of proxy servers, which often mask the actual IP address of the requesting browser, this method no longer worked.

Another approach involved appending extra information to the URL in the query string. This "extra information" might include some ID number to uniquely identify the user as well as any user-specific data—perhaps such things as the choices the user had made when using the shopping cart application. Obviously, this approach required more work for developers because they needed to make sure that all session-related data was passed with every request to the server. Moreover, query strings have a size limitation, so they couldn't be used to pass large amounts of data, nor could they be used to pass anything but simple data types.

Although these early approaches to state maintenance are available to JSP programmers, JSP also provides more advanced features that make it possible to maintain state, including the state of complex objects associated with an individual session, across requests.

It is important to note, however, that despite the variety of approaches to maintaining state, they all depend on the cooperation of the browser. One way or another, it must pass some information to the server with every request to identify itself to the server.

Using the Session Scope

JSP provides a generalized, simple way to help automate the task of tracking individual user sessions. There are two components to the session services in JSP:

- *A unique session ID that is assigned to a user when he first requests a page from the site*—This session ID is generated by the system and is the key that makes session maintenance work. By default, the server sends the session ID to the browser as a "cookie" (a small piece of server data that is stored by the browser on the client side). For each subsequent request, the browser passes this cookie back to the server. It is this session ID that tells the server who is making the request. (It is also possible to pass the session ID on in the query string, which we'll examine later in the chapter. For the current discussion, we'll assume the user's browser has been set to accept cookies from the server.)

- *A session object that is maintained on the server*—The session object is keyed to the session ID—each unique session ID maps to a unique session object.

Although the HTTP server retains no memory of a request after it has been fulfilled, the JSP engine persists unique session objects across requests. JSP uses the session ID to look up the

10

unique session object and makes it, and its related data, available to the JSP page. This means that instead of trying to pass all the user-specific data back and forth between browser and server, JSP simply passes around the session ID and stores the session-specific data on the server side.

NOTE

Although JSP implements `session` as an object, it is sometimes referred to as a "scope." "Scope" is used to describe the area in which a particular variable is visible. For example, variables defined within a block of code in Java are only available within that code block. Its "scope" is the block of code.

Values assigned to the `session` object have the entire session as their scope—they are visible within the session. It is not uncommon to see "session" referred to both as an object and as a scope.

The `session` object is an implicit object that is made available automatically to JSP developers and implements the `javax.servlet.http.HttpSession` interface. The following section describes how to use the `session` object.

Setting Simple Values into the Session Scope

To see how the `session` object works, let's begin by storing and then retrieving a simple data type in the `session` object. Listing 10.1 contains a basic form that asks the user to type in his favorite color.

LISTING 10.1   A Basic Form to Get a User's Favorite Color

```
<!---
File:          SetColor.jsp
Author:        david aden (david@wwstudios.com)
Date:          7/4/00
Description:   Sets the chosen color into the session object and then
               forwards to DisplayColor.jsp to show the selected
               color.
Notes:
--->
<!DOCTYPE HTML PUBLIC "-//W3C//DTD HTML 4.0 Transitional//EN">

<html>
<head>
    <title>FirstSessionVars</title>
</head>

<body>
```

LISTING 10.1 Continued

```
<form name="AskColor" method="post" action="SetColor.jsp">
<center>
<table width="400" border="1">
    <tr>
        <th colspan="2" valign="middle">
            Color Chooser<br><br>
        </th>
    </tr>
    <tr>
        <td>Favorite Color</td>

        <td><input type="text" name="FavColor" size="30" value="">
        </td>
    </tr>
    <tr>
        <td colspan="2" align="center">
            <input type="submit" name="Submit" value="Submit">
        </td>
    </tr>
</table>
</center>
</form>

</body>
</html>
```

This template contains a basic HTML form that asks the user to enter his favorite color. Figure 10.1 shows what this template displays. Submitting the form sends the data to another JSP, SetColor.jsp, which is in Listing 10.2.

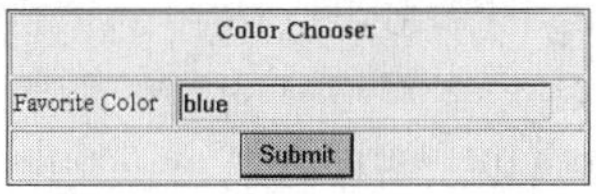

FIGURE 10.1
A simple form for entering a color preference.

TIP

Listing 10.2 is a JSP file but, as it is currently written, it could be an HTML file because it contains no JSP code or tags. In many cases, it is a good idea to make even simple files JSPs because as you build the site you may decide to add functionality to a page that originally only contained HTML code. It is often easier to make most of your site into JSPs while building the site rather than having to rename scattered links to your pages if you later decide to add dynamic functionality to what were originally static HTML files.

An exception to this may be your site's home page. High traffic sites will sometimes make their home pages static HTML. That way, even if the JSP server is down, users will still be able to access the home page. Also important is the fact that static HTML will always serve up faster than any dynamically generated page.

LISTING 10.2   Setting Data into the Session Scope

```
<!---
File:            SetColor.jsp
Author:              david aden (david@wwstudios.com)
Date:            7/4/00
Description:    Set the chosen color into the session object.

Notes:
--->

<%
    // Set the session variable "FavColor" to the value passed in
    //  from the form.
    session.setAttribute( "FavColor", request.getParameter("FavColor") );

%>

<!--- Let's just forward to the next page. —->
<jsp:forward page="DisplayColor.jsp"/>
```

Listing 10.2 doesn't display anything back to the user—it simply uses the `setAttribute()` method of the `session` object to create a session-scope variable called `FavColor` that contains the value passed from the form. Although this variable is named the same as the value passed in from the form, it is stored and accessed differently, so it will not be confused with the form variable.

TIP

For more information on using HTML forms and using JSP to access form data, see Chapter 7, "Working with Forms."

We then use the `jsp:forward` command to forward the user to `DisplayColor.jsp`. The forward command invokes `DisplayColor.jsp` without making a trip back to the browser. This allows us to set the user's choice of favorite color into the session scope and then immediately call a page to display the choice without incurring the network traffic overhead of returning the intermediary page to the browser. `DisplayColor.jsp` is shown in Listing 10.3.

LISTING 10.3   Displaying the Value of the `session` Variable

```
<!---
File:            DisplayColor.jsp
Author:              david aden (david@wwstudios.com)
Date:            7/4/00
Description:     Displays the value set into the session variable.

Notes:
--->

<!DOCTYPE HTML PUBLIC "-//W3C//DTD HTML 4.0 Transitional//EN">

<html>
<head>
    <title>DisplayColor.jsp</title>
</head>

<body>

Your favorite color is: <%=session.getAttribute("FavColor")%>!

</body>
</html>
```

This is a simple JSP that outputs the value contained in the `session` variable we set in `SetColor.jsp`. It uses the session method `getAttribute("FavColor")` to access the variable's value.

TIP

If you try using `getAttribute()` to access a `session` variable that doesn't exist, it will return `null`, which is an easy way to check whether a `session` variable exists before you attempt to use it. You can use a construct like the following to verify whether a variable exists in the session scope:

```
if ( session.getAttribute("blah") == null ) {
    // The variable does NOT exist
    out.println("not exist");
} else {
    // The variable DOES exist
}
```

10

Although the session scope is useful for saving simple values and making them available to a series of pages, the power of the session scope becomes more clear as you begin to use it to maintain state for entire objects.

Saving Complex Data Types in the Session Scope

One of the great advantages of the session object is that it accommodates maintaining more than simple variables, and the syntax for storing complex data types (objects) is basically the same as it is for storing simple values.

For example, suppose we want to create a Vector to store a set of selections made by a user. Vectors are part of the `java.util` package and are basically arrays that can grow or shrink as needed. (Arrays cannot change size once set; with Vectors, Java internally adjusts the Vector's size as needed.) The individual elements of a Vector are objects themselves that can be as simple as a string or as complicated as instances of user-defined classes.

The JSP code for creating a Vector is in Listing 10.4.

LISTING 10.4   Creating and Populating a Vector

```
<%@ page import="java.util.Vector" %>

<%
    // Create and populate a vector
    Vector java.util.vec = new java.util.Vector();

    vec.addElement("My first choice");
    vec.addElement("My second choice");
    vec.addElement("My third choice");
%>
```

Listing 10.4 creates a new Vector object and then adds several elements to it. Remember that strings are actually objects in Java, so we have effectively added three objects to the Vector named vec.

Assigning this object to the session scope is as simple as

```
session.setAttribute("MyVec", vec);
```

Now, for the duration of the session, our Vector object will be available to any page called by the user. Retrieving the object value into a variable local to the page is accomplished with the following:

```
Vector vec = (Vector) session.getAttribute("MyVec");
```

Because the `getAttribute()` method returns an object of class `Object`, the superclass of all objects in Java, we need to cast what it returns to the specific type of object we're actually retrieving. In the previous code, we've cast the return with (`Vector`).

We could also access values within our Vector object without creating a local reference to it, but the syntax tends to be harder to read:

```
String str = (String) ((Vector) session.getAttribute("MyVec")).elementAt(1);
```

Again, we've used `getAttributes()` to get the object that is cast to type Vector. We then invoke the `elementAt()` method of the Vector object to return the second element of the Vector. This returns an object that we cast to a `String`.

> ### TIP
>
> Casting is the process of changing the data type of a variable. Java allows you to cast objects to any of their subclasses—because `Object` is the top of the hierarchy, objects of type `Object` can be cast to any other class. In this case, we knew that the session scope variable contained a Vector, so we cast it to that type and were then able to invoke Vector methods on it.

Any type of Java object, whether a standard part of the Java runtime environment or a user-defined object, can be instantiated and saved into the session scope using the `session.setAttribute()` method.

Managing the Session

The `session` object also provides methods for managing the contents of the session itself and the objects stored within it. For example, to get a list of all the objects currently stored in the session scope, use the `getAttributeNames()` method. The following retrieves a list of all the attributes in the current session and prints out their names:

```
String s = "";
// Get a list of all the variables in the Session scope
Enumeration enum = session.getAttributeNames();

// Loop through the Enumeration
while ( enum.hasMoreElements() ) {
    s = (String) enum.nextElement();
    out.println( "<br>  Session variable name: " + s );
}
```

`getAttributeName()` returns an instance of `java.util.Enumeration`, so accessing it requires importing `java.util.Enumeration` at the top of your page. The loop uses the enumeration methods `hasMoreElements()` and `nextElement()` to loop through all the items in the enumeration and output them.

To find out when `session` was last accessed, use the `getLastAccessedTime()`:

```
out.println( "<br><br>Last Accessed: " + session.getLastAccessedTime() );
```

Of course, running a page to check when a session was last accessed involves a session access, thereby updating the value returned by `getLastAccessedTime()`.

More important than checking when a session was last accessed is checking how long the session is set to persist and adjusting its time-out interval. The time-out is set by specifying the number of seconds of session inactivity after which the server will invalidate the session. To see what the current time-out period is for the current session, use the following:

```
out.println( "Time-out: " + session.getMaxInactiveInterval() );
```

Setting the inactivity interval is also straightforward:

```
session.setMaxInactiveInterval(60*100);
```

This sets the time-out interval to 6000 seconds (100 minutes). After the time-out interval has elapsed with no activity from the client, the JSP engine automatically invalidates the session and unbinds any objects that have been tied to it. You can also invalidate a session programmatically with the `invalidate()` method:

```
session.invalidate();
```

When a session is invalidated, or times out, all the references to objects that were bound to it are lost. When the user next requests an application page, the JSP engine creates a new instance of the `session` object and makes it available to all subsequent JSP pages.

To determine if a session was just started (to do initialization or other setup), use the `session.isNew()` method, which returns a Boolean `true` if the session is new; otherwise, it returns `false`.

By default, the client browser needs to accept cookies for session management to work—if cookies are disabled, session management becomes much less automatic and more difficult. It is possible to establish and use sessions by passing session ID information on the URL, but this requires additional work on the part of the developer (how to do this is covered in the next section).

TABLE 10.1   Useful Methods in the `HttpSession` Interface

Method Name	Description
getAttribute(String name)	Returns the object bound to the specified name in this session or `null` if no object is bound to the name.
getAttributeNames()	Returns an enumeration of `String` objects containing the names of all the objects bound to this session.
getCreationTime()	Returns a long value that represents the date and time when the session was created.
getID()	Returns the session ID. This is used internally to identify a single session.
getLastAccesssedTime(long)	Returns a long integer that represents the time the session was last accessed.

TABLE 10.1 Continued

Method Name	Description
getMaxInactiveInterval(int)	Returns an int that represents the maximum number of seconds the session can remain inactive (without any requests) before timing out.
invalidate()	Invalidates this session and unbinds any objects bound to it.
isNew()	Returns a Boolean true if the session is new; Boolean false if the session is not new.
removeAttribute(String)	Removes (unbinds) the attribute of the specified name from the session.
setAttribute(String name, Object value)	Binds the object specified by value into the session scope identified by name.
setMaxInactiveInterval (int interval)	Specifies the maximum time in seconds that the session can remain inactive without being invalidated.

Using Embedded URLs (Rewriting)

As mentioned, the default way for a session to maintain state is by creating and storing a unique session ID in a cookie stored by the browser. However, it is also possible for the session ID to be passed with the URL in the query string. This might be needed in those cases when a browser is configured so it does not accept cookies. As an alternative to using cookies, you can put the session ID into a variable that is passed with the URL whenever any pages in the application are requested. This is a far more tedious and less reliable method of maintaining state as it involves additional overhead for the developer, who must make sure that every anchor in the site passes the session ID.

JSP helps to automate this process. This is useful to know about, although it has liabilities as a means for maintaining state. Hopefully, you won't have to use the approach often because it is more difficult to work with and has additional security problems that cookies do not have—for one thing, the session ID is in plain view in all requested URLs.

The session object is designed to take a session ID from either a cookie (if the user's browser supports cookies) or from a session ID passed with the URL. In fact, you can find where the session ID was taken from with the following methods of the request implicit object:

```
// Find out if the session id came from a cookie or a url variable
out.println( "<br><br>Session from cookie? " +
    request.isRequestedSessionIdFromCookie() );

out.println( "<br>Session from the URL? " +
    request.isRequestedSessionIdFromUrl() );
```

If you are working with a browser that doesn't accept cookies, a method of the response object can be used to rewrite all URLs so that they include the session ID if one doesn't already exist as a cookie. Instead of writing internal links to your site as normal HTML, as in the following

```
<a href="URLReWriting.jsp">Link to myself</a>
```

the same link would be coded as

```
<a href="<%=response.encodeURL("URLReWriting.jsp")%>">Link with Session ID</a>
```

In the second code line, the JSP engine determines if it already has a session variable associated with this user. If a session ID already exists in a cookie passed by the browser, the link is unchanged. If, however, no cookie exists containing a session ID, a session ID is created and appended to the URL. If no cookie session ID exists but a session was passed as part of the query string, the session ID received in the query string is added to the link.

To maintain a session for the whole site using this method, all links on the site need to be rewritten using the encodeURL() method.

Using Cookies

In addition to the previously described behind-the-scenes use of cookies for specifically maintaining a session, it is also possible to use cookies to maintain individual pieces of data from one page to another. Although it is generally preferable to store personalized data in the session object, it is possible to store simple data in a cookie. The browser will return the cookie to the server for each subsequent page request.

As with everything else in Java, cookies are implemented as a class that exposes methods used to get and set information within an instance of the Cookie class. First, let's look at how to create and set a cookie:

```
// Create a new cookie
Cookie myCookie = new Cookie("TestCookie", "Jason");

// Add it to the response scope to send it back to the user's browser
response.addCookie(myCookie);
```

The first line creates a new Cookie object with the name "TestCookie" and the value "Jason". The second line adds the cookie to the response object so that the cookie will be returned to the user's browser with the rest of the response. When the browser receives the response (including the cookie), the cookie is set.

Unfortunately, there is no method to get the value of a single cookie. Instead, you have to get an array of all the Cookie objects and then loop through the array to find the one you want.

```
Cookie cook = null;

// Get the cookie value back out.
Cookie[] aCookies = request.getCookies();

// Find the cookie we're interested in
for ( x=0; x < aCookies.length; x++ ) {

    // find the cookie and print it
    if ( aCookies[x].getName().equals("TestCookie") ) {
        // We found the right cookie -- let's set it to a local var
        //   to hold it.
        cook = aCookies[x];

        // Show the cookie's name
        out.println( "<br>  Cookie name: " + cook.getName() );

        // Show the value
        out.println( "<br>  Cookie name: " + cook.getValue() );

        // Show the maximum age of the cookie
        out.println( "<br>  Cookie Max Age: " + cook.getMaxAge() );
        break;
    }
}
```

This code uses the request object's getCookies() method to get all the available cookies into an array of Cookie objects named aCookies[]. The if statement checks to see if the name of the current cookie matches the one we are looking for. If so, it runs the enclosed block of code. The block of code stores the cookie into a local variable named cook. This block of code outputs the name of the cookie using the getName() method. The next lines output the cookie's value with getValue() and the cookie's maximum age getMaxAge(). This returns how soon after its creation (in seconds) it will expire.

TIP

For sites with relatively low security requirements, it is possible to store usernames and passwords in a cookie. When the user returns to your site from a browser that has the cookie, you use it to automatically log in the person. If the user comes to the site from a browser that doesn't have a cookie, you can provide a standard login screen.

10

Table 10.2 contains a full list of the available methods for `Cookie` objects.

TABLE 10.2   Useful Methods of the `Cookie` Class

Method Name	Description
getName()	Returns the name of the cookie as a string.
getValue()	Returns the value of the cookie as a string.
getMaxAge()	Gets the maximum age of the cookie in seconds. After the specified number of seconds, the cookie expires. A value of -1 indicates the cookie will persist until the browser shuts down.
setMaxAge(int expiry)	Sets, in seconds, the length of time the cookie will persist.
setValue(String s)	Sets the value of the cookie.
clone()	Makes a copy of the cookie and returns it as an object.

After you have made changes to a `Cookie` object, remember that you need to add it to the response object with the `addCookie()` method. Without this step, the updated cookie is never returned to the requesting browser.

Using Hidden Form Fields

Hidden form fields are another common way to pass data from one page to another. Although it is unrealistic to use hidden form fields as a method for maintaining session state (because not all application pages will be submitted), it is possible to persist data from one page to another using hidden form fields.

The same method used to find the value of variables passed with the URL also works to extract information passed as form variables. For example, if a form is submitted with a hidden field called `UserID`, the receiving page would access the value of `UserID` with the following:

```
request.getParameter("UserID")
```

JSP does not distinguish between data that is passed by a form submission and data that is passed as part of the URL in the query string. In a test with the JRun engine, creating two variables with the same name—one submitted as a form variable, the other passed as part of the URL—the JRun engine found and used the URL variable, ignoring the one passed in a form. Other engines may behave differently, so it is better to simply avoid duplicating names of variables passed as form variables and those submitted on the URL.

For developers accustomed to other environments where form field values and values passed in the query string are accessed differently, such as ASP, this may take some getting used to.

Summary

In this chapter, we examined the idea of maintaining state between a client browser and a JSP engine. The trick of it is that we needed to accomplish this over a network protocol that is essentially stateless. In fact, the problem of maintaining state in a Web application is not particular to JSP but is an problem for all Web application development, no matter which technology is used.

To make it possible to maintain state, Web developers have used a variety of tricks over the years—all of which enlist the cooperation of the browser to send some piece of data to the server to distinguish individual sessions. JSP provides server support for those "tricks," making state management a relatively easy and transparent part of Web development.

Unless your application has unique requirements or you need to cater to a user base that is unable to accept cookies, most session management is accomplished using cookies.

By using cookies to just store the session ID and maintaining the session-specific data on the server, JSP makes it possible for developers to write code as if a formal session exists and to take advantage of the object-oriented design of Java.

Integrating with Email

IN THIS CHAPTER

Electronic mail is the one of the most widely used Internet services. It is difficult to imagine a major Internet site that didn't provide some form of email interaction. Major Internet portals provide Web-based email services, and online retailers automate basic emailing tasks such as confirmation of order placement and sending out forgotten passwords. Integrating email functionality is an element of all major Web sites.

Thankfully, we can use the Sun Microsystems JavaMail API to incorporate email functionality into JSP pages. In this chapter we will look at how to automatically send and receive mail from a JSP page. The final example involves writing a Web-based email system similar in function to Yahoo! Mail or Microsoft Hotmail that will enable a user to log in and log out of any POP3 or IMAP mail server, as well as send and retrieve messages, all from a JSP-based Web interface.

Getting Started

The JavaMail API is a standard Java Extension API. Sun Microsystems provides a free reference implementation and some utilities for the most common protocols and standards, including SMTP, POP3, and IMAP. In addition, the API is designed so that independent software vendors can easily implement other protocols.

To get started, you will need to download the latest JavaMail implementation from JavaSoft at `http://java.sun.com/products/javamail/`. At the time of this writing, the most recent JavaMail implementation is JavaMail 1.1.3, released February 22, 2000. Unzip the files to a directory on your computer. The JavaMail class files are stored in a file called `mail.jar`. Ensure that the file is included in the classpath of both your Java server and your compiler.

Before getting into all the details of the JavaMail API, we'll write a simple Java program that performs the seemingly complicated task of connecting to a mail server and sending a message.

LISTING 11.1   `SendMail.java`—Send an Email Message Using the JavaMail API

```
import javax.mail.*;
import javax.mail.internet.*;

public class SendMail
{
    public static void main(String args[]) throws MessagingException
    {
        if (args.length <3)
        {
            System.out.println("Usage: java SendMail
                                    recipient sender mailServer");
            System.out.println("Example: java SendMail
                            joe@foo.com  dave@foo.com  mail.foo.com");
```

LISTING 11.1 Continued

```
            System.exit(1);
    }

    String to = args[0];
    String from = args[1];
    String mailServer = args[2];

    // Make a session
    java.util.Properties properties = System.getProperties();
    Session session = Session.getInstance(properties, null);

    // Make a message
    MimeMessage message = new MimeMessage(session);
    message.setFrom(new InternetAddress(from));
    message.addRecipient(Message.RecipientType.TO,
                                    new InternetAddress(to));
    message.setSubject("My First JavaMail Example");
    message.setText("JavaMail is Easy!");


    // connect to the transport
    // (if required, insert your username and password)
    Transport transport = session.getTransport("smtp");
    transport.connect(mailServer, "","");

    // send the message
    transport.sendMessage(message, message.getAllRecipients());
    transport.close();
    }
} // EOF
```

Compile the SendMail application and, to execute it from a command prompt, type the following:

```
java SendMail recipient sender mailserver
```

where `recipient` and `sender` are properly formatted email addresses and `mailserver` is the name of your outgoing mail server. Contact your network administrator or Internet service provider if you do not know the name of your outgoing mail server.

The actual JavaMail code in the SendMail program is very short. We see that the basic process of sending an electronic mail message requires the following steps:

1. Create a mail session

2. Using the session, create a message and set the various message properties

3. Connect to a mail transport system

4. Use the mail transport system to send the message

Now that you have seen just how easy it is to send mail from a Java application, we will talk about the JavaMail API itself.

Using the JavaMail API

The JavaMail API provides a set of abstract classes that model an Internet mail system. It allows Java developers to write software using the same JavaMail API method calls to send, receive, and store messages regardless of the underlying message-content type, message store, or message transport protocol, consistent with Java's "write once, deploy anywhere" programming philosophy.

The core functionality of the JavaMail API is contained in just a few main classes. This section presents the main classes and their most commonly invoked methods. It may seem like a considerable amount of material to remember, but the good news is twofold:

1. Email processing is not difficult, as you shall soon see.

2. There are numerous freely available JSP tag extension libraries that abstract all of the Java code so that you can send and receive email without writing any Java code.

Creating `javax.mail.Session`

This class is the top-level class of the JavaMail API, representing a mail session. It collects properties and defaults used by the mail APIs. It provides the capability to load and control the various classes for different mail protocols. This is not to be confused with the implicit JSP `Session` object, which is associated with a user's HTTP session.

In the SendMail example, we first create a session as follows.

```
// Make a session
java.util.Properties properties = System.getProperties();
Session session = Session.getInstance(properties, null);
```

First obtain a `Properties` object by calling the static `System.getProperties()` method. A `Properties` object is a hashtable that contains information about your system such as the operating system, Java Runtime Environment, classpath, and much more. This `Properties` object is then passed to the static `Session.getInstance()` method, which returns a new `Session` object, required to get things started.

Note that the second argument passed to the `Session.getInstance()` method was a null value. If the example required robust security, you would specify a reference to an Authenticator, instead.

The most commonly invoked methods of this class are related to obtaining references to the provider, store or transport associated with the current session, which are required to send and receive email, all of which will be discussed.

Using `javax.mail.Transport`

The Internet has several different mail transport protocols, of which the most common by far is the Simple Mail Transfer Protocol (SMTP). `javax.mail.Transport` is an abstract class that models a message transport, abstracting away the low-level details of the underlying message delivery system. Subclasses written by service providers provide the actual implementations.

The `Transport` class defines a static `send(Message msg)` method that can be used for sending electronic mail using the registered default mail transport. However, an alternative way of sending mail would be as follows:

```
String mailServer = "...";  // your outgoing mail server name
// connect to the transport
// (if required, insert your username and password)
Transport transport = session.getTransport("smtp");
transport.connect(mailServer, "","");

// send the message & close transport.
transport.sendMessage(message, message.getAllRecipients());
transport.close();
```

In this case, `session` and `message` are references to `javax.mail.Session` and `javax.mail.internet.MimeMessage` objects, respectively. Rather than simply invoking the static `send()` method, we specifically obtain the transport by asking the top-level `session` object for the SMTP `Transport` object by calling `session.getTransport("smtp")`. Then we connect to the specified mail server by calling the `connect()` method, which takes as arguments the name of the mail server and the username and password if required. Once connected, we invoke a `sendMessage()` method, which requires the message to be sent and the recipient list as arguments. Finally, it is important to close the message transport when it is no longer in use by calling the `close()` method.

Composing `javax.mail.Message`

This is an abstract class that models the characteristics of an electronic mail message, including To, From, Cc, Bcc, and Subject headers, as well as the message body content. Messages also have a set of flags that describe its state within the folder. `Message` objects are either newly instantiated by a client or obtained from a folder. Subclasses written by service providers provide the actual implementations.

The SendMail example illustrates the most common way to send a message: instantiate a `MimeMessage` (which directly extends `Message`), set the various header and content attributes, and invoke the `Transport.sendMessage()` method.

The most commonly used methods of `Message` involve getting and setting the various message attributes, as shown in SendMail. Another interesting method is `reply(boolean replyToAll)`, which creates a message and sets the recipient address fields appropriately.

Connecting to `javax.mail.Store`

This is an abstract class that models a message store and its access protocol for storing and retrieving messages. Subclasses are implemented by service providers, such as a software vendor developing a POP3 or IMAP mail service.

It also enables Read, Write, Monitor, and Search capabilities for a particular mail protocol. The following code fragment connects to an IMAP store; it could just as easily connect to a POP3 store by specifying pop3 instead.

```
// connect to store
Store store = session.getStore("imap"); // throws NoSuchProviderException
store.connect(inMailServer, user, password); // throws MessagingException
```

Because `Store` extends the `Service` class, like the `Transport` class, `Store` has many common methods for connecting to stores and listening to connection events. The `javax.mail.Folder` class is accessed through this class.

> **NOTE**
>
> IMAP stands for Internet Message Access Protocol. It is a method of accessing electronic mail and newsgroup messages kept on a mail server. IMAP permits a client email program to access remote message stores as though they were local. For example, email stored on an IMAP server can be manipulated from a desktop computer at home, a workstation at the office, and a notebook computer while traveling, without the need to transfer messages or files back and forth between those computers.
>
> While POP3 remains the dominant mail store used by ISPs today, it is inconvenient for those who access mail from different locations, because a POP3 mail client typically downloads the mail from the mail server, deletes it from the server, and stores a copy on the local file system. This was designed to accommodate offline mail access but has a tendency to sprinkle mail messages across all of the different computers used for mail access. IMAP's capability to access messages (both new and saved) and organize them into logical folders on the server from any terminal has become extremely important as reliance on electronic messaging and use of multiple computers increase. For example, IMAP has enjoyed tremendous support in college settings because mail is typically accessed from numerous terminals on campus or from home.

Using `javax.mail.Folder`

This is an abstract class that represents a folder in a mail message system. Depending on the specific implementation, a `Folder` can contain zero or more `Message` objects and possibly zero or more `Folder` objects, too, thus providing a tree structure hierarchy rooted at the `Store`'s default Inbox. Remember that the idea of folders is an IMAP concept; POP3 stores all mail in a single folder called `inbox`, and `inbox` is a case-insensitive reserved word for both IMAP and POP3 stores, referring to the primary folder for the current user and mail server. Subclasses implement protocol-specific `Folders`.

The following code fragment opens the Inbox and obtains an array of messages:

```
// open the inbox
Folder folder = store.getFolder("inbox");
folder.open(Folder.READ_ONLY); // throws messaging exception.

// get and list the messages.
Message[] messages = folder.getMessages();
```

As you can see, a `Folder` is obtained from a `Store` by calling the `getFolder()` method, which requires the name of the `Folder` as a parameter. The message listing, represented as an array of messages, is obtained by invoking the `Folder`'s `getMessages()` method.

NOTE

Message objects obtained from a `Folder` are just lightweight references to the actual message. The JavaMail API makes use of the Lazy Initialization design pattern, commonly used in distributed systems to accommodate limited bandwidth. This means that when you open an Inbox, initially you are given only a listing of message headers and not the actual `Message` objects. The individual `Message` objects are instantiated on demand, thus improving performance.

Now that you have had an introduction to some of the various classes involved with the JavaMail API, let's take a look at some of the possibilities for integrating email functionality into your JSPs.

ColdMail.com: A JSP and JavaMail Case Study

You are the principal software engineer for a relatively new startup Internet portal. To compete with the major players in this industry, your manager, a true Internet visionary, has dreamed up the idea of ColdMail.com (no relationship to Microsoft Hotmail), a mail portal feature to attract site traffic. Rather than duplicating existing mail portals, ColdMail.com is simply a

Web-based interface into any POP3 or IMAP mail store. The nature of the site requires flashy presentation layout, and so the company staff is comprised of mainly HTML layout and content editors. It is therefore imperative that your program achieve a clean separation of business and presentation logic so that the production staff can go about their work without having to deal with massive amounts of Java code.

Before we dive into the code, let's take a quick look at how the finished application will look. Initially, the user will be asked to provide information about his username, his password, and his inbound and outgoing mail servers. Upon successful login, he will be presented with a page such as that seen in Figure 11.1, which displays a listing of an email folder. Clicking on the message's hyperlink in the Subject: column will display the contents of the message on a new page.

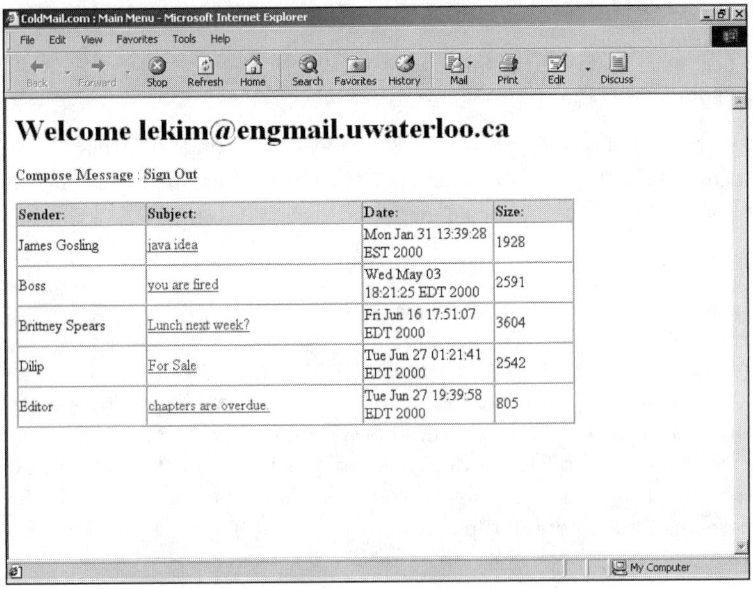

FIGURE 11.1
Browsing an email folder on the Web.

In addition to reading messages, the user can compose new messages, as seen in Figure 11.2.

One of the greatest challenges in writing such an application is choosing among the many different program architectures. As you develop more complex JSP applications, you will become familiar with numerous architectures to choose from, and you'll become painfully aware of the tradeoffs among them.

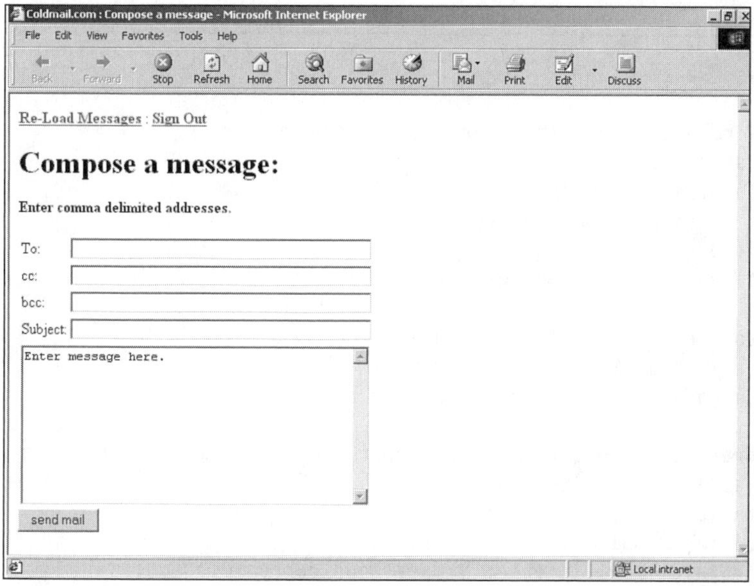

FIGURE 11.2

Composing a message.

For example, maximizing performance and efficiency will likely affect the ease with which the code base can be maintained. Another factor to consider is the extent to which your code has the potential for reuse. For example, some applications are written as servlets and JSP, so cutting and pasting code fragments constitutes code reuse. Other approaches achieve such a clean separation of business and presentation logic that the client could have been written as a Java Swing client or JSP without modifying any of the business logic.

In this example we choose a JavaBean/JSP approach. This is by far the easiest approach and does a good job of separating business and presentation logic.

The core of the program is in the `MailBean.java` file. The `MailBean` class encapsulates the various properties and methods that a user would need in order to interact with a mail server, including logging in, checking and reading mail, as well as composing new messages. The methods and properties are themselves self-explanatory and are commented in the code.

LISTING 11.2   `MailBean.java`—A JavaBean That Encapsulates a User's Interaction with a Mail Server

```
import javax.mail.*;
import java.util.*;
import javax.mail.internet.*;
```

LISTING 11.2   Continued

```
public class MailBean
{
    // information about the user & mail servers
    private String user;
    private String password;
    private String outMailServer;
    private String inMailServer;
    private boolean loginSuccessful=false;

    // data representing the user's session
    private java.util.Properties properties;
    private javax.mail.Session session;

    // representing mail store, transport, folders & message being read
    private javax.mail.Store store;
    private javax.mail.Folder folder;
    private javax.mail.Message[] messages;
    private javax.mail.internet.MimeMessage currentMessage;
    private javax.mail.Transport transport;

    // data representing a new message about to be sent.
    private javax.mail.internet.MimeMessage newMessage;
    private String to;
    private String cc;
    private String bcc;
    private String subject;
    private String body;

    public MailBean()
    {
      // a no-argument constructor.
    }

    // note: this example opens an imap store, change if necessary.
    public void login() throws NoSuchProviderException, MessagingException
    {
        // start session
        properties = System.getProperties();
        session = Session.getInstance(properties, null);

        // connect to store

        // throws NoSuchProviderException
```

LISTING 11.2   Continued

```
    store = session.getStore("imap");

    // throws MessagingException
    store.connect(inMailServer, user, password);

    // temp variable used by jsp the page.
    this.setLoginSuccessful(true);      }

public void openInbox() throws MessagingException
{
    // open the inbox
    folder = store.getFolder("inbox");
    folder.open(Folder.READ_ONLY); // throws messaging exception.

    // get and list the messages.
    messages = folder.getMessages();
}

public void readMsg(String s) throws
            MessagingException, NumberFormatException
{
    int msgNumber = Integer.parseInt(s);
    currentMessage = (MimeMessage)this.messages[msgNumber];
}

public void signout() throws MessagingException
{
    folder.close(false);
    store.close();
}

public void sendMsg() throws
            AddressException, SendFailedException, MessagingException
{
    properties = System.getProperties();
    properties.put("mail.smtp.host", outMailServer);
    session = Session.getInstance(properties, null);

    // Fill in the message headers
    newMessage = new MimeMessage(session);
    String from = new String(user + "@" + inMailServer);
    newMessage.setFrom(new InternetAddress(from));
    newMessage.setSubject(subject);
    newMessage.setText(body);
```

LISTING 11.2   Continued

```java
    Address[] toAddresses =  InternetAddress.parse(to);
    newMessage.setRecipients(Message.RecipientType.TO, toAddresses);

    Address[] ccAddresses =  InternetAddress.parse(cc);
    newMessage.setRecipients(Message.RecipientType.CC, ccAddresses);

    Address[] bccAddresses =  InternetAddress.parse(bcc);
    newMessage.setRecipients(Message.RecipientType.BCC, bccAddresses);

    // connect to the transport (if required, insert username and password)
    Transport transport = session.getTransport("smtp");
    transport.connect(outMailServer, "","");

    // send the message
    transport.sendMessage(newMessage, newMessage.getAllRecipients());
    transport.close();
}


// get & set methods, included for completeness.

public void setUser(String s) { user = s; }
public String getUser() { return user; }

public void setPassword(String s) { password = s; }
public String getPassword() { return password; }

public void setOutMailServer(String s) { outMailServer = s; }
public String getOutMailServer() { return outMailServer; }

public void setInMailServer(String s) { inMailServer = s; }
public String getInMailServer() { return inMailServer; }

public void setLoginSuccessful(boolean b) { loginSuccessful = b; }
public boolean getLoginSuccessful() { return loginSuccessful; }

public void setMessages(Message[] msg) { messages = msg; }
public Message[] getMessages() { return messages; }

public void setCurrentMessage(MimeMessage msg) { currentMessage = msg; }
public MimeMessage getCurrentMessage() { return currentMessage; }
```

LISTING 11.2   Continued

```
    public void setNewMessage(MimeMessage msg) { newMessage = msg; }
    public MimeMessage getNewMessage() { return newMessage; }

    public void setTo(String s) { to = s; }
    public String getTo() { return to; }

    public void setCc(String s) { cc = s; }
    public String getCc() { return cc; }

    public void setBcc(String s) { bcc = s; }
    public String getBcc() { return bcc; }

    public void setSubject(String s) { subject = s; }
    public String getSubject() { return subject; }

    public void setBody(String s) { body = s; }
    public String getBody() { return body; }
}
```

The MailBean in Listing 11.2 simply throws any exceptions that might occur into the context of the JSP page. They are then caught by a standard JSP error page, which tells the user that something has gone wrong and to contact the Webmaster if the problem persists. Also, all of the methods are written to minimize the number of scriptlets present in the various JSP files. Clearly, the majority of this code consists of accessor and mutator methods for the various JavaBean properties, which are included for the sake of completeness.

The entry into the mail portal is through an index.html file, which is shown in listing 11.3. It is simply a form that asks for a user's information including username, password, and outgoing and inbound mail servers.

LISTING 11.3   index.html—An HTML File That Challenges a User for His Email Credentials

```
<html>
<head>
    <title>Welcome to ColdMail.com, a Web-based email service.</title>
</head>
<body>
<h1>Welcome to ColdMail.com</h1>
<h4>Please enter your account information:</h4>
<form action="mainpage.jsp" method="post" />
<table cellspacing="0" cellpadding="0" border="0">
```

LISTING 11.3 Continued

```
<tr>
    <td width="150">Username:</td>
    <td><input type="text" name="username" /></td>
</tr>
<tr>
    <td>Password:</td>
    <td><input type="password" name="password" /></td>
</tr>
<tr>
    <td>outgoing SMTP server:</td>
    <td><input type="text" name="outgoing" /></td>
</tr>
<tr>
    <td>Incoming mail server:</td>
    <td><input type="text" name="incoming" /></td>
</tr>
<tr>
    <td></td>
    <td><input type="submit" value="Login" /><input type="reset" /></td>
</tr>
</table>
</form>
</body>
</html>
```

There is nothing dramatic about this page; it is simply a form that invokes the mainpage.jsp file from Listing 11.4 when invoked. If an error occurs (an invalid username or password, mail server unavailable, and so on), the user will be directed to the error.jsp file, a standard JSP error page, which is shown in Listing 11.9 and discussed later.

LISTING 11.4 mainpage.jsp—Logging In to a Mail Server with User-Provided Credentials

```
<%@ page language="java" errorPage="errorpage.jsp"%>
<html>
<head>
    <title>ColdMail.com : Main Menu</title>
</head>
<body>
<jsp:useBean id="mb" scope="session" class="MailBean" />
<%     if (!mb.getLoginSuccessful())
    {
```

LISTING 11.4   Continued

```
        mb.setUser(request.getParameter("username"));
        mb.setPassword(request.getParameter("password"));
        mb.setOutMailServer(request.getParameter("outgoing"));
        mb.setInMailServer(request.getParameter("incoming"));
        mb.login();
    }
    mb.openInbox();
%>

<h1>Welcome <%= mb.getUser() %>@<%= mb.getInMailServer() %></h1>
<a href="compose.jsp"><b>Compose Message</b></a> :
<a href="signout.jsp"><b>Sign Out</b></a><br><br>
<table width="800" border="1" cellspacing="0" cellpadding="1">
<tr  BGCOLOR="#dcdcdc">
    <td><b>Sender:</b></td>
    <td><b>Subject:</b></td>
    <td><b>Date:</b></td>
    <td><b>Size:</b></td>
</tr>

<%      for (int i = 0; i < mb.getMessages().length; ++i)
    {
%>
<tr>
    <td width="180"><%= mb.getMessages()[i].getFrom()[0] %></td>
    <td width="260"><a href="viewmsg.jsp?msgnum=<%= i %>">
    <%= mb.getMessages()[i].getSubject() %></a></td>
    <td width="180"><%= mb.getMessages()[i].getSentDate() %></td>
    <td width="90"><%= mb.getMessages()[i].getSize() %></td>
</tr>
<%
    }
%>
</table>
</body>
</html>
```

The first time a new user reads `mainpage.jsp`, it instantiates an instance of a `MailBean` that has session scope and thus exists throughout the duration of the current HTTP session. Next it attempts to log in to the mail store and open the user's Inbox. Subsequent requests for `mainpage.jsp` only require opening the Inbox, since the user will have already logged in successfully. This is accomplished by setting a Boolean flag upon successful login as shown in the `MailBean` in Listing 11.2. Finally, the contents of the Inbox, including the Sender, Subject,

Date, and Size message headers, are printed out to the page in table layout. A hyperlink on each message's Subject text will invoke viewmsg.jsp?msgmum=x, which displays the contents corresponding to message x. Let's take a closer look at the viewsg.jsp file that performs the task of displaying a specified message.

LISTING 11.5   viewmsg.jsp—A JSP That Displays a Specified Message from a Mail Folder

```
<%-- viewmsg.jsp  --%>
<%@ page language="java" errorPage="errorpage.jsp"%>
<html>
<head>
    <title>ColdMail.com : View Message</title>
</head>
<body>
<jsp:useBean id="mb" scope="session" class="MailBean" />
<% mb.readMsg((String)request.getParameter("msgnum")); %>

<a href="mainpage.jsp"><b>Re-Load Messages</b></a> :
<a href="signout.jsp"><b>Sign Out</b></a><br><br>
<table cellspacing="0" cellpadding="0" border="0">
<tr>
    <td><b>Date:</b></td>
    <td><%= mb.getCurrentMessage().getSentDate() %></td>
</tr>
<tr>
    <td><b>To:</b></td>
    <td><%= mb.getCurrentMessage().getAllRecipients()[0] %></td>
</tr>
<tr>
    <td><b>From:</b></td>
    <td><%= mb.getCurrentMessage().getFrom()[0] %></td>
</tr>
<tr>
    <td><b>Subject:</b></td>
    <td><%= mb.getCurrentMessage().getSubject() %></td>
</tr>
</table>
<p>
<%= mb.getCurrentMessage().getContent() %>
</body>
</html>
```

The code for viewmsg.jsp as shown in Listing 11.5 attempts to read the message corresponding to the number that was encoded on to the request URL. For example, viewmsg.jsp?msgnum=5 attempts to view the contents of message number 5 of the current folder. Note that each message in a folder has a unique message number corresponding to its place in the folder. Now that we've looked at browsing email folders and individual messages, let's take a look at composing email messages. Listing 11.6 shows the JSP page used to compose a message.

LISTING 11.6   compose.jsp—A JSP Used to Compose New Email Messages

```
<%-- compose.jsp  --%>
<%@ page language="java" errorPage="errorpage.jsp"%>
<html>
<head><title>Coldmail.com : Compose a message</title></head>
<body>
<a href="mainpage.jsp"><b>Re-Load Messages</b></a> :
<a href="signout.jsp"><b>Sign Out</b></a><br><br>
<h1>Compose a message:</h1>
<h4>Enter comma delimited addresses.</h4>
<form action="sendmail.jsp" method="post" />
<table>
<tr>
    <td>To:</td>
    <td><input type="text" name="to" size="50" /></td>
</tr>
<tr>
    <td>cc:</td>
    <td><input type="text" name="cc" size="50" /></td>
</tr>
<tr>
    <td>bcc:</td>
    <td><input type="text" name="bcc" size="50" /></td>
</tr>
<tr>
    <td>Subject:</td>
    <td><input type="text" name="subject" size="50" /></td>
</tr>
<tr>
    <td colspan="2"><textarea name="body" rows="20" cols="60">
    Enter message here.</textarea></td>
</tr>
</table>
<input type="submit" value="send mail" />
</form>
</body>
</html>
```

Composing a message is simply a matter of filling out the form of listing 11.6. This form was illustrated earlier on in the chapter in Figure 11.2. Submitting the form invokes the sendmail.jsp, which obtains all of the form parameters and takes care of instantiating and firing off a new message. Let's take a look at the sendmail.jsp file from Listing 11.7.

LISTING 11.7   sendmail.jsp—Sends an Email Message Using the Parameters Passed to It from a Form

```
<%-- sendmail.jsp  --%>
<%@ page language="java" errorPage="errorpage.jsp"%>
<html>
<head>
    <title>Coldmail.com : Your message was sent </title>
</head>
<jsp:useBean id="mb" scope="session" class="MailBean" />
<%    mb.setTo(request.getParameter("to"));
    mb.setBcc(request.getParameter("bcc"));
    mb.setCc(request.getParameter("cc"));
    mb.setSubject(request.getParameter("subject"));
    mb.setBody(request.getParameter("body"));
    mb.sendMsg();
%>
<body>
<a href="mainpage.jsp"><b>Re-Load Messages</b></a> :
<a href="signout.jsp"><b>Sign Out</b></a><br><br>
<h1>Your message has been sent.</h1>
</body>
</html>
```

Listing 11.7 shows that invoking the sendmail.jsp uses the MailBean associated with the current HTTP session to set the message headers as well as the message body in the bean's property fields. It then invokes the MailBean's sendMsg() method, which takes care of connecting to the mail transport and firing off the message.

Next we need to log out of the mail server when finished so that the next person using the terminal won't have access to your email. Logging out can be done from anywhere in the application by clicking on the logout hyperlink located on the top left corner of every page. Clicking on the hyperlink will invoke the signout.jsp file shown in Listing 11.8.

LISTING 11.8   signout.jsp—A JSP to Log the Current User Out of the Mail Server and Invalidate the Current HTTP Session

```
<%-- signout.jsp  --%>
<%@ page language="java" errorPage="errorpage.jsp"%>
```

LISTING 11.8   Continued

```html
<html>
<head>
    <title>Thank you for using ColdMail.com</title>
</head>

<body>

<jsp:useBean id="mb" scope="session" class="MailBean" />
<h1>Thank you for using ColdMail</h1>

<%   mb.signout();
     session.invalidate();
%>

click <a href="index.html">here</a> to log-in again.
</body>
</html>
```

Signing out is simply a matter of calling a signout() method in the MailBean associated with this session, which closes the folder and store associated with the session. In addition, the session is explicitly invalidated from within the JSP page.

The last thing we need to do is to handle exceptions such as invalid passwords, network failures, and so on. This is done using a JSP error page, as shown in Listing 11.9.

LISTING 11.9   errorpage.jsp—A Standard JSP Error Page

```jsp
<%-- errorpage.jsp  --%>
<%@ page language="java" isErrorPage="true"%>
<html>
<head>
    <title>ColdMail.com : An error has occurred.</title>
</head>
<body>
<h2>ColdMail.com regrets to report that an error has occurred.</h2>
<h4>Error:</h4>
<%= exception.toString() %><br>
Please contact the <a href="mailto:Webmaster@yourcompany.com">
Webmaster</a> if this problem persists.
</body>
</html>
```

As shown in Listing 11.9, all exceptions are caught by errorpage.jsp, which is preferable to having a user accidentally stumble into an HTTP error or see some stack-trace message. Further, it provides a method for users to report problems that may have slipped past the development process or are the result of an external system (perhaps a mail server) going down.

Throughout this case study, we see that the majority of the code in the JSP files is HTML presentation logic. This demonstrates how a well-written bean can achieve good separation of presentation and business logic, allowing content editors to design flashy pages without having to deal with so much Java code. This is one of the principal benefits of JSP, which then enables startup companies such as ColdMail.com to go public and make millions.

Introduction to Tag Extensions

Earlier we talked briefly about choosing among the different application architectures available to JSP programmers. It is quite possible that current JSP programming styles will be radically changed by advancements in the JSP specification, tag extensions (sometimes referred to as *custom tags*), and tag extension libraries in particular. Later chapters are dedicated to the topic of tag extensions, but as an example of how programming styles might change, we present a tag extension that encapsulates JavaMail email functionality. This is a possible alternative to the approach taken in the SendMail program that was presented at the beginning of this chapter. In this case, the tag extension is simply a tag-based abstraction to methods available in the JavaMail API. The JSP code is as follows:

```
<%-- mailtag.jsp --%>
<%@ taglib uri="jruntags" prefix="jrun" %>
<jrun:sendmail host="mail.yourserver.com"
sender="yourname@yourcompany.com"
recipient="bob@othercompany.com"
cc="dave@othercompany.com"
subject="JavaMail and custom tags">
Custom Tags Make JSP development easier.
</jrun:sendmail>
```

This is an actual working <sendmail> tag that can be found in the JRun Tag Library, one of several JSP tag libraries available for download on the Internet. The tag has parameters such as host, sender, recipient, and subject. The body of the email message is located between the opening and closing tags. The effect is to create a very short, simple, reusable tag that removes even more scriptlet code from the JSP file than in the JSP/bean approach. Further, because the JSP 1.1 specification defines a standard way of writing these tag libraries, they are portable across application servers. A more in-depth explanation of how to write tag handlers (the classes that make this tag work) will be presented in the next chapter.

Summary

In this chapter we discussed the JavaMail API as an easy means of adding interactive function-ality to your site. Note that it wouldn't difficult to beef up the functionality of the MailBean.java file, such as adding support for viewing or downloading attachments that are not plain text. There's still considerable work needed to make the code secure and more robust, but we have seen that the JavaMail API is very easy to use because all of the low-level details of implementation are handled for us. Finally, we briefly introduced the possibility of encapsu-lating JavaMail functionality into JSP tag extensions, as an alternative way of creating similar programs. This will be the subject of later chapters.

Developing Custom Tags

IN THIS CHAPTER

This chapter gives an overview of custom JSP tags or "custom actions" as they are also called. A general discussion of tag-based language features precedes an introduction to JSP custom tags and tag handlers. Examples are given of some of the different types of custom tags you can author under the JSP 1.1 specification. The process of packaging and writing an XML tag library descriptor for deployment of tags is covered. The chapter ends with references to some existing tag libraries and brief coverage of what they offer.

Custom tag development is an advanced topic requiring skills more usually found in Java developers rather than content developers. This book is aimed squarely at content developers wanting to learn how to use JSP to enhance their dynamic Web pages. We realize that there are a lot of people who do both or who are interested in developing their Java skills more. While this chapter is by no means a complete or deep coverage of developing custom tags for JSP (we feel no single chapter could do that, rather, a whole volume could and should be dedicated to it), we hope it is a sufficient start for those interested in pursuing the topic further.

Understanding Custom Tags

So you've been hearing about custom tags and tag libraries in this book and elsewhere. What's all the hype about? What are these things? Why would you want to use them? Those are the kinds of questions we're going to answer in this section.

First off, what's a tag? If we want to talk about custom tags, we should first know what a regular tag is, right? I'm sure we all have an intuitive understanding of what a tag is, but let's make our intuitions explicit in words.

Defining a Tag

A *tag* is a significant unit of code in a tag-based language. Tag-based computer languages include things like the mother (directly or indirectly) of all tag-based markup languages—SGML (Standard Generalized Markup Language), HTML, XML (and its offspring, XSL, WML, XHTML, and so on), and CFML. Tag-based languages are typically concerned with "marking up" other content, usually text, with tags. The key idea behind SGML-derived markup languages is the separation of form and content; that is, tags are often used to structure and format data (in the case of HTML) or to provide meta-information about data (in the case of XML).

NOTE

There are other, non-tag-based languages for marking up text, such as PostScript and LaTeX.

Tags typically come in opening and closing pairs, such as `<html>` and `</html>`. Tags typically follow the convention, inherited from SGML, of separating themselves from the surrounding content by being enclosed in angle brackets, also known as less-than and greater-than symbols. Tags are interpreted by the software reading the file in which they are contained. Typically the tag itself is not rendered and displayed to the user's screen. Instead, the content contained between the begin tag (`<Tag>`) and the end tag (`</Tag>`) is rendered using the interpretation of the tag (or tags if nested) as well as the attributes of the tag.

HTML should be very familiar to the audience for which this book is intended. The normal situation for HTML is that it is used to mark up plain text documents with the intent that the HTML will be evaluated by specialized software called a Web browser. (I know this is all obvious, but please bear with me.)

Web browsers read HTML documents and render the tags by substituting something else for the tags. What gets substituted depends on several factors, including but not limited to the version and capabilities of the browser, the particular tag being rendered, the values of its attributes, and the tag's relation to other tags in the document.

Tags can typically be nested. For instance, all HTML tags are (optionally) nested within opening and closing `<html>` tags. Nesting tags is sometimes a requirement of the tag-based syntax. For example, to build tables in HTML, you have to nest (at minimum) `<table>`, `<tr>`, and `<td>` tags properly. Other types of nesting can achieve formatting effects that are cumulative. For example, nesting a header `<h1>` tag between `<b>`, `<i>`, `<u>`, and `<center>` tags as shown in the following code has a cumulative effect on one section of text:

```
<b><i><u><center><h1>Hello</h1></center></u></i></b>
```

…yielding something like

Hello

Some tags have an effect only if there is something contained between the opening and closing of the tag elements, such as the `<b>` for bold text. If there's no text between the opening and closing `<b></b>`, there's nothing rendered. Other tags, such as the HTML `<img>` tag, take no body content.

Finally, tags often have attributes. Tag attributes go within the angle brackets of the tag and are used to provide information relevant to the function of the tag, such as the following example:

```
<img src="images/foo.jpg" height="200" width="40" alt="The foo" />
```

To summarize, tag-based languages usually have the following features:

- Opening and closing tags like `<foo></foo>`, unless the tag is empty, in which case a forward slash closes it (`<foo />`).

- Enclosed in angle brackets <...>.
- Can be nested.
- When tags are processed, they are substituted with formatting information, content, or otherwise translated into information used to process or display the document and associated resources.
- Can be processed by client- or server-side software, depending on the tag language and its purpose.
- Can be used to enclose content and affect its presentation or meaning, or use enclosed content as input to the tag's processing.
- Can be used without enclosing any content (empty tags).
- Can take attributes to provide additional information used in processing the tag.

CFML Tags

A tag language like ColdFusion Markup Language (CFML) capitalizes on these features of tag-based languages, but is designed such that an application server rather than a Web browser processes the tags. As such, CFML tags are geared to server-side dynamic content generation, including tags for making SQL queries, sending and retrieving email, manipulating XML data, and so on. Yet CFML employs all the same features and concepts of other tag-based languages. Similar to HTML, CFML encapsulates a lot of powerful functionality in easy-to-use tags. The custom tag concept of the JavaServer Pages technology is similar to the server-side tag concept of CFML. CFML is a proprietary language of the Allaire Corporation, developed long before JSP custom tags came into existence. For quite some time, users have been able to extend Allaire's CFML by writing their own CFML tags in C++ and Java.

A significant difference between JSP custom tags and CFML is that JSP custom tags are written to comply with a public standard (the JSP 1.1 Specification), which was developed under the Java Community Process. Interestingly, Allaire has been an active and influential contributor to the JSP specification.

Developing Simple Tags: No Attributes or Body Content

The backend implementations of custom JSP tags (also known as "custom actions") are Java classes called *tag handlers*. These are what you will write when you create your custom tags. Tag handlers are similar to JavaBeans in that they are specialized yet reusable components with public accessor/mutator methods. We'll see in the next section that the implementation of tag attributes in tag handler classes is borrowed directly from the GET and SET property methods of JavaBeans.

The simplest type of custom tag you can write in JSP is a tag that takes no attributes and that does not evaluate any body content. In this section, we will develop and deploy such a tag.

Obtaining the JSP and Servlet APIs

The Servlet 2.2 API (and Servlet 2.3, when those appear sometime in 2001) classes from JavaSoft contain all the classes needed for coding and compiling custom tags. No separate JSP development kit or set of classes apart from the Servlet API classes are needed. All you need are the J2EE classes that come with the Java 2 Enterprise Edition (in j2ee.jar), or the servlet.jar or jsdk.jar that came with your JSP 1.1-compliant servlet container.

Most containers that support the Servlet 2.2 APIs keep the Servlet API classes in a separate JAR file for ease of use and maintenance. Orion (as of Orion 1.0) does not, so you can use the ones in the orion.jar file. When in doubt, you can always acquire your own set of the latest Servlet API library from Sun at http://java.sun.com/products/servlet.

Make sure you have the JAR file in your classpath or your IDE's classpath while you are compiling these examples and developing your own tags.

12

> **NOTE**
>
> An easy way to add a class to your classpath with a Java 2 installation, both for compilation and for runtime, is simply to add the class's JAR file(s) to your <JAVA_HOME>/jre/lib/ext directory. Any classes in that directory will be discovered automatically by the JVM. It's worth mentioning here that the Servlet 2.3 specification requires JDK 1.2, and all related specifications (JSP and J2EE) will require JDK 1.2 or higher.

Understanding a Basic Tag Handler

The basicTagClass in Listing 12.1 shows a skeleton of a simple custom JSP tag. This skeleton can be used as a template for future development. Listing 12.1 illustrates the basic methods, import statements, and exceptions common to every tag handler class.

LISTING 12.1 basicTagClass.java—A Skeleton for Tag Handlers with No Attributes or Body Content

```
import javax.servlet.jsp.*;
import javax.servlet.jsp.tagext.*;

public class basicTagClass extends TagSupport
{
```

LISTING 12.1   Continued

```
public int doStartTag() throws JspException
{
    try
    {
        /** your code goes here */
        return SKIP_BODY;
    }
    catch(Exception e)
    {
        throw new JspException(e.getMessage());
    }
}

public int doEndTag() throws JspException
{
    try
    {
        /** more of your code goes here if you decide to
            implement this optional method */
        return EVAL_PAGE;
    }
    catch(Exception e)
    {
        throw new JspException(e.getMessage());
    }
}
}
```

All custom tag handlers are required to implement one of two interfaces: `javax.servlet.jsp.tagext.Tag` or `javax.servlet.jsp.tagext.BodyTag`. `Tag` is the granddaddy of all tag handlers; its only parent is `java.lang.Object`. `BodyTag` extends `Tag`. Both of them are interfaces, which means you must implement them using the `implements` keyword in your class declaration. Instead of going into that now, we will take an easier route.

Understanding the `Tag` and `BodyTag` Interfaces

The Servlet 2.2 API includes ready-made implementations of the `Tag` and `BodyTag` interfaces: `javax.servlet.jsp.TagSupport` and `javax.servlet.jsp.BodyTagSupport`. These will save you a lot of trouble. This convenience of ready-made utility classes is similar to how the standard Servlet API library helps servlet developers. That is, the Servlet API includes a `Servlet` interface that users can implement if they want to, but also provides a `GenericServlet` class that implements the `Servlet` interface and even provides a protocol-specific extension of

GenericServlet called HttpServlet. Nine out of ten servlet programmers will develop their servlets by extending the HttpServlet class rather than implementing the Servlet interface from ground zero.

Don't worry too much about what an interface is or whether we're glossing something over. Simply put, an *interface* is a special type of Java program that defines some methods, and potentially some constants, but does not include an implementation of the methods. Interfaces define protocols, really, and the classes implementing them are free to do so in their own way, as long as the ground rules set in the interface are followed.

Interfaces are another way Java can interrelate classes without requiring the direct ancestral relationship of extension. Partly it's a workaround for avoiding multiple inheritance (an error prone feature of C++ eliminated from Java by design) while allowing for class definitions to be interrelated. Note that interfaces are not classes because they cannot be instantiated as objects and they do not include the class keyword in their declarations. For more on interfaces, please refer to a good Java language reference. See also abstract classes, which in many ways are similar to interfaces.

Understanding the `TagSupport` and `BodyTagSupport` Classes

We can just subclass TagSupport any time we want to write a basic tag handler that does not evaluate body content. That's what the class is intended for. Likewise for BodyTagSupport, when we want to write a tag handler that processes body content. TagSupport has a few methods beyond those implemented from the Tag interface, but the main Tag methods are enough for basic tags:

- doEndTag(), returns int
- doStartTag(), returns int
- getParent(), returns Tag
- release(), returns void
- setPageContext(PageContext), returns void
- setParent(Tag), returns void

Note that as long as the TagSupport class implements all these methods (and it does), we only have to follow suit when we subclass TagSupport. It only takes one method to do the work in a simple tag handler, but we must follow the rules of the interface and implement all the methods, even if they don't do anything. We must use one of either doStartTag() or doEndTag() when implementing our tag handler, or we can use both.

doStartTag() is executed as soon as the custom tag is instantiated and initialized by the JSP container. doEndTag() is executed as soon as the doStartTag() completes. Both these methods, as well as the processes of loading and initializing custom tag handlers, are automatically invoked and handled by the JSP container.

The doStartTag() and doEndTag() methods return int values. The int values they return are, to human eyes, short phrases, such as SKIP_BODY and EVAL_PAGE. You may not have seen integers like this before! The return values that matter to the JSP container are the integer values of these human-readable text messages. These ints send a flag to the JSP container about what to do next, based on a limited set of options. The human-readable equivalents of the ints are made to signify to programmers what the tag does at the source code level. This is a common practice not unique to JSP development.

The following are the int values that doStartTag() can return:

- EVAL_BODY_INCLUDE   Means include the body between the opening and closing tags into the existing output stream, but do not create a new BodyContent object. This return value is only valid for classes extending TagSupport and/or implementing the Tag interface. These tags cannot process body content, but they can include it in the existing output stream.

- EVAL_BODY_TAG   Means create a new BodyContent object and process the body of the tag. Naturally, this return value is only valid for classes extending BodyTagSupport and/or implementing BodyTag. This is because only those tag handlers can do anything with tag body content other than passively including it in an existing output stream.

- SKIP_BODY   Means do not process the body of the tag if there is one. This is a valid return for a doStartTag() method in either type of tag handler.

The following are the int values that doEndTag() can return:

- EVAL_PAGE   Continue to process the rest of the JSP.
- SKIP_PAGE   Skip evaluating the rest of the JSP.

Writing Our First Tag Handler

There are four kinds of sophistication that can be layered in a variety of ways to create tags. The first kind is the simple tag with no attributes, optional body content, and no custom scripting variables. The second kind adds one or more attributes. Attributes in JSP tags, like HTML tags, are used to pass extra data or processing information to the tag. The third kind adds the ability to process body content in the tag. This includes the feature of being able to nest tags and perform iterations over tag content, perhaps dynamically changing the action performed on body content each time it is processed through the loop. The fourth kind of sophistication is the addition of custom scripting variables in the JSP. Custom scripting variables require an additional type of special class called a TagExtraInfo class.

Extending the `TagSupport` Class

Let's look at a simple extension of the `TagSupport` class. Listing 12.2 shows `SimpleTag`, a tag handler for a custom tag with no attributes and no fancy programming logic. In other words, a simple tag to get us started with writing tag handlers.

LISTING 12.2   `SimpleTag.java`—Simple Tag Handler for a Custom Tag with No Attributes

```java
import javax.servlet.jsp.*;
import javax.servlet.jsp.tagext.*;

public class SimpleTag extends TagSupport
{
    public int doStartTag() throws JspException
    {
        try
        {
            JspWriter jw = pageContext.getOut();
            jw.print("<html>\n");
            jw.print("<head><title>SimpleTag Example</title></head>\n");
            jw.print("<body bgcolor=\"#ffffff\">\n");
            jw.print("<h1 align=\"center\">SimpleTag</h1>\n");

            return EVAL_BODY_INCLUDE;
            //We return the "EVAL_BODY_INCLUDE" value to indicate to the
            //container that any text between the opening and closing tags
            //of this custom tag should be included in the response output
            //stream.  We can't do anything to the body content because this
            //class does not extend BodyTagSupport, but we can include body
            //content.
        }
        catch(Exception e)
        {
            throw new JspException(e.getMessage());
        }
    }

    public int doEndTag() throws JspException
    {
        try
        {
            JspWriter jw = pageContext.getOut();
            jw.print("<center><p>Copyright <a href=\"mailto:jdoe@acme.com\">" +
                    "John Doe</a> &copy; 2000</p></center>\n");
            jw.print("</body></html>");
```

LISTING 12.2   Continued

```
        return SKIP_PAGE;
        //We returned the int value "SKIP_PAGE" to indicate that the rest
        //of the JSP should be skipped.  This is because we don't want
        //anyone to add any HTML output after the tag completes.  However,
        //this will also prevent any scriptlet code from being evaluated
        //after this point in the page.
    }
    catch(Exception e)
    {
        throw new JspException(e.getMessage());
    }
}

public void release()
{
    /* This method is totally optional, but it's a good habit to include
     * it so you don't forget it when you really need it.
     */
}
}
```

Using Our Basic Tag Handler in a JSP

Listing 12.3 is a simple JSP used to call this tag. The tag handler prints out some text from its doStartTag() method and then prints some more from its doEndTag() method. It allows you to put content in its body, although it does not evaluate the content. The body content is evaluated for scripting code by the JSP container, but the tag handler itself ignores it.

LISTING 12.3   simpleTagExamp.jsp—JSP to Call Our First Simple Tag a Couple of Times

```
%@ taglib prefix="custom" uri="/simpleTag" %>
<custom:simple>
<h4>Here is some non-evaluated text in the middle</h4>
<p>Here is a JSP expression, untouched by the custom tag:<font color="red">
 <%= new java.util.Date(); %></font></p>
</custom:simple>
```

Remember, classes extending TagSupport or implementing Tag directly cannot evaluate body content, but they can include it. A very natural use of tag handlers is for HTML generation of reusable Web content components, such as headers and footers, as shown here, or other components such as menus, toolbars and sidebars. Figure 12.1 shows the output of a request to simpleTagExamp.jsp.

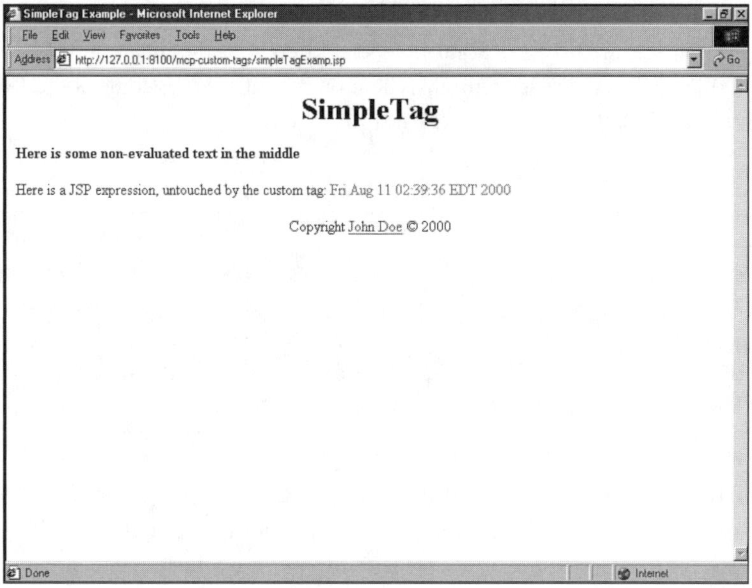

FIGURE 12.1

`simpleTagExamp.jsp`'s result, showing dynamically generated output.

Reviewing the `taglib` Directive

Note the use of the `taglib` directive to call our custom tag in Listing 12.3. The `taglib` directive must appear before any tags associated with it are used in the page. It's good practice to put your `taglib` directives at the top of the page.

The `taglib` directive takes two attributes. One is a user-defined `prefix` that is used on the page as a prefix to the custom tag. The main reason for having prefixes is to prevent situations where you have multiple tags with the same name but different functionality (a likely possibility when using a variety of third-party tags). The prefix keeps them in their own namespace. The prefix can be anything you or your content developers or your boss like, except for seven special cases reserved by Sun Microsystems—`jsp`, `jspx`, `java`, `javax`, `servlet`, `sun`, and `sunw`. There is no hard-coded tie between the tag handler class and the `prefix` attribute of the `taglib` directive.

The second attribute is a URI (uniform resource identifier) pointing to the JAR file containing the tag handler being used and associated in this page with that prefix. If you package your tag handler classes in a JAR file with a `META-INF` directory containing a special XML file named `taglib.tld` (which we cover next), you can refer to them collectively by their `<taglib>` definition in the `web.xml` for your Web application. Otherwise, you can extract the tag library descriptor (TLD) file and keep it in a directory in your Web application (such as WEB-INF), in which case the taglib directive's uri attribute should point to the location of the tld file. You could also put the tag library descriptor anywhere on the Internet, as long as the JSP container can access it via the URI you specify in the uri attribute.

NOTE

Note that the taglib tag attribute uri is lowercase, as it must appear when used in a taglib directive. The acronym URI is uppercase in the paragraph above because it stands for *uniform resource identifier*, which is a class of resource identifiers that includes URLs (all URLs are URIs, but not all URIs are URLs). Just remember that, unlike HTML, JSP tags are case sensitive, and the attribute name uri is lowercase.

Understanding the Tag Library Descriptor

The tag library descriptor is an XML deployment descriptor that is part of the JSP 1.1 standard. Its purpose is to describe the characteristics of your tag library. The JSP container uses it to help instantiate and initialize your tag handlers. As we've said, the most portable way to package your tag handlers is in JAR files with the tag library descriptor named taglib.tld and placed into the META-INF directory of the JAR file. The taglib.tld for our current example is shown in Listing 12.4.

LISTING 12.4   taglib.tld—Tag Library Descriptor for Our First Example

```
<?xml version="1.0" encoding="ISO-8859-1" ?>
<!DOCTYPE taglib
        PUBLIC "-//Sun Microsystems, Inc.//DTD JSP Tag Library 1.1//EN"
        "http://java.sun.com/j2ee/dtds/web-jsptaglibrary_1_1.dtd">
<taglib>
    <tlibversion>1.0</tlibversion>
    <jspversion>1.1</jspversion>
    <shortname>MCP JSP Samples</shortname>
    <tag>
        <name>simple</name>
        <tagclass>SimpleTag</tagclass>
        <bodycontent>JSP</bodycontent>
    </tag>
</taglib>
```

And the web.xml entry for the tag library is as follows:

```
    <taglib>
        <taglib-uri>/simpleTag</taglib-uri>
        <taglib-location>/WEB-INF/lib/simpleTag.jar</taglib-location>
    </taglib>
```

To use a custom tag in a Web application, the servlet/JSP container must be able to find the tag's handler class(es) and TLD file. Doing so requires that you add an entry to the container's web.xml for the tag or tag library in question and then make the tag library classes and deployment descriptor known to the container. The easiest way to do this is as previously outlined, putting the tag library's JAR file into the Web application's WEB-INF/lib directory. Then your content developers can easily access it using the uri attribute value shown above in Listing 12.4.

Now is a good time to go over the syntax of the tag library descriptor XML file. The official document type definition (DTD) for the TLD file can be found online at http://java.sun.com/j2ee/dtds/web-jsptaglibrary_1_1.dtd. Here we will go over it briefly, using the empty but complete list of elements in Listing 12.5 as our reference.

LISTING 12.5 taglib.tld.example — Tag Library Descriptor for Our First Example

```
<!DOCTYPE taglib
        PUBLIC "-//Sun Microsystems, Inc.//DTD JSP Tag Library 1.1//EN"
        "http://java.sun.com/j2ee/dtds/web-jsptaglibrary_1_1.dtd">
<taglib>
    <tlibversion></tlibversion>
    <shortname></shortname>
    <info></info>
    <jspversion></jspversion>
    <uri></uri>
    <tag>
        <name></name>
        <tagclass></tagclass>
        <bodycontent></bodycontent>
        <info></info>
        <teiclass></teiclass>
        <attribute>
            <name></name>
            <required></required>
            <rtexprvalue></rtexprvalue>
        </attribute>
    </tag>
</taglib>
```

First, like any good XML document with a public DTD, the DOCTYPE declaration is listed at the top. Some containers may require this to be there, others do not. The root element of every tag library descriptor is the <taglib> element. There must be only one <taglib> element in which all other elements are nested. The <taglib> element has three required sub-elements and three optional elements. The optional elements are <jspversion>, <uri>, and <info>. The default value for `<jspversion>` is `1.1`. `<jspversion>` can be used to indicate the minimum version of JSP the container must support to use this tag library. The `<uri>` element can be used to indicate a public URI that uniquely identifies the version of this tag library. The `<info>` element can contain any arbitrary string that provides some description of the tag library. The optional elements can all be omitted or left empty in the tag library descriptor. Each of these optional elements can only be used per tag library descriptor.

The first required sub-element of `<taglib>` is `<tlibversion>`, which is used to identify the version of this tag library and differentiate it from other versions of the same tag library. A `<shortname>` element is required to define a default (preferably short) name for tag instances and variables created by this tag library. It must follow the syntax rules for names of Java variables (cannot start with digits or underscores, and no whitespace allowed). Finally, one or more `<tag>` elements must be included. Each tag handler in your tag library (which could be as small as one, or infinitely large), that is each custom JSP tag, must have one `<tag>` entry in the `<taglib>` definition.

The `<tag>` element has several required and optional sub-elements. The required elements are `<name>` and `<tagclass>`. The `<name>` element defines the canonical name of the tag being defined. This is where you define the name of the tag to be used by content developers. The *canonical name* is a name you make up for reference purposes, just like a variable name, preferably a short but meaningful name. The `<tagclass>` element defines the full name of the tag handler class. So if your tag handler is `com.fiddle.sticks.CoolTag`, its `<tagclass>` is `com.fiddle.sticks.CoolTag` and its canonical name could be something like `cool`.

The optional sub-elements of `<tag>` are `<info>`, which serves exactly the same descriptive purpose it does as a sub-element of `<taglib>`, `<teiclass>`, `<bodycontent>`, and zero or more `<attribute>` elements. The `<teiclass>` element is used to name an optional subclass of `javax.servlet.jsp.tagext.TagExtraInfo` for this tag.

A `TagExtraInfo` (`TEI`) class is used to provide supplemental translation time information relevant to the processing of a tag handler. You would write such a class, if needed, and include it in the JAR file with this tag library. We won't get into too much detail on `TEI` classes in this chapter. The `<bodycontent>` element is used to give the JSP container a "hint" as to the type of body content this tag can contain. This element is primarily intended to be informative to JSP development tools. The `<bodycontent>` element can take one of three values—`tagdependent`, `JSP`, or `empty`. `JSP` is the default value if unspecified. The last optional element of `<tag>` is `<attribute>`. If you write a tag handler that can or must accept one or more attributes (attributes can be optional, as we'll see), you must include an `<attribute>` tag for each of them. If your tag handler takes no attributes, its corresponding `<tag>` element does not require an `<attribute>` element.

Every non-empty `<attribute>` element must have one `<name>` element that names the attribute being defined. The name in the `<name>` element must match that of the attribute because it will be used in JavaServer Pages, which also matches the attribute's definition in the tag handler class. The attribute element may contain a `<required>` element, which indicates whether the attribute is required or not when the tag is used. The possible values are `true`, `yes`, `no`, or `false`. `True` and `yes` are interchangeable and equivalent, as are `no` and `false`. The default is for attributes to be optional unless otherwise indicated with this element. Finally, each attribute element can take one `<rtexprvalue>` sub-element, which indicates whether the value of the attribute can be specified in the JSP as a scriptlet expression or whether the attribute's value must be static. The possible values of this element are the same as for the `<required>` element, and the default is `false`.

Understanding the `web.xml` Deployment Descriptor

The `web.xml` deployment descriptor requires a lengthier discussion beyond the scope of this chapter. It has been mentioned several times, and examples have been given when necessary. Just as the `taglib.tld` tag library descriptor describes a tag library to a JSP container, the `web.xml` deployment descriptor describes a Web application to a Servlet container. Because a Web application can include zero or more tag libraries, there is a `<taglib>` element for indicating the presence of tag libraries. The Servlet container will use the sub-elements of the `<taglib>` element to locate the tag library and its descriptor. The syntax of the `<taglib>` element of `web.xml` is as follows:

```
<taglib>
    <taglib-uri></taglib-uri>
    <taglib-location></taglib-location>
</taglib>
```

Both sub-elements of the `<taglib>` element are required. The `<taglib>` element itself must be a sub-element of the root `<web-app>` element of `web.xml`. The `<taglib-uri>` element specifies a URI, relative to the location of the `web.xml` file (which must always be in the root of the Web application's `WEB-INF` directory), which identifies a tag library to be used in the Web application. The `<taglib-location>` element specifies the location of the tag library descriptor XML file, relative to the `web.xml` document. An example of using the `<%@ taglib %>` directive in a JSP and how it relates to the `<taglib>` element in `web.xml` follows:

In the JSP

```
<%@ taglib uri="/myTagLib" prefix="mytags" %>
```

In the `web.xml`

```
<taglib>
<taglib-uri>/myTagLib</taglib-uri>
<taglib-location>/WEB-INF/tlds/myTagLib.tld</taglib-uri>
</taglib>
```

12

DEVELOPING CUSTOM TAGS

Recall that if we do not put a `taglib.tld` file in the META-INF directory of the tag library's JAR file, we can name the tag library descriptor anything we like and refer to it in this way. Otherwise, if we use the more portable method of putting a `taglib.tld` file in the META-INF of our tag library JARs, we would have something like the following example (this is how we designed our `simpleTag` example as well):

In the JSP

```
<%@ taglib uri="/myTagLib" prefix="mytags" %>
```

And in the `web.xml`

```
<taglib>
    <taglib-uri>/myTagLib</taglib-uri>
    <taglib-location>/WEB-INF/lib/myTagLibrary.jar</taglib-location>
</taglib>
```

NOTE

All this XML fun is probably more than you bargained for, although if you have HTML experience, it should be pretty easy to get used to. Unfortunately, the whole J2EE platform is relatively very young compared to a lot of Internet technologies. As a result, there are a lot of configuration files and other steps for preparing and deploying applications that are still rather raw. As better and more sophisticated tools for J2EE development and deployment become available, you should find it less and less necessary to ever have to edit an XML deployment descriptor by hand.

Developing Complex Tags: Adding Attributes and Evaluating Body Content

There are two main ways to pass data to a tag for processing. One way is to pass data as an attribute to the tag, such as in the src attribute of the HTML <img> tag. The location of an image file can be passed to the tag via the src attribute (for example, <img src="/images/foo.png" />. The second way is to include content in the body of the tag. The space between the opening and closing tags of a tag element is its *body*. An example of passing data to a tag in its body is the HTML <em> tag (for example, <em>Here is emphasized text</em>). An HTML browser will render the text in the body of an <em> tag as emphasized (in reality, most browsers will italicize the text). When you are designing and creating your tag handlers, you should consider whether it makes better sense to pass data to the tag as an attribute or as body content. Consider the content developer's perspective: which design makes the most sense for when the tag will be used in JSP development?

In the next examples, we will be adding attributes and body content processing to tag handlers.

A Tag for Retrieving and Formatting Syndication Content

The example that follows shows Web syndication and XML style sheet transformation. Syndication is a very popular technique for building news and topic-oriented Web content out of what's available on the Web. Many Web sites that maintain news and message boards (such as the popular computer geek site—one of my favorites—http://www.slashdot.org) or are related to or are providers of news service (such as http://www.cnn.com) make their headlines available to others for free or for a price. There are also meta-services that collate news sources from all over the Web and sell or give away news feeds from their sites.

There are two XML document formats that are the most commonly used formats for publishing headlines for syndication. One is *Rich Site Summary* (RSS). The other is *Resource Description Framework* (RDF). Usually you can just send an HTTP request for a site's latest RDF or RSS file. When you get it back, you can do what you want with it. Because RDF and RSS are both XML formats, the first thing most people want to do with it is convert it into something more readable and attractive, such as HTML. Many Web sites use RSS and RDF news feeds to enrich their site. Some sites are built almost entirely from collections of news feeds from other sites.

12

DEVELOPING
CUSTOM TAGS

NOTE

You can find out more about RSS and RDF by simply searching the Web, but some particularly useful resources are the O'Reilly Network DevCenter on RSS (http://www.oreillynet.com/topics/rss/rss) and the RDF specification recommendation at the World Wide Web Consortium (http://www.w3.org/TR/REC-rdf-syntax).

In the example JSP in Listing 12.9, we use Slashdot's RDF URL (http://www.slashdot.org/slashdot.rdf) and two free syndication services on the Web, O'Reilly's Meerkat Open Wire Service (http://www.oreillynet.com/meerkat/) and Moreover's "webfeed" service (http://www.moreover.com/).

To use raw syndication content for building Web pages, we have to transform it into something with a friendlier user interface, such as HTML. To do that, we are going to rely on Extensible Stylesheet Language Transformation (XSLT), which is an XML-based technology (read about XSL and XSLT at http://www.w3.org/Style/XSL/). XSLT uses XSL style sheets (which are themselves XML documents) to transform XML into other data, including HTML, PDF, SQL, Java code, other programming languages, and other XML formats.

I'm going to focus on the JSP end of things and assume you can find out more about XSL and XSLT on your own. This example uses two String attributes in the custom tag, rdfURL and xslURI. The XSL transformation will be relatively effortless, thanks to the open source Xalan Java and Xerces Java projects at http://xml.apache.org. We'll be relying on the Xerces XML parser in combination with the Xalan XSLT processor to parse and transform our XML for us.

> **NOTE**
>
> You'll need to download Xalan Java (which includes the Xerces Java parser) from http://xml.apache.org/xalan to compile and run this example. Both JAR files (xalan.jar and xerces.jar) must be in your CLASSPATH to compile the example, and then they must be in your JSP container's CLASSPATH to run the example. As of this writing, Xalan Java was in version 1.2.D01.

Adding Attributes to a Custom Tag

Custom tag attributes are implemented as standard JavaBean GET and SET methods. Please review Chapter 5, "Using Beans," for an overview of JavaBeans. Each attribute you create for a custom JSP tag will have corresponding instance variables and GET and SET methods in the tag handler class.

> **TIP**
>
> The rules for converting attribute values from their String representation to primitive types, shown in Table 5.1 of Chapter 5, apply for the attribute values of custom tags as well as the standard tags (<jsp:useBean> and the like).

For each attribute, add GET and SET methods and an instance variable to the tag handler. When you're ready to deploy your tag handler, declare the attributes to the JSP container using the <attribute> element in the taglib.tld file. See the first few lines after the import statements of RdfTag.java in Listing 12.6. After the first line of the class declaration, we declare a JavaBean-style no argument constructor. Then follow the private instance variable declarations and their corresponding GET and SET methods for the tag attributes rdfURL and xslURI.

LISTING 12.6   RdfTag.java—Custom Tag Handler with Attributes

```
import java.io.InputStreamReader;
import java.net.URL;
```

LISTING 12.6   Continued

```
    }

    // Note there's no doEndTag() implemented because we don't need one.
    // We could do more processing in the doEndTag() method, but we don't
    // have anything to do so we don't have to override the default
    // implementation provided by TagSupport.

    public void release()
    {
        // There's nothing to release, so we don't need this method either.
        // The XSLTProcessor's reset() method should release any resources
        // it had used.  The release() method is similar to the destroy()
        // method of the Servlet API.
    }
}
```

In the doStartTag() method, we do a number of things. First, we get a reference to the
ServletContext object of this Web application. We will use that later to retrieve the XSL file
specified in the xslURI attribute:

```
        ServletContext context = pageContext.getServletContext();
```

The J2EE specification and platform were designed with portable component development and
deployment architecture in mind. The most portable way to use XSL sheets for a tag like this
is to keep them in the Web application itself. You could keep them anywhere on your network
or file system, but thanks to the way the architecture and APIs of J2EE are designed, we can
guarantee that as long as the XSL files are kept in the Web application, we can get at them.

The next preparatory step is to create a URL based on the value of the rdfURL passed in from
the JSP. This URL object will be passed to the XSLTProcessor as one of the parameters it needs
(an input XML file):

```
        URL url = new URL(rdfURL);
```

Next, following the API documentation that comes with the Xalan XSLT processor, we create
an instance of the processor class and then create instances of the input and output objects we
will need to complete our transformation:

```
        XSLTProcessor proc = XSLTProcessorFactory.getProcessor();

        XSLTInputSource inputXml =
            new  XSLTInputSource( new
                            InputStreamReader( url.openStream() ) );
```

```
XSLTInputSource inputXsl =
        new  XSLTInputSource( context.getResourceAsStream( xslURI ) );

XSLTResultTarget target =
        new XSLTResultTarget( pageContext.getOut() );
```

Now we call the XSLTProcessor's process method by passing it the encapsulated objects it requires—an XML input document, an XSL sheet to apply, and output location for the result:

```
proc.process(inputXml, inputXsl, target);
```

Then we reset the processor so it frees its resources and is ready to be used again if needed:

```
proc.reset();
```

There isn't much to the rest of the tag handler. We SKIP_BODY, just to do something different. We don't implement doEndTag() because we don't need to unless we want to use it to do something. We put the release() method in for practice, but we don't rely on it for anything. If this were an SQL tag and we had a database connection or ResultSet we wanted to make sure got closed, the release() method would be used for that. The XSLTProcessor's reset() method frees us from needing to do any manual cleanup.

We have two XSL files for this example. One (Listing 12.7) is tailored to the RDF 0.92 version format of Slashdot's news feed, and the other (Listing 12.8) is an XSL sheet for RSS version 0.91. Both XSL sheets specify rules for converting XML input into HTML output. You shouldn't find it too difficult to modify these for your preference, even if you don't know XSL. The places to change font size, color, and other HTML elements are pretty obvious. Keep in mind that you need to find out ahead which XSL sheet you will need for a particular news feed. There are ways to find this out dynamically, but we haven't implemented them here.

LISTING 12.7   rdf092.xsl—XSL Sheet for Use with RDF 0.92 Files Retrieved by Our RdfTag

```
<?xml version="1.0"?>
<xsl:stylesheet
  version="1.0"
  xmlns:simple="http://my.netscape.com/rdf/simple/0.9/"
  xmlns:xsl="http://www.w3.org/1999/XSL/Transform"
  xmlns:rdf="http://www.w3.org/1999/02/22-rdf-syntax-ns#">

<xsl:output method="html" indent="yes" omit-xml-declaration="yes"/>

<xsl:template match="/">
  <xsl:apply-templates select="rdf:RDF"/>
</xsl:template>

<xsl:template match="rdf:RDF">
  <xsl:element name="table" namespace="">
```

LISTING 12.7 Continued

```
      <xsl:attribute name="border">1</xsl:attribute>
      <xsl:attribute name="cellpadding">2</xsl:attribute>
      <xsl:attribute name="cellspacing">0</xsl:attribute>
      <xsl:apply-templates select="simple:channel"/>
      <xsl:element name="tr" namespace="">
        <xsl:element name="td" namespace="">
          <xsl:apply-templates select="simple:item"/>
        </xsl:element>
      </xsl:element>
    </xsl:element>
  </xsl:template>

  <xsl:template match="simple:channel">
    <xsl:element name="tr" namespace="">
      <xsl:attribute name="bgcolor">#006666</xsl:attribute>
      <xsl:element name="td" namespace="">
        <xsl:element name="a" namespace="">
          <xsl:attribute name="href"><xsl:value-of select="simple:link"/>
➥</xsl:attribute>
          <xsl:attribute name="target">_top</xsl:attribute>
          <xsl:element name="font" namespace="">
            <xsl:attribute name="color">#ffffff</xsl:attribute>
            <xsl:attribute name="size">+1</xsl:attribute>
            <xsl:element name="b" namespace="">
              <xsl:value-of select="simple:title"/>
            </xsl:element>
          </xsl:element>
        </xsl:element>
      </xsl:element>
    </xsl:element>
  </xsl:template>

  <xsl:template match="simple:item">
    <xsl:element name="li" namespace="">
      <xsl:element name="a" namespace="">
        <xsl:attribute name="href"><xsl:value-of select="simple:link"/>
➥</xsl:attribute>
        <xsl:attribute name="target">_top</xsl:attribute>
        <xsl:value-of select="simple:title"/>
      </xsl:element>
    </xsl:element>
  </xsl:template>
</xsl:stylesheet>
```

LISTING 12.8   `rss-html.xsl`—XSL Sheet for Use with RSS 0.91 Files Retrieved by Our `RdfTag`

```xml
<?xml version="1.0"?>
<xsl:stylesheet
  version="1.0"
  xmlns:xsl="http://www.w3.org/1999/XSL/Transform">

  <xsl:output method="html" indent="yes" omit-xml-declaration="yes"/>

  <xsl:template match="channel">

    <table border="1" cellpadding="2" cellspacing="0">
      <tr bgcolor="#aa0000">
        <td>
          <b>
            <font size="+1" color="#ffffff">
              <xsl:value-of select="title"/>
            </font>
          </b>
        </td>
      </tr>

      <tr>
        <td>
          <xsl:apply-templates select="item"/>
        </td>
      </tr>
    </table>
  </xsl:template>

  <xsl:template match="item">
      <li>
        <a>
          <xsl:attribute name="href">
            <xsl:value-of select="link"/>
          </xsl:attribute>
          <xsl:value-of select="title"/>
        </a>
      </li>
  </xsl:template>
</xsl:stylesheet>
```

Listing 12.9 shows an example of a JSP, rdfTag.jsp, that uses the RdfTag. This JSP is very plain and simple. It just calls the RdfTag three times and prints the results to a browser. A real example would use the RdfTag to enrich a page with nicer formatting and more content, perhaps to retrieve a sidebar of news headers. Note that the RDF URLs are very different for each service. The Meerkat service has a very cool query language that gets appended to the URL as request parameters. Using this query syntax with Meerkat, one can request all sorts of different content including content delimited by time ranges, document format, and subject.

LISTING 12.9   rdfTag.jsp—Example Usage of Our RdfTag

```
<%@ taglib prefix="synd" uri="/rdfTag" %>
<% response.setHeader("Pragma", "no-cache"); %>
<html>
<head><title>RDF Tag Test</title>
<style type="text/css">
<!--
body { background-color: #ffffff; }
h1   { text-align: center;
       color: #008888;
       text-decoration: underline; }
-->
</style>
</head>
<body>
<h1>Output of RDFTag</h1>
<synd:rdf rdfURL="http://www.slashdot.org/slashdot.rdf"
          xslURI="xml/rdf092.xsl"/>

<synd:rdf rdfURL="http://meerkat.oreillynet.com/?t=ALL&_de=0&s=java&_fl=rss"
          xslURI="xml/rss-html.xsl"/>
<synd:rdf rdfURL="http://www.moreover.com/cgi-local/page?index_java+rss"
          xslURI="xml/rss-html.xsl"/>
</body>
</html>
```

Note the use of the taglib directive at the top of the page. As long as it appears before the tag library it identifies is used in the JSP, you'll be okay. We give it the arbitrary prefix synd as short for "syndication." In Figure 12.2, you can see the output from a particular run. You can't see much of the Moreover results in the screen shot, but they are there below the frame.

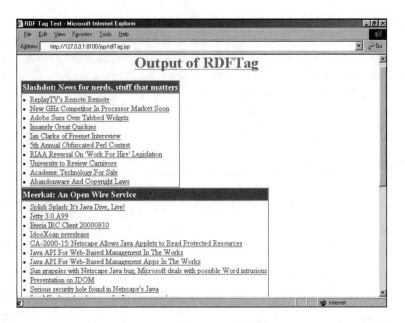

FIGURE 12.2

rdfTag.jsp's result, showing dynamically generated HTML after processing the XML via XSLT.

The tag library descriptor in Listing 12.10 contains `<attribute>` element entries for the tag handler's attributes. The value of the `<name>` element must match the name of the attribute as it will be used in the JSP. We list both of these attributes as `<required>true</required>` because they are both necessary for the proper function of the `RdfTag`. One is listed as being capable of taking its value from a runtime JSP expression and one isn't. It doesn't really matter in the case of the `RdfTag` tag, but other tags could require or prohibit a runtime expression value for good reason. For example, a tag that required a value to be set dynamically from a user's implicit `session` object might need to use a JSP expression. Another example when a runtime expression might be necessary is when HTML FORM fields are used to populate a tag's attributes. Then the JSP developer would probably want to use the implicit `request` object's methods for obtaining its parameters.

LISTING 12.10   `taglib.tld`—TLD File for the `RdfTag`

```
<?xml version="1.0" ?>
<!DOCTYPE taglib
        PUBLIC "-//Sun Microsystems, Inc.//DTD JSP Tag Library 1.1//EN"
        "http://java.sun.com/j2ee/dtds/web-jsptaglibrary_1_1.dtd">
<taglib>
  <tlibversion>1.0</tlibversion>
  <jspversion>1.1</jspversion>
  <shortname>MCP Syndication Tag</shortname>
  <tag>
```

LISTING 12.10   Continued

```
    <name>rdf</name>
    <tagclass>RdfTag</tagclass>
    <bodycontent>empty</bodycontent>
    <attribute>
        <name>rdfURL</name>
        <required>true</required>
        <rtexprvalue>true</rtexprvalue>
    </attribute>
    <attribute>
        <name>xslURI</name>
        <required>true</required>
        <rtexprvalue>false</rtexprvalue>
    </attribute>
  </tag>
</taglib>
```

Existing JSP Tag Library Projects

There are numerous JSP tag libraries beginning to pop up around the Internet. Some are small and specialized; others more comprehensive or general purpose. We have chosen to include here three custom tag projects because of three positive features they all share. They are all freely available and at least somewhat robust. They should all run on any JSP 1.1–compliant container.

JRun Tag Library from Allaire Corporation

```
http://devex.allaire.com/developer/gallery/
```

This is without doubt the finest tag library currently on the market. Allaire has brought to JSP its years of skill and experience with developing server-side tags for ColdFusion. The Allaire JSP tag library is free and currently bundled with the JRun application server (which is free for development). In the future, the tag library will be on its own development and release cycle and will be available as a separate download. Currently there are tags for SQL queries, sending/receiving email, form validation, JNDI lookups, JTA transactions, XSL transformations, and flow control. The JRun application server itself comes with hundreds of pages of bleeding edge documentation, including tutorials on writing and deploying custom JSP tags.

Orion Tag Libraries from Orionserver

```
http://www.orionserver.com/
```

This is two tag libraries: one for EJB lookups and interaction, another for various time-saving utilities such as currency and time localization. The Orion application server is very fast, low-cost for production licensing, and freely available for development.

Taglibs Project from Jakarta

`http://jakarta.apache.org/taglibs`

This includes a few tags for XSL, SQL, two examples implemented from the JSP 1.1 specification, and two tags for using the IBM Bean Scripting Framework (which allows the use of more scripting languages in JSP). The Jakarta tag library project has taken off slowly. Although not too much has been done yet, this is a project to watch. The tags that are included are well documented, so they make good examples to learn from.

Summary

This chapter gave an overview of understanding, writing, and deploying basic custom JSP tags. We started off with an informal history of tag-based languages, demonstrating that tag languages have been used on the client and server since long before JSP. We wrote a couple of tags and showed all the attendant configuration work required to deploy and then use tag classes in a JSP. We wrapped up with references to some of the leading JSP tag libraries.

In developing custom JSP tags, it's hard not to notice the amount of work involved. Much of the effort involved in creating and using custom tags is XML file configuration, packaging, and then linking between a JSP, web.xml, and the tag library descriptor and its tag handler classes. Eventually this should all get easier as the technology and the tools mature.

Imagine if, to edit Word documents and use the spellchecker, you had to link the Word software to the spell-checker module, ensure that the spell-checker's configuration file was complete, and then reference the spellchecker module in your documents. That's essentially the process you have to go through with custom tags (albeit the analogy is from a client-side tool to a server-side tool, but the basis for a comparison is there, I believe). In reality, the Word software is preconfigured with the spellchecker enabled and automatically available to all your documents without special configuration (except to point and click to run it). That's kind of how JRun works, due to the fact that its default application comes deployed with the Allaire JSP tags ready to be used.

These kinds of problems with configuration files and linking between application components are one of the main headaches of J2EE application development and deployment. Developing JSPs, for instance, should be easier when tools can auto-generate TLDs from tag handler classes. Deploying will be easier when J2EE app servers provide tools for linking a new component into a running application without requiring a person to edit an XML file and restart the server.

Two of the main reasons for these problems are that everything in J2EE is designed to be componentized, and everything must be platform and vendor neutral. These benefits have to be weighed against costs in terms of developer productivity and application fragility. In midyear,

Microsoft unveiled its plans for the .NET framework, including the extremely JSP-like (custom tags and all) ASP+ (ASP-plus). I think J2EE is a great concept, and JSP has wonderful potential. It will be a good thing if the competition between J2EE and Microsoft results in better tools for developing and deploying custom JSP tags and the rest.

Interacting with Enterprise JavaBeans

IN THIS CHAPTER

An *Enterprise JavaBean* (EJB) is a standard for developing server-side components that make network-enabled applications easier to create and manage. It is a thin-client, server-side solution that takes care of the low-level details for you. EJB provides an architecture that manages state and transaction management, resource pooling, data persistence, and multithreading itself in order to allow the developer to focus on the business logic. The component nature provides for a portable, reusable, and cross-platform application.

This chapter is a brief look at Enterprise JavaBeans. There are many books entirely focused on the subject that cover all the details you could ever want. We will focus only on a brief explanation of what an EJB is, how to build your own beans, and how to use them with JSP.

To do this, we will build a simple JSP application for a small Internet storefront. We will use EJBs to do authentication, create a shopping cart, and keep track of customer information.

Understanding EJB

First we must have a clear understanding of what an EJB is. An Enterprise JavaBean is code sitting on the server ready to do its thing. Client programs interact with it, or it can interact with other beans. Each EJB is created as a remote object using RMI. An Enterprise JavaBean has three parts: the Home Interface, the Remote Interface, and the bean implementation itself.

To develop and deploy an EJB application, you must have the EJB API and an EJB server. Java 2EE includes the EJB API and can be downloaded from `www.java.sun.com` `/j2ee/` `download.html`. There are many EJB servers available. Search the Internet for *EJB Servers*, and you will be presented with a plethora of options. The examples in this chapter will use BEA Weblogic Server 5.1.0. An evaluation version can be downloaded from BEA's Web site at `www.beasys.com/download.html`.

NOTE

In EJB 1.0, EJB servers were required to support only Session beans. EJB 1.1 requires that compliant servers support both Session beans and Entity beans. If you are using an older server, you want to upgrade to an EJB 1.1–compliant server.

The Container

The *container* is what differentiates EJB objects from regular RMI objects. At deployment, the EJB server will create the container and the various classes the container uses to manage the bean. The container is what handles resource pooling, data persistence, and transaction management for you.

One of the best things about the container is that you really don't need to know much about it to use EJBs. You just need to know that it is there and that certain methods must be made available to it. These methods will be pointed out as we go through our examples.

Another important point is that the server uses the *deployment descriptor* to govern the actions of the container. You will define what kind of bean you are using and many properties of the bean in the deployment descriptor.

The Remote Interface

The *Remote Interface* is the typical development starting point. This is where you specify the business methods available to the client. The Remote Interface is how the client interacts with the bean. The container pools stubs of the Remote Interface that the client makes function calls on. The container is responsible for directing these function calls on to an instance of the bean on the server.

> **NOTE**
>
> Naming conventions for EJB development are based from the Remote Interface. For example, if we were making a Person bean, the Remote Interface would be named `Person.java`, the Home Interface would be named `PersonHome.java`, and the bean itself would be named `PersonBean.java`.

We will start our little store by building the Remote Interface for our Authentication bean. Listing 13.1 is the complete code for the Remote Interface for `AuthenticationBean.java`. The Remote Interface must extend `javax.ejb.EJBObject`, which extends `java.rmi.Remote`. This enables the bean to be exported as an RMI object. The `isAuthentic()` function is the bean's only business logic. Thus, it is the only method defined in the Remote Interface.

LISTING 13.1 Authentication.java

```java
package ejbs.authentication;

import javax.ejb.*;
import java.rmi.RemoteException;

public interface Authentication extends EJBObject {
  public boolean isAuthentic(String userName, String password)
    throws RemoteException;
}
```

The Home Interface

The *Home Interface* is the client's starting point. It describes how a client creates, finds (for Entity beans only), and removes beans from the container. The Home Interface's create() method returns a reference to a stub that implements the bean's Remote Interface. Each create() method must have a corresponding ejbCreate() method in the bean implementation.

The client finds the Home Interface using JNDI. The client will use the JNDI name that the Home Interface is registered as in the deployment descriptor.

Continuing with our example, let's take a look at the Home Interface for our Authentication bean, AuthenticationHome.java. Listing 13.2 is our Home Interface. Notice that AuthenticationHome.java extends javax.ejb.EJBHome, which in turn extends java.rmi.Remote. Again, this is done in order to export it as an RMI object.

LISTING 13.2 AuthenticationHome.java

```java
package ejbs.authentication;

import javax.ejb.*;
import java.rmi.RemoteException;

public interface AuthenticationHome extends EJBHome {
  public Authentication create()
    throws CreateException, RemoteException;
}
```

The Bean Implementation

This is where the action takes place! Here, all the method listed in the Remote Interface and in the Home Interface must be defined. The bean must implement javax.ejb.EnterpriseBean.

Normally, this is done by extending `javax.ejb.SessionBean` or `javax.ejb.EnterpriseBean`. The bean does not need to implement the Remote Interface because the container will take care of that. Also, the bean must implement `ejbActivate()`, `ejbPassivate()`, `ejbCreate()`, and `ejbRemove()`. Entity beans must also implement `ejbPostCreate()`, `ejbStore()`, `ejbLoad()`, and `isModified()`. The bean must also be public in order to allow the container to introspect.

Our `AuthenticationBean.java`, shown in Listing 13.3, demonstrates how this is done. The bean must implement `javax.ejb.EnterpriseBean`. This is done by implementing `javax.ejb.SessionBean`. The bean implements the `isAuthentic()` function specified in the Remote Interface and implements `ejbCreate()` to correspond with the Home Interface. For simplicity, our authentication is hard coded to require the same username (`Elvis`) and password (`lives`) from everyone. You can enable the bean to read from a database or to access another EJB to do the database read, but I will leave this for you to do yourself.

LISTING 13.3   AuthenticationBean.java

```java
package ejbs.authentication;

import javax.ejb.*;
import java.rmi.RemoteException;

public class AuthenticationBean implements SessionBean {

  private SessionContext ctx;

  public boolean isAuthentic(String userName, String password)
    throws RemoteException {
    return "Elvis".equals(userName) && "lives".equals(password);
  }

  public void ejbCreate()
    throws CreateException, RemoteException {
  }

  // Methods used by the container
  public void setSessionContext(SessionContext ctx)
    throws RemoteException {
    this.ctx = ctx;
  }
  public void ejbRemove() throws RemoteException { }
  public void ejbActivate() throws RemoteException { }
  public void ejbPassivate() throws RemoteException { }

}
```

13

Session Beans

A *Session* bean is an Enterprise bean that represents a business activity. There are two types of Session beans: stateless and stateful. A Session bean is accessed by a single client and lives only as long as the session is active. The bean represents a conversation with the client. In the case of stateful Session beans, the bean's fields contain the state of the conversation. We will go into more detail about stateful and stateless Session beans next.

A Session bean must implement javax.ejb.SessionBean and include the function setSessionContext(). The container calls setSessionContext() just after the bean is created to send the bean its javax.ejb.SessionContext, which is a javax.ejb.EJBContext and represents the runtime context for the bean.

The deployment descriptor must specify to the container whether the Session bean is stateful or stateless.

Stateless Session Beans

A *stateless* Session bean is just what it says: a Session bean that does not maintain state. It is always the same regardless of when it is called or by whom. Therefore, multiple clients can use the same stateless bean, because there is no stored or shared data that could be corrupted. Put simply, there are no class variables in the bean that can be changed by the client. This bean performs one activity and is done.

Stateless Session beans are pooled and reused. Each stateless bean's Home Interface must have a single create() method with no parameters and a corresponding ejbCreate() method in the bean implementation. This allows the container to create and pool these beans as needed. Also, stateless Session beans do not need a passivated() method, because the bean holds no resources to be released.

Our AuthenticationBean.java is an example of a stateless Session bean. Looking back to Listing 13.3, we can see that there are no class variables that can be changed and that there is a single create() method with no parameters. The container can create as many instances of the bean as it needs by calling create() over and over again. The isAuthentic() function will perform the same service for whomever calls it.

Stateful Session Beans

You might have already guessed this, but a *stateful* Session bean is a Session bean that does maintain state. The definitions of these beans are amazingly intuitive, aren't they? A stateful Session bean has fields that can be accessed and changed by the client. This bean represents a continuing conversation with the client in which the bean's fields contain the state of the conversation.

The next part of our storefront is to create a shopping cart. We will use the stateful Session bean ShoppingCartBean.java, shown in Listing 13.4. The code for the Home and Remote Interfaces is available on the CD-ROM provided with this book. We will not go through those now, but remember that the Home Interface must have create() methods to match the ejbCreate() methods defined in the bean implementation. Also, all the business methods must be listed in the Remote Interface.

LISTING 13.4 ShoppingCartBean.java

```java
package ejbs.shoppingcart;

import javax.ejb.*;
import java.io.Serializable;
import java.util.*;
import java.text.NumberFormat;

public class ShoppingCartBean implements SessionBean {
  public Hashtable cart;
  public String cartName;
  private SessionContext cxt;
  protected NumberFormat formatter;

  // ** Business methods ** //
  /**
   * Adds an item to the cart if the
   * item's quantity is greater than zero
   *
   * @param title        String title of the movie
   * @param price        double price of the movie
   * @param quantity     int number of movie order
   */
  public void addItem(String t, double p, int q) {
    Hashtable item = createCartItem(t, p, q);
    if (cart == null) {
      cart = new Hashtable();
    }
    if (cart.containsKey(t)) {
      cart.remove(t);
    }
    if (q > 0) {
      cart.put(t, item);
    }
  }
```

LISTING 13.4   Continued

```java
/**
 * Returns the requested item
 * from the shopping cart.
 *
 * @param key         String title of the movie
 */
public Hashtable getItem(String key) {
  if (cart != null) {
    return (Hashtable)cart.get(key);
  }
  return null;
}

/**
 * Returns an array of all the
 * items in the shopping cart.
 */
public Hashtable[] getItems() {
  Hashtable[] retVal = null;
  int i = 0;

  if (cart != null) {
    retVal = new Hashtable[cart.size()];
    Enumeration keys = cart.keys();
    while (keys.hasMoreElements()) {
      retVal[i] = (Hashtable)cart.get(keys.nextElement());
      i++;
    }
  }
  return retVal;
}

/**
 * Returns the total cost of a
 * particular item in the cart.
 *
 * @param item         Hashtable item of cart
 */
public String getItemsTotalCost(Hashtable item) {
  int q = ((Integer)item.get("quantity")).intValue();
  double p = ((Double)item.get("price")).doubleValue();
  formatter = NumberFormat.getCurrencyInstance();
  return formatter.format(p*q);
}
```

LISTING 13.4   Continued

```java
/**
 * Returns the total cost of all
 * the items in the cart.
 */
public String getCartsTotalCost() {
  double retVal = 0;

  if (cart != null) {
    Enumeration keys = cart.keys();
    while (keys.hasMoreElements()) {
      Hashtable item = (Hashtable)cart.get(keys.nextElement());
      int q = ((Integer)item.get("quantity")).intValue();
      double p = ((Double)item.get("price")).doubleValue();
      retVal += p*q;
    }
  }
  formatter = NumberFormat.getCurrencyInstance();
  return formatter.format(retVal);
}

/**
 * Creates an item to put into the cart
 *
 * @param title         String title of the movie
 * @param price         double price of the movie
 * @param quantity      int number of movie order
 */
private Hashtable createCartItem(String title, double price, int quantity) {
  Hashtable h = new Hashtable();
  h.put("title", title);
  h.put("price", new Double(price));
  h.put("quantity", new Integer(quantity));
  return h;
}


// ** Container methods ** //
public void ejbCreate(String cartName) {
  this.cartName = cartName;
  if (cart == null) {
    cart = new Hashtable();
  } else {
    cart.clear();
```

13

LISTING 13.4   Continued

```
  }
   }

   public void setSessionContext(SessionContext ctx) {
     this.cxt = cxt;
   }

   public void ejbActivate() {}
   public void ejbRemove() {}
   public void ejbPassivate() {}


}
```

This is a pretty good-sized chunk of code, so let's walk through it a bit. The first thing to point out is that we implement `javax.ejb.SessionBean`. Next we list our class variables. These are where we keep track of the session information. The main class variable is a `java.util.Hashtable` called `cart`. This keeps the state. The same `cart` object is available for the entire session or the life of the bean. Again, this is what makes it a stateful Session bean: the capability to store and retrieve information in these objects throughout the life of the bean.

The business methods of the bean manipulate or return the contents of the `Hashtable`. The methods that are listed in the Remote Interface and defined here are `addItem()`, `getItem()`, `getItems()`, `getItemsTotalCost()`, and `getCartsTotalCost()`. Each of these methods performs different functions on `cart`. The comments in the code should help you understand the purpose of each method. The bean also implements `ejbCreate()` to create a new instance of the bean.

Entity Beans

An *Entity bean* implements a business entity. An Entity bean represents data that is stored, can be accessed by multiple clients, and is persisted. It represents the data in a database and the methods to act on the data. Another way to think of it is that an Entity bean represents a row in a database table. Entity beans persist across the life of the server. They outlive client sessions and even server crashes. As long as the data exists in persisted storage, the Entity bean lives on. Passivation disassociates the bean from the persisted data it represents to allow the bean to be pooled.

Each Entity bean has a unique identifier that is used to look up the same bean across multiple clients. That way the bean will always reflect the current state of the data. Multiple clients can access the same Entity bean at the same time, and the container will manage the concurrent transactions for you.

The unique identifier used to find the Entity bean is called the *primary key*. The primary key class includes all the information needed to uniquely identify an item in persisted storage. It is a public identifier that clients use to access data items and must implement `java.io.Serializable`. The bean gains access to the primary key from the `java.ejb.EntityContext` passed to it in the `setEntityContext()` method.

The Entity bean we will create is `CustomerBean.java`. It represents the customer's information in the database. The primary key will use the first name to find the record in the database. Because we are using only the first name as the primary key, we can use `java.lang.String` as our primary key class. If we were to use a more complex primary key, for example both the first and last names, we would have to create a class for the primary key. In most cases, using a person's first name as a primary key is a bad idea. In this case, however, I am going to take a little creative license and assume that none of our customers will have the same first name.

The Home Interface for Entity beans must include finder methods with corresponding finder methods in the bean. For example, to create a method to find a bean by a user's first name, we would create a method called `findByFirstName()` in the Home Interface and a corresponding `ejbFindByFirstName()` method in the bean implementation. These methods are needed to find existing instances of the bean. A finder method must return an instance of the Remote Interface or a collection of Remote Interface instances of beans that meet the find criteria. The function `findByPrimaryKey()` is the default finder and must be implemented in all Entity beans.

13

INTERACTING WITH ENTERPRISE JAVABEANS

NOTE

EJB specification 1.0 specifies that `finder` methods can only return the Remote Interface or an `Enumeration`. In 1.1, a `Collection` is added to the list of objects that `finder` methods can return.

The Home Interface for our `CustomerBean.java` is shown in Listing 13.5. The only `finder` method we list is the default `findByPrimaryKey()`. We could have included `findByFirstName()` or `findByLastName()`, but we are not going to use them, so we'll leave them out. The `create()` method creates a new entry in the database. In this case, we pass in the first name because it is our primary key. This creates a specific instance of the bean that represents a new row in the table for this customer.

LISTING 13.5   CustomerHome.java

```
package ejbs.customer;

import javax.ejb.*;
import java.rmi.RemoteException;

public interface CustomerHome extends EJBHome {
  public Customer create(String firstName, String lastName)
    throws CreateException, RemoteException;
  public Customer findByPrimaryKey(BonusPK key)
    throws FinderException, RemoteException;
}
```

There are two ways to deal with persisting data in Entity beans. Either you can do all the work in the bean itself or you can have the container take care of all that for you. To spell it out in the bean is *bean-managed* persistence. To allow the container to do it for you is *container-managed* persistence.

Container-Managed Persistence

When the container does the persisting for you, the data mapping is done in the deployment descriptor. You define your data elements as your class variables in the bean implementation and the remote interface. You then list these variables where they should be mapped to and in the deployment descriptor. The container will automatically generate an ejbFindByPrimaryKey() for you based on the information given in the deployment descriptor. You will need to tell the container how to deal with any other find methods you list in the Home Interface. Refer to you server's specs for information on how this is done.

> **CAUTION**
>
> For complicated data mapping, defining the finder methods in the deployment descriptor can quickly get ugly. It is usually best to use bean-managed persistence in those cases.

A container-managed Entity bean must be public, have a public default constructor, and have public data members. The primary key must have the all the same data members as are being stored by the bean.

Bean-Managed Persistence

Bean-managed persistence requires the database calls and connection to be specified by the bean. The finder methods should contain all the necessary code to query the database and create the primary key with the results.

Having the bean manage the persistence gives the programmer complete control of all persisted data and finder methods. For complicated data mapping, this is an advantage over container-managed persistence, where the data mapping is done in the deployment descriptor.

An Entity Bean Example

To help all this Entity bean stuff make sense, let's build one. Since we have already covered JDBC (see Chapter 8, "Interacting with Databases"), we will take advantage of the EJB architecture and let the container manage the persistence for us. For our little storefront, we want to keep track of our customers. We will create an Entity bean to give us access to each customer's information. Our `CustomerBean.java` will keep track of only the customer's first and last name. Obviously, this bean could be expanded to include a lot more information; we will keep it simple.

LISTING 13.6 Customer.java

```java
package ejbs.customer;

import javax.ejb.*;
import java.rmi.RemoteException;

public interface Customer extends EJBObject {
  public String getFirstName()
    throws RemoteException;

  public void setFirstName(String firstName)
    throws RemoteException;

  public String getLastName()
    throws RemoteException;

  public void setLastName(String lastName)
    throws RemoteException;

}
```

13

Our Remote Interface is shown in Listing 13.6, and the bean itself is in Listing 13.7. The bean would look a lot different if its persistence were bean managed. All the JDBC code and database calls would be included for each of the getter, setter, and finder methods. However, since it is container-managed, we leave all that work to the container!

LISTING 13.7   CustomerBean.java

```java
package ejbs.customer;

import javax.ejb.*;
import java.rmi.RemoteException;

public class CustomerBean implements EntityBean {
  public String firstName = "";
  public String lastName = "";
  private boolean isDirty;
  protected EntityContext ctx;

  // Business methods
  // getters and setters
  /**
   * Returns the customers first name
   */
  public String getFirstName() {
    return firstName;
  }

  /**
   * Sets the customers first name
   *
   * @param firstName          String First Name
   */
  public void setFirstName(String firstName) {
    this.firstName = firstName;
    setModified(true);
  }

  /**
   * Returns the customers last name
   */
  public String getLastName() {
    return lastName;
  }

  /**
```

LISTING 13.7 Continued

```
 * Sets the customers last name
 *
 * @param firstName          String Last Name
 */
public void setLastName(String lastName) {
  this.lastName = lastName;
  setModified(true);
}

// Container methods //
/**
 * Sets the EntityContext for the EJBean.
 *
 * @param ctx               EntityContext
 */
public void setEntityContext(EntityContext ctx) {
  this.ctx = ctx;
}

/**
 * Unsets the EntityContext for the EJBean.
 */
public void unsetEntityContext() {
  this.ctx = null;
}

/**
 * Returns whether the EJBean has been modified or not.
 *
 * This method must be public for the container to be able to invoke it.
 *
 * @return                  boolean isDirty
 */
public boolean isModified() {
  return isDirty;
}

/**
 * Sets the EJBean's modified flag.
 *
 * @param flag              Modified Flag
 */
public void setModified(boolean flag) {
  isDirty = flag;
```

13

**INTERACTING WITH
ENTERPRISE
JAVABEANS**

LISTING 13.7   Continued

```java
  }

  /**
   * Sets the EJBean's modified flag to false.
   * set to false to "reset" the variable for the next transaction.
   */
  public void ejbStore() {
    setModified(false);
  }


  /**
   * This method corresponds to the create method in the home interface
   * "CustomerHome.java".
   *
   * @param firstName         String First Name
   * @param lastName          String Last Name
   * @exception               javax.ejb.CreateException
   *                          if there is a problem creating the bean
   */
  public String ejbCreate(String firstName, String lastName)
    throws CreateException {
    this.firstName = firstName;
    this.lastName  = lastName;
    return null;  // See 9.4.2 of the EJB 1.1 specification
  }

  // These methods are required by the EJB Specification,
  // but are not used by this example.
  public void ejbPostCreate(String firstName, String lastName) { }
  public void ejbActivate() { }
  public void ejbPassivate() { }
  public void ejbLoad() { }
  public void ejbRemove() throws RemoveException { }

}
```

The first two fields in `CustomerBean.java` are the information we will be persisting. We have mapped these variables to the database in the deployment descriptor. The third field, `boolean isDirty`, is used by the container to determine if the data has changed. The container will call the `isModified()` method to retrieve this variable to find out if it should persist the data.

Of course, there are a few methods that the container requires. Notice that `ejbCreate()` returns a null. This is because we are using container-managed persistence. For bean-managed persistence, the `ejbCreate()` method must return the primary key. Also, the `ejbPostCreate()` method has the same parameters as the `ejbCreate()` method, as required by the EJB 1.1 spec.

Implementing Enterprise JavaBeans

Now that we have built all the Enterprise JavaBeans that we will need for our store, it's time put it all together with some JavaServer Pages. We will build pages to add a new user to the database, handle a user's login, and do a little shopping. Of course, we will use the Enterprise beans we have created to perform all the business logic. We will look at the code for most of the JSPs and show some screen captures of the final results. We will not go through all the code and JSPs involved in our store, but everything is included on the accompanying CD-ROM. This example is in no way intended to be a complete storefront; it is intended only to show examples of how to interact with EJBs from JSPs. All examples are run using BEA's Weblogic Server 5.1.0.

Interacting with an Entity Bean

The Entity bean we have already built, `CustomerBean.java`, will be instantiated to represent a specific customer in the database. For every new customer we add, we will need a new `Customer` object. For every existing customer, we need to find the corresponding `Customer` object that already exists.

Our scenario will start by adding a new customer to our database by creating a new `Customer` object. After the object is created, we will add the customer's information to the database. We will then view the customer's information by finding the corresponding `Customer` object and getting the information back from it.

The first page in this process is a simple HTML form asking for the customer's first and last names. The form is submitted to `NewbyCreate.jsp`. Listing 13.8 shows just the Java code for `NewbyCreate.jsp`. Figure 13.1 shows what `NewbyCreate.jsp` looks like.

LISTING 13.8   `NewbyCreate.jsp`—Using `CustomerBean`

```
<%@ page errorPage = "ErrorPage.jsp" %>
<%@ page import = "ejbs.customer.*" %>
<%@ page import = "javax.ejb.*" %>
<%@ page import = "javax.naming.*" %>
<%@ page import = "java.util.Properties" %>

<%! String firstName, lastName; %>
<%
```

LISTING 13.8 Continued

```
lastName = request.getParameter("lastName");
firstName = request.getParameter("firstName");

try {
  /* Get context */
  Properties env = new Properties();
  env.put(Context.INITIAL_CONTEXT_FACTORY,
  ➥"weblogic.jndi.WLInitialContextFactory");
  Context ctx = new InitialContext(env);

  /* Get Customer */
  CustomerHome custHome = (CustomerHome)ctx.lookup("customer.CustomerHome");
  Customer customer = custHome.create(firstName,lastName);
  customer.setFirstName(firstName);
  customer.setLastName(lastName);
} catch (Exception e) {
  /* didn't work */
}

%>
```

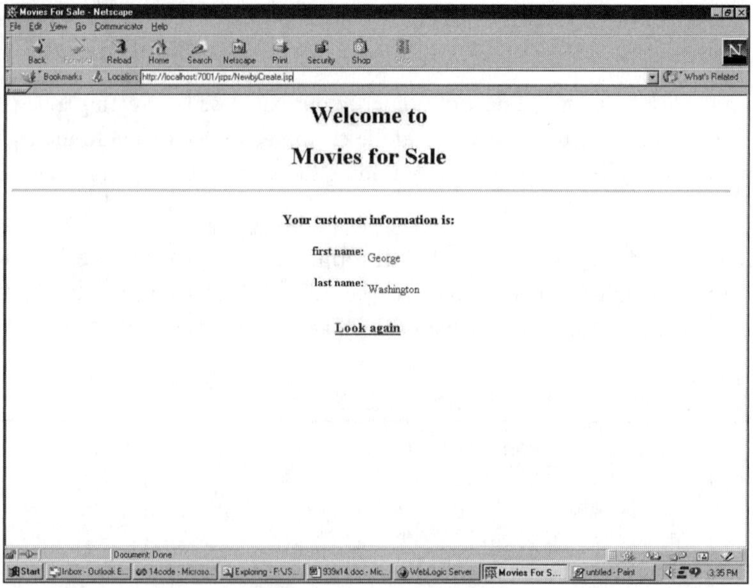

FIGURE 13.1

NewbyCreate.jsp, *displaying the selected customer's first and last names.*

The process `NewbyCreate.jsp` uses to get a reference to the bean is similar regardless of whether we are using a Session bean or an Entity bean. First, we get `javax.naming.Context` by using a `java.util.Properties` object that contains environment information. From `Context` we can look on the server to find a reference to the bean's Home Interface. The Home Interface's `create()` method returns a reference to the bean's Remote Interface, which gives us access to the bean's business logic. In this case, we are accessing `setter` methods on the bean to add a new customer to the database.

The link at the bottom of `NewbyCreate.jsp` sends us to `NewbyFind.jsp`, shown in Listing 13.9. Notice that the link sends the customer's first name as a parameter. We will use the first name to find the bean again. In `NewbyFind.jsp`, we use the `findByPrimaryKey()` method to get a reference to the bean we just created. Once we have found the `Customer` object we are looking for, we get the information we want and show it off in the page. Figure 13.2 proves that it worked.

LISTING 13.9   `NewbyFind.jsp`—Using `CustomerBean`

```
<%@import = ejbs.customer.* %>
<%@import = javax.ejb.* %>
<%@import = java.util.Properties %>

<%! String firstName, lastName; %>
<%

  try {
    /* Get context */
    Properties env = new Properties();
    env.put(Context.INITIAL_CONTEXT_FACTORY,
➥ "weblogic.jndi.WLInitialContextFactory");
    Context ctx = new InitialContext(env);

    /* find Customer */
    String rFirstName = request.getParameter("firstName");
    CustomerHome custHome = (CustomerHome)ctx.lookup("customer.CustomerHome");
    Customer customer = custHome.findByPrimaryKey(rFirstName);
    firstName = customer.getFirstName();
    lastName = customer.getLastName();
  } catch (Exception e) { }
%>
```

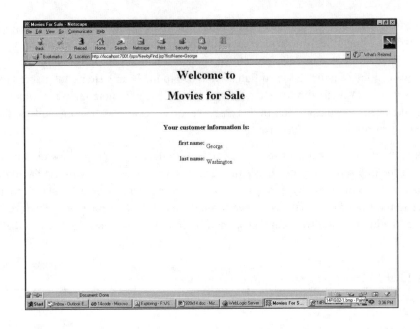

FIGURE 13.2

NewbyFind.jsp *displays the customer information returned from* CustomerBean.java*.*

Interacting with a Stateless Session Bean

For an existing customer, our first step is to authenticate the user's login information. Of course, we will use our AuthenticationBean.java. Listing 13.10, LoginConfirm.jsp, is the code used to access the Authentication bean and verify the user's login information. Login.jsp gathers the login information for us and sends it to LoginConfirm.jsp. We go through the same steps to get an Authentication object that we did to get a Customer object in our previous example. We get the IntitialContext and from there look up a reference to AuthenticationHome from the server. Our stateless Session bean will be used to check for authentication and then will be gone (see Chapter 10, "Managing Session States," to find out how to keep the return value around). If the username and password are not correct (that is, if they are not Elvis and lives, respectively, in this case), we send them back to Login.jsp to try again.

LISTING 13.10   LoginConfirm.jsp—Using AuthenticationBean.java

```
<%@ page errorPage="ErrorPage.jsp"%>
<%@ page import = "ejbs.authentication.*"%>
<%@ page import = "javax.ejb.*"%>
```

LISTING 13.10   Continued

```
<%@ page import = "javax.naming.*"%>
<%@ page import = "java.util.Properties"%>

<%
  String userName = request.getParameter("userName");
  String password = request.getParameter("password");

  try {
    /* Get context */
    Properties env = new Properties();
    env.put(Context.INITIAL_CONTEXT_FACTORY,
➥"weblogic.jndi.WLInitialContextFactory");
    Context ctx = new InitialContext(env);

    /* get Authentication */
    AuthenticationHome authHome = (AuthenticationHome)
➥ctx.lookup("authentication.AuthenticationHome");
    Authentication check = authHome.create();

    boolean isAuthentic = check.isAuthentic(userName, password);
    if (!isAuthentic) {
      /* Redirect back to the login page... */
      response.sendRedirect("Login.jsp?loginError=IncorrectLogin");
    }
  } catch (Exception e) {}
%>
```

Interacting with Stateful Session Beans

It's finally time to do some shopping! `Storefront.htm` is a frameset that lists the movies that are available in `MoviesAvailable.htm` and gives an introduction in `MoviesIntro.jsp`. `MoviesIntro.jsp` is shown in Listing 13.11 because that is where we get a reference to our `ShoppingCart` object. We put the cart in the session so that we can get to it while we shop.

LISTING 13.11   MoviesIntro.jsp—Using ShoppingCartBean

```
<%@import = ejbs.shoppingcart.* %>
<%@import = javax.ejb.* %>
<%@import = java.util.Properties %>

<%

try {
  // Get context //
```

LISTING 13.11   Continued

```
    Properties env = new Properties();
    env.put("java.naming.factory.initial",
➥   "com.ejbhome.naming.spi.rmi.RMIInitCtxFactory");
    Context ctx = new InitialContext(env);

    // Get ShoppingCart //
    ShoppingCartHome cartHome = (ShoppingCartHome)ctx.lookup("shoppingcart");
    ShoppingCart cart = cartHome.create(userId);
    session.put("shoppingCart", cart);

} catch (Exception e) {}

%>
<html>
<head>
<title>Intro</title>
<meta http-equiv="Content-Type" content="text/html; charset=iso-8859-1">
</head>

<body bgcolor="#FFFFFF">
<h4>Select which movies you would<br>
  like to ad to your shopping cart!</h4>
</body>
</html>
```

Each of the movie pages looks pretty much the same as far as the Java code goes. Listing 13.12 shows one of the pages, ArmyOfDarkness.jsp, to show how we add items to the shopping cart.

LISTING 13.12   ArmyOfDarkness.jsp—Using ShoppingCartBean

```
<%@import = ejbs.authentication.* %>
<%@import = ejbs.shoppingcart.* %>

<%@ page errorPage = "../ErrorPage.jsp" %>
<%@ page import = "ejbs.shoppingcart.*" %>


<%! String title = "Army of Darkness"; %>
<%! int quantity = 0; %>

<%
```

LISTING 13.12 Continued

```
String strQuantity = request.getParameter("quantity");
if (strQuantity != null) {
  try {
    quantity = Integer.valueOf(strQuantity).intValue();

    ShoppingCart cart = (ShoppingCart)session.getAttribute("shoppingCart");
    if (cart != null) {
      cart.addItem(title, 10.95, quantity);
    }
  } catch (Exception e) {
    title += "<p>Please enter a valid quantity for \"how many?\"";
  }
}
%>
```

We had to throw a little logic into this one to make sure that there is a valid quantity entered. Clicking the Add Item button on the page returns the same page but adds the new item to the shopping cart. Figure 13.3 shows us buying some copies of *Army of Darkness*.

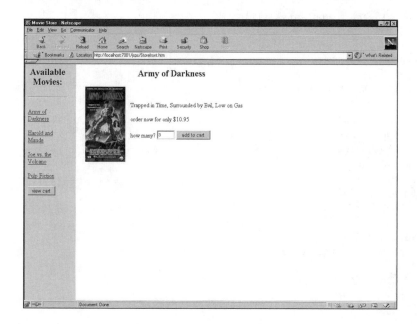

FIGURE 13.3

`Storefront.htm`, *showing our storefront and how to order products.*

After doing some serious movie shopping, we might want to view everything in our cart. We can do this from the frame with `MoviesAvailable.htm` in it. Clicking the View Cart button launches `ViewCart.jsp`, which is displayed in Listing 13.13.

LISTING 13.13   `ViewCart.jsp`—Using `ShoppingCartBean`

```
<%@ page errorPage = "ErrorPage.jsp" %>
<%@ page import = "ejbs.shoppingcart.*" %>
<%@ page import = "java.util.Hashtable" %>

<%! Hashtable[] items; %>
<%! ShoppingCart cart; %>

<%

  cart = (ShoppingCart)session.getAttribute("shoppingCart");
  items = cart.getItems();

%>
<html>
<head>
<title>shopping cart contents</title>
</head>

<body bgcolor="#FFFFFF">
<div align="center">
  <h1>Items in Shopping Cart</h1>
  <hr>
  <table width="500" border="0">
    <tr align="center" valign="bottom">
      <td width="100">
        <h4>Title</h4>
      </td>
      <td width="70">
        <h4>Quantity</h4>
      </td>
      <td width="65">
        <h4>Price<br>per movie</h4>
      </td>
      <td width="65">
        <h4>Total<br>
          Cost</h4>
      </td>
    </tr>
<%
```

LISTING 13.13 Continued

```
   for (int i=0; i<items.length; i++) {
%>
     <tr>
       <td width="150"><%=items[i].get("title") %></td>
       <td width="70" align="center"><%=items[i].get("quantity") %></td>
       <td align="right" width="65"><%="$"+items[i].get("price") %></td>
       <td align="right" width="65"><%=cart.getItemsTotalCost(items[i]) %></td>
     </tr>
<% } %>
     <tr align="center">
       <td width="150">
         <h4> </h4>
       </td>
       <td width="70">
         <h4> </h4>
       </td>
       <td align="center" width="65">
         <h4> </h4>
       </td>
       <td align="right" width="65">
         <h4> </h4>
       </td>
     </tr>
     <tr align="center">
       <td width="150">
         <h4> </h4>
       </td>
       <td width="70">
         <h4> </h4>
       </td>
       <td align="center" width="65">
         <h4>Total</h4>
       </td>
       <td align="right" width="65">
         <h4><%=cart.getCartsTotalCost() %></h4>
       </td>
     </tr>
   </table>
   <p> </p>
   <h3>Thanks for shopping with us!</h3>
</div>
</body>
</html>
```

13

INTERACTING WITH
ENTERPRISE
JAVABEANS

The Java code is pretty short and simple. We just get our cart and call the getItems() method. We iterate through the items in the cart and display them for review. What is important to notice here is that the same ShoppingCart object is still around and has all our selections in it. Figure 13.4 shows the movies I am going to buy.

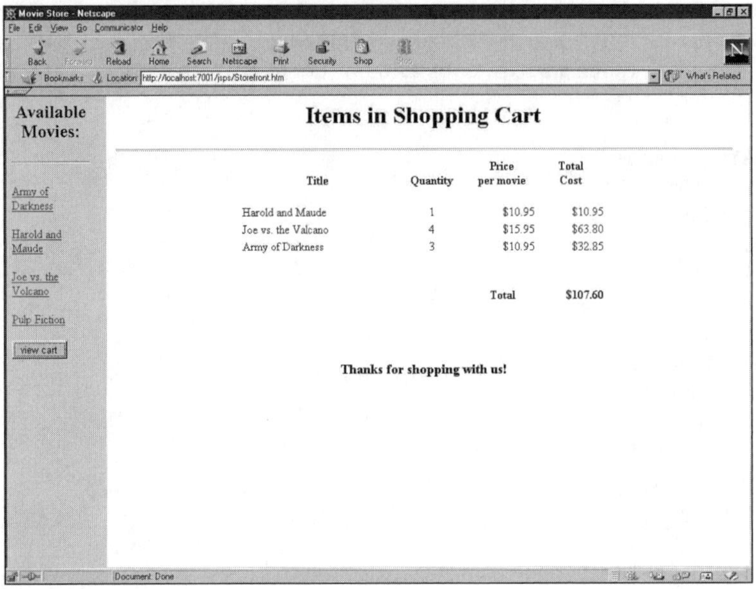

FIGURE **13.4**

ViewCart.jsp *displays the results of our shopping spree.*

Summary

Enterprise JavaBeans is a powerful technology for server-side Java applications. EJB architecture allows developers to focus on business logic and let Java take care of all the system details. Using Enterprise JavaBeans with JavaServer Pages provides a robust solution that is easy to build and maintain. This combination is a key example of the power and ease of Java's enterprise solutions.

Handling Errors

IN THIS CHAPTER

The wise Jedi Master Yoda once said, "do or do not, there is no try." As wise as Yoda was, he obviously didn't do much programming. In the programming world we have to deal with errors, and this means trying some things that might not always work right. It is impossible to completely eliminate errors from software, so instead we just deal with them. The process of recognizing errors and anticipating them is something that every JSP programmer will have to learn.

In this chapter, we will learn what error handling is, how to implement it, and how to use JSP's error page. The first part will cover Java basics about what errors there are and what we can do about them. Next is how to deal with errors (we will go into detail on how to make your program continue to run smoothly even when an error occurs). Finally, we will dive right into what JSP has to offer in the way of error handling and how to use a JSP error page for debugging and user direction.

Understanding Error Handling

When we say "error," there are many things we could mean, such as compile-time errors, which are errors that the Java compiler finds while trying to create a class file. These are usually listed by whatever program you are using to compile the file. Most JSP servers produce an HTML page that lists the errors you must fix in order for the page to compile. If we tried to run a JSP with the following code

```
<%

  String s;
  int slength = s.length();


%>
```

BEA's Weblogic Server would produce the following JSP compile error statement:

```
D:\weblogic\myserver\jsps\compiled\jsp_servlet\_15jsps\_errorexample.java:77:
➥ Variable s may not have been initialized.
➥probably occurred due to an error in /15jsps/ErrorExample.jsp line 6:
➥int slength = s.length();
```

Another error that can happen is java.lang.Error. These are unrecoverable errors—things like linkage problems or Virtual Machine problems. You don't need to give these any thought, because there isn't much you can do about them. They will normally cause the application to display a message and die.

The kind of error we will be talking about is normally called an *exception*. An exception is an instance of java.lang.Exception, which extends java.lang.Throwable. An exception is a message that is sent in response to an error during runtime execution that tells you that something didn't go quite right or that an error happened. Java's exceptions provide a neat and clean way to handle errors. Exceptions allow you to separate error-handling code from normal code and deal with errors in the normal flow of the application without having to deal with odd return values.

Java is so serious about handling errors that declaring what errors a method can throw is just as important as specifying a method's return value and parameters. Every method that throws an exception or passes one along must declare that it can throw this exception or deal with the exception itself. If the exception is not declared or dealt with, a compile-time error will occur.

At the point an error occurs, an `Exception` object is created. This object and the flow of the program are then passed to the block of code that handles the exception. An `Exception` object is said to be "thrown" from one point and "caught" at another.

> **TIP**
>
> The Java API gives a complete listing of all the subclasses of `java.lang.Error` and `java.lang.Exception`. Sun's Web site gives a tree view of the subclass at `http://www.java.sun.com/j2se/1.3/docs/api/java/lang/package-tree.html`. It is useful to review this list to familiarize yourself with what errors and exceptions can be thrown.

Implementing Exception Handling

Now that I've got you all excited about how well Java deals with error handling, I bet you're dying to know how to do it. Actually, you have already seen error handling in some of the examples in this book. The syntax starts by declaring that you want to *try* a block of code. If an exception is thrown in the process of trying the code, you want to *catch* the exception and deal with it accordingly. These are discussed in the following sections.

The `try` Block

In your applications, there are going to be things you want to do that might throw exceptions. Regardless of the risk, you want to try.

That's what `try` is about; it's the code you really want to run. A `try` block is code that will deliver an exception to its corresponding `catch` clause, stopping execution where the exception is thrown. Knowing this is handy because it guarantees that everything prior to the exception was executed correctly. For example

```
String activity = request.getParameter("activity");
String answer = "I like " + activity + " too!";
```

```
try {
  doSomething(activity);
} catch (Exception e) {
  answer = "I don't like " + activity;
}

int length = activity.length();
```

Here we can use the variables `activity` and `answer` whenever we want because they were instantiated before an exception could occur. This would not compile if we had tried to instantiate them inside the `try`, like so:

```
String activity;
String answer;

try {
  activity = request.getParameter("activity");
  answer = "I like " + activity + " too!";
  doSomething(activity);
} catch (Exception e) {
  answer = "I don't like " + activity;
}

int length = activity.length();
```

We would have gotten a compile-time error when we attempted to use `activity` outside the `try`. This is because there is a chance that `activity` has not been instantiated. It is often wise to keep as little code as possible in the `try` statement, in order to keep track of exactly where the exception occurred and to know what was executed successfully. The circumstances of your own code will dictate how much should take place in the `try` statement.

The catch Clause

A `catch` clause (also called an *exception handler*) is called only if an exception occurs. The `catch` clause resembles a method, with the `Exception` object it is looking for as its only parameter. A `catch` clause can look for any exception specified as the parameter. This parameter is called the *exception parameter*. Each `try` block can have as many `catch` clauses as needed. In the event of an exception, each `catch` clause will be evaluated in order. Every exception is a child of `java.lang.Exception`, so just specifying `Exception` will catch any exception. In this case, we have been catching an exception by writing

```
} catch (Exception e) {
```

However, we could look for more detail as follows:

```
String activity = request.getParameter("activity");
```

```
String answer = "I like " + activity + " too!";

try {
  doSomething(activity);
} catch (DidntDoSomethingException e) {
  answer = "I don't like " + activity;
} catch (Exception e) {
  System.out.println(e.toString());
  System.out.print(e.printStackTrace());
}

int length = activity.length();
```

In this case, we go through the exceptions we know are possible and respond to each accordingly. We include Exception as a default to catch anything we might have missed. Although we have multiple catch clauses, only the one with the exception parameter that matches the kind of exception thrown will be run. Then the flow will go back to normal or wherever directed by the catch clause.

The finally Block

We can also add a finally block to our try statement to take care of any cleanup that is needed. A finally block performs any necessary tasks regardless of what happens in the try statement. The finally block will be executed no matter what, regardless of how the try block executes or how control leaves the try block. It looks like this:

```
String activity = request.getParameter("activity");
String answer = "I like " + activity + " too!";

try {
  doSomething(activity);
} catch (Exception e) {
  answer = "I don't like " + activity;
} finally {
  // cleanup stuff
}
```

We can even use the finally clause without a catch clause. If there is no catch, the flow will go straight to the finally clause, and the exception will continue to bubble up until it is caught.

```
try {
  doSomething();
  return; // or break or continue or whatever
} finally {
  // cleanup stuff
}
```

Bubbling Up

Exceptions that are not caught are said to "bubble up." This means that the exception is thrown to the method that called the function that threw the exception. This continues until the exception either is caught or reaches the top and kills the application with an error message. Methods that create exceptions that are not caught in the method must declare that the exception is thrown. This means that another function is going to have to catch it.

Runtime Exceptions

There is always an exception to the rule; in this case it is *runtime exceptions*. Exceptions known as *general exceptions* must always be caught. This is what we have been talking about—things like not being able to find a file (`FileNotFoundException`) and such.

Runtime exceptions are given a little more leeway. These are things that can legitimately occur in any application. Runtime exceptions do not have to be caught in order for the file to compile, and methods do not have to declare that they can throw them. Just for the sake of being good programmers, we should make sure that these exceptions do not occur. However, we do not have to wrap everything in a `try` statement to prevent these exceptions.

An `ArrayIndexOutOfBoundsException` is a runtime exception. Instead of having to wrap every array in a `try` statement, we can just check to make sure that we are asking for a legitimate index. For example, if we had a `String` array named `months` that contained the months of the year, and we wanted to get an element out of it at a given index named `index`, we could do it in either of two ways.

```
String month;
try {
  month = months[index];
} catch (ArrayIndexOutOfBoundsException e) {
  System.out.println("Invalid index")
}
```

This would work, but it would eat up a lot of resources unnecessarily. Instead, we should do it like this:

```
String month;
if (index <= months.length) {
  month = months[index];
} else {
  System.out.println("Invalid index")
}
```

Throwing Exceptions

If we really want to have fun with exceptions, we can go around throwing them whenever we want! We can even make up our own. Of course, they must be instances of Exception or one of its subclasses. In these cases, we simply instantiate our chosen exception and throw it with the throw statement. Our doSomething() method could look something like this:

```
public void doSomething(String activity)
  throws DoSomethingException, Exception{
  if ("".equals(activity))
    throw new DoSomethingException();
  throw new Exception();
}
```

The method doSomething() is useless, but it illustrates quite well how to throw exceptions. The DoSomethingException will have to be defined elsewhere and must extend java.lang.Exception. Notice that we can list as many exceptions as are needed after the throws keyword by separating them with commas. Then we tell when to throw the appropriate exception with the throw keyword.

This statement will stop the execution of the method and send control to the nearest applicable catch clause. We can include useful information in the exception by providing a descriptive string as a parameter, or we can create our own exception that will let us know what happened (as we did with DoSomethingException above).

Using Error Pages

Because exceptions are pretty common and often predictable, the good folks at Sun supplied JSP with a convenient way to deal with exceptions. It's a simple concept called an *error page*, which is a page that is called if an exception occurs. An error page has access to the predefined Exception object that was created when the exception occurred. The error page shows up only if and when an exception is thrown. It can be used to display information to the user to guide him in correcting the problem. It also can be used for debugging, to tell a JSP programmer what's wrong with an application.

Each JSP page must specify which error page it will use. It does so with the errorPage attribute in the page directive, like this:

```
<@ page errorPage="ErrorPage.jsp" %>
```

You can specify only one error page for each JSP page, but each JSP page can have its own error page. How many error pages you have is completely up to you and the needs of your application. It is a good practice to have at least one error page. If you don't, the browser will come up with one of those unfriendly HTTP error pages that make no sense. The error will be logged with the JSP engine, but the user's experience is not a good one.

Creating an error page is a relatively simple task. To do so, set the `isErrorPage` attribute in the page directive to `true`.

```
<@ page isErrorPage="true" %>
```

The default for this attribute is `false`, so every page that is not declared is set to `false`. By setting `isErrorPage` to `true`, we now have use of the `Exception` object.

The error page should never be called directly. It should be served only if an exception has been thrown from another JSP page. If the error page is called directly, the `Exception` object will be `null`.

As previously explained, `Exception` objects are derived from `java.lang.Throwable`. As a result, all the methods inherited from `Throwable` come with the `Exception` object that the JSP engine provides. `exception.toString()` and `exception.printStackTrace()` are among the most common. `exception.toString()` displays the exception's class name and `exception.printStackTrace()` displays the exception's stack trace. These can be displayed in the JSP page like this:

```
<%= exception.toString() %>
<% exception.printStackTrace(); %>
```

This is all we need to know to create an error page. A straightforward error page that displays the class name of the exception and its stack trace could look like this:

```
<%@ page isErrorPage="true" %>

<html>
<head><title>JSP Error Page</title></head>

<body bgcolor=#ffffff>

<h2><font color=#FF0000>JSP Error Page</font></h2>
<hr>

<p> An exception was thrown: <b> <%= exception.toString() %>

<p> With the following stack trace:
<pre>

<%
    ByteArrayOutputStream ostr = new ByteArrayOutputStream();
    exception.printStackTrace(new PrintStream(ostr));
    out.print(ostr);
%>
</pre>
```

```
<p>
<hr>
</body>
</html>
```

As handy as it is for the JSP programmer to know the exception's class and stack trace, the odds are that these things will mean nothing to the common Web surfer. As a result, most error pages will have to provide more useful information to guide the user toward solving the problem. To make an error page that is friendlier to the end user, we should provide more useful messages, as illustrated in the following:

```
<%@ page isErrorPage="true" %>

<html>
<head><title>JSP Error Page</title></head>

<body bgcolor=#ffffff>

<font face="Helvetica">

<h2><font color=#FF0000>JSP Error Page</font></h2>
<hr>

<% if ( exception instanceof java.lang.NullPointerException ) { %>
<p> Please make sure that you have responded
    to all the required fields.

<% } else if ( exception instanceof java.lang.NumberFormatException ) { %>
<p> Please make sure that you have responded
    with correct values for all numbers.

<% } else { %>
<p> An unexpected error occured of type:
    <b><%= exception.toString() %></b>

<p> With the following stack trace:
<pre>

<%
    ByteArrayOutputStream ostr = new ByteArrayOutputStream();
    exception.printStackTrace(new PrintStream(ostr));
    out.print(ostr);
%>

</pre>
<% } %>
```

```
<hr>
</body>
</html>
```

In this example, we check to see what kind of exception we are getting and try to respond logically to guide the user in fixing the problem. This could be used as a form-handling error page. If we get a `NullPointerException`, we assume that a field was left blank, and we direct the user to fix the problem accordingly. If we are thrown a `NumberFormatException`, we assume that an invalid value was entered where we were expecting a number. We ask the user to check all the number values to make sure that they are appropriate. If it is neither of these problems, we resort to the good old stack trace for debugging.

Summary

Because no program will run perfectly 100% of the time, we should all give thanks to the good people at Sun for making it so easy to handle exceptions. With Java's exception handling and JSP's error page, making smooth-running applications is a snap! All we really have to do is just try.

Debugging and Troubleshooting

IN THIS CHAPTER

There are a lot of things that can go wrong in developing, deploying, and maintaining Web applications. There are many possible points of failure, including the software you are using to run your application (Web server, JSP container, Java Virtual Machine), your application code (JSPs, JavaBeans, servlets), and the configuration of your software (web.xml, property files), not to mention your overworked, caffeine-addled brain. We cover many of the potential pitfalls in this chapter and provide solutions for several. For problems that don't fall into a neat category or easy answer, we provide proven troubleshooting techniques.

Container Problems

The JSP container itself is a potential source of trouble. If a feature doesn't seem to be acting as it should, if an API function seems to be broken or misbehaving, or if something that worked before (with an earlier version or another product) suddenly breaks, there may be a bug in the JSP container.

Always make sure you have the latest and greatest production release of the software you are using. This guideline applies equally to the other components in your application, such as your JDBC drivers, JVM, Web server, and operating system. Software vendors regularly release patches for bugs in their software. Unfortunately, bugs are a natural and frequently encountered part of software development.

Besides keeping up-to-date with bug patches for the software you are using, make sure you report bugs to your vendor if you find them. The end user frequently finds bugs that were never caught in development or QA. Most software vendors have a "developer" section on their sites, where hard-core users can report and track bugs.

Besides reporting bugs, end users can help improve software greatly by making enhancement requests to vendors. Believe me, software developers want your input. If there's a bug or an intelligent feature that should be added to the software, they especially appreciate hearing about it from users. Some typical container problems follow, with their recommended solutions.

Non-Compliant Containers

You would think this sort of problem would decrease, since servlets and JSP have been around for a while now. But consider that there is currently a whole new wave of servlet and JSP containers out there (supporting the JSP 1.1 and Servlet 2.2 APIs), which means a whole new cycle of development, QA, and release has finished. There are likely to be some bugs in this area for a while. In part this is due to the fact that every time a new API is released, some old things get deprecated and new things must be supported.

The number one thing to do if your JSP container is not acting in compliance with expected APIs is to check for a bug patch at the vendor's Web site. If a relevant patch is not available, the vendor may not be aware of the bug. You might wonder why no one else has reported it. The reason may be that someone else has experienced the bug but didn't believe the software could be broken. I tend to think that if something doesn't work as it should, it's my fault, and usually it is. But it's also possible that a bug wasn't reported for several other reasons:

- A user found a workaround for the bug and didn't tell anyone. A savvy user can often work around a bug, and he may not report the bug he found if he's too busy, lazy, or just not nice (see the next point).

- Another user was too lazy to report the bug, or the bug was not enough of a showstopper to merit pursuit from his perspective. In this case no workaround is implemented; the feature is just dropped from consideration, and the user moves on without mentioning it to anyone in a newsgroup, an online forum, or a bug tracker facility. Remember this the next time you find a bug! Report bugs to other users and to vendors!

- No one else has tried that feature yet (some complex or esoteric feature of an API may be rarely used, and those who use it might be more likely to find their own workarounds).

- Other users switched to another product because of the bug but, again, didn't bother to report the bug.

When reporting a bug, you will usually be asked for a template or test case that reproduces the buggy behavior. The best thing you can do to help ensure that the bug will be reproduced and fixed is to provide a simple, reproducible test case. Bugs in an API are usually easy to reproduce in a test case. Either it behaves according to spec or it doesn't.

Another possible origin of an API support problem is an overlooked problem in your environment. For example, if the JSP container depends on environment variables, such as your PATH or CLASSPATH, but you have them set such that they are incompatible with the JSP container, then you could have problems. A good example of this is if you have an older version of the Java binary executable in your PATH when you install the JSP container. The JSP container may try to use that version of Java and its corresponding lib directory for its runtime classes. If the JSP container is expecting classes from the Java 2 runtime libraries (for example, the Java 2 Collections classes) to be available but can't find them, you will get runtime exceptions (probably NoClassDefFound or AbstractMethodError). The solution is to make sure the latest JDK/JRE libraries are available to the JSP container.

A similar problem could occur if you are using Java 2 and at some time in the past you put an older servlet.jar (such as one supporting the Servlet 2.1 API) in your JAVA_HOME/jre/lib/ext directory. Since the JAR files in the ext directory will take precedence in the JVM over any loaded by your JSP container on startup, you will run into problems, because the Servlet 2.1 classes are going to be used instead of the Servlet 2.2 classes that the JSP container probably needs.

> **NOTE**
>
> The JAVA_HOME/jre/lib/ext directory has a special function related to the loading of classes into the JVM. Basically, any JAR files you put in that directory are automatically available to the JVM without making any changes to your CLASSPATH environment variable. It is part of the *Extension Mechanism* introduced in Java 2. To read more about it, check out the documentation for the Java 2 platform at JavaSoft, in particular the JDK's "Guide to Features" section at http://java.sun.com/products/jdk/1.3/docs/.

One rather drastic but highly possible solution to a spec compatibility problem is to borrow a spec-compliant component from another vendor and use that in your broken JSP container. For example, you should be able to take the jsp.jar from Tomcat 3.0 and use it in any Servlet 2.2–compliant servlet container to enable JSP 1.1.

Deploying Your JSPs, Beans, and Servlets

Figuring out where to deploy your application's files is less of a hassle than it was in the days prior to the Servlet 2.2 specification. In earlier versions of the specification, there was no standard directory structure for the deployment of servlet- and JSP-based Web applications. The Servlet 2.2 specification fixed that. Now we have the WEB-INF directory, the *WAR* file format, and web.xml, all of which are standards aimed at making application deployment easier and more universal across JSP/servlet container implementations.

Basically, Web application deployment boils down to putting your loose supporting classes (JavaBeans and servlets) in the classes directory, your JSPs, HTML, and other static content in the root directory or your Web server's documents directory, and any JAR files in the lib directory. Most servlet engines released prior to the Servlet 2.2 specification followed somewhat similar conventions, but in a standards-compliant servlet container of the 2.2 generation, deployment practices are universal.

Where each servlet/JSP container keeps its default WEB-INF directory is dependent on the implementation. For example, JRun 3.0 keeps its WEB-INF directory under servers/default/ default-app. Resin 1.1, on the other hand, keeps it under the doc directory. Tomcat puts its under webapps/examples. Orion's is under the default-web-app directory. ServletExec 3.0 put it under Examples/exampleWebApp.

Eventually, what you should do is deploy your applications using the WAR file format. A WAR file is essentially a Java archive of a WEB-INF directory. WAR files are covered in Chapter 1, "Understanding JSP," but you should also see your JSP container's documentation for vendor-specific information. All containers ship with some sort of utility, even if only a batch or shell script, to assist you in creating deployable WAR files from your Web application files.

Port Conflicts

Any given JSP container requires at least one dedicated port to listen on for client requests. That's if the JSP container is embedded in a Java-based HTTP server, such as Resin 1.1, Tomcat, and Orion can be. That's also true for in-process JSP/servlet containers like ServletExec, which run (optionally) within the process space of a native Web server.

> **NOTE**
>
> Do not confuse an in-process JSP/servlet container such as ServletExec with an in-process *connector* that just filters requests to a JSP/servlet container running in a separate process, such as is possible with combinations such as Tomcat and Apache, Resin and IIS, or JRun and IIS. The threads of an in-process container share a single memory and address space with the Web server. This can be a great performance boost, primarily due to the fact that there's no extra overhead for the operating system in communicating between servlet container and Web threads. Also, there's no TCP/IP overhead such as is required when sending requests via a proprietary (TCP/IP–based) protocol to a separate process. But it can also be a stability problem, since a thread deadlock in the container will crash the Web server, and vice versa. There are other plusses and minuses to each approach that we won't go into here.

Many JSP container configurations require two or more ports to run correctly. For example, there may be a special port reserved for sending administrative commands like restart or shutdown. In JRun 3.0 there is an admin server that runs on one port, and then at least one regular server that can run standalone or out-of-process with a native Web server. In the latter case there are three ports you have to be aware of:

•The admin port

•The standalone port

•The port through which JRun and the native Web server communicate

If you run other network services in a multi-tier, distributed environment (as most people do these days), you also have the Web server port(s) (default port 80 for HTTP and default port 443 for HTTPS), the database port, and maybe even a port for your EJB server. You have to watch out for all these ports and make sure you don't trample on other applications (or let your vendors' applications trample them) by stealing their ports. If one application grabs a port that another application needs, whichever application got started second will never get the port.

Virtually all of the JSP/servlet containers out there use ports in the 7000 and 8000 ranges. For example, Tomcat and Resin use port 8080 as the default for incoming HTTP requests. JRun uses port 8000 as the default for standalone requests and uses port 8081 as the default for communicating with its native Web server connector. If you are running multiple JSP/servlet containers or multiple instances of the same JSP/servlet container on the same machine, make sure you follow the instructions in the product documentation for configuring the containers to run on unique ports.

If you have a port conflict such that your JSP/servlet container cannot start because it cannot open a socket on a port it needs, look in your logs for more information. Typically you will see a BindException in your error log, with an error message printed out. To debug port conflicts, it's sometimes easiest to just try another port in the high numbers (you have from 1024 to 65,535 to choose from).

If you really want to find out what's going on, use the near-universal netstat command. For example, opening a DOS shell (cmd.exe on NT or command.exe on Windows 9x) and running netstat /a on Win32 systems will tell what ports are in active use on the local machine. On Linux, netstat -a -p will tell you the same thing, except Linux will show you the PID (process identification number) of the process using each port. Most UNIX systems have versions of netstat that work more or less like the Linux version. Once you've narrowed down the port conflict to the two applications competing for the same port, you must reconfigure them to listen on unique ports. Every servlet and JSP container out there now has a configuration file that allows you to do this.

Properties and Configuration Files

Fortunately, the Servlet 2.2 specification has settled a standard deployment descriptor for all J2EE Web applications. The web.xml file is the standard file that must be present in your application's WEB-INF directory and must adhere to Sun's Web Application Document Type Definition (DTD) syntax (http://java.sun.com/j2ee/dtds/web-app_2_2.dtd).

According to "Java Servlet Specification Version 2.2" (`http://java.sun.com/products/servlet/`), the purpose of the `web.xml` deployment descriptor is to configure the following types of information:

- `ServletContext` Init Parameters
- Session Configuration
- Servlet/JSP Definitions
- Servlet/JSP Mappings
- Mime Type Mappings
- Welcome File List
- Error Pages
- Security

But there is a lot of other configuration information that you can use to customize your JSP container. Every JSP container has its own implementation of configuration property files. Some use plain old Java property files, and others use XML files. There is no standard to rely on as there is for the Web application deployment descriptor.

Here are some of the properties your JSP container is likely to expose through implementation-specific property files:

- Java Virtual Machine settings
- Application-specific `CLASSPATH` settings
- Performance tuning parameters
- Logging preferences
- JSP Compiler settings
- Built-in JDBC pooling or connection settings
- EJB feature settings
- Other vendor-specific add-ons and services

One might argue that implementations should follow the example set in the Jakarta project's Tomcat, which is the official reference implementation of the Servlet and JSP specifications. But the specs don't say anything about how a container's properties must be exposed. In fact, it is essential that vendors be allowed to implement their configuration files in their own way. One of the chief value-adds of a production implementation versus a reference implementation is that the production implementation may have extra features not accounted for in the spec.

See Appendix B, "Using Popular JSP Servers," for more on vendor specifics regarding configuration files. The bottom line is to get familiar with the configuration files of your favorite JSP container.

Using Logs

Logs are your friends. Use them. Every JSP container has some sort of logging capability. Since several of the latest and greatest containers out there are forged from the fires of the first generation of JSP containers, they should have pretty good logging mechanisms (a lesson learned during the first wave of servlets and JSPs). At the time of this writing, many actually *do not* have very good logging mechanisms, but they should in the future.

A good logging mechanism should allow you to set different levels of logging (for example, info, warn, error, debug), depending on your needs. It should also allow you to customize the log output somewhat, such as letting you specify the format of the timestamps in log entries. Ideally, the logging apparatus should make log rotations easy for the administrator of the application.

It's amazing how many people have a problem with their software but never look in the logs to see what the problem might be, let alone turn on Debug mode in the logging configuration to really see what's wrong. Allaire's JRun 3.0 excels in logging, primarily because its logging interface is so customizable and flexible. This flexibility was highly driven by customer demand. It's nice to have robust logging capabilities built into your JSP container.

On the other hand, you have the power to log a lot of information yourself from a JSP without relying on the logging capabilities of your particular container. The Servlet API has had a couple of log() methods in place since at least Servlet 2.0. In Servlet 2.x, the built-in log() methods are both specified in the abstract javax.servlet.GenericServlet class.

The first method logs a user-specified string, automatically prepended with the servlet name:

```
public void log(java.lang.String msg)
```

The second method does the same thing as the first but takes an instance of Throwable as an argument. It prints the name of the Throwable object it was passed, followed by the exception's stack trace:

```
public void log(java.lang.String message, java.lang.Throwable t)
```

Remember that Throwable is one of the fundamental Java classes, like String or Class. All Exceptions and Errors in Java are subclasses of Throwable, so typically if you are using the second log() method, you are going to be passing an Exception or Error object as the second parameter to the method. As an example, Listing 15.1 is a JSP called LogTest.jsp. The purpose is to show you how these methods are used, with some examples of the default location of log messages in some popular JSP containers. It also logs some strings to System.out and System.err, which typically go to different locations separate from the output of the Servlet log() method.

LISTING 15.1 LogTest.jsp—Testing Logging Capabilities Using a JSP

```
<html>
<head><title>Log Test JSP</title></head>
<body>
<h1>Hello</h1>
<% System.out.println("[info] Hi, I am in System.out!"); %>

<% application.log("This is from LogTest.jsp at " + new java.util.Date()); %>

<%
    try
    {
        int illegal = 1 / 0;
    }
    catch (Exception e)
    {
        application.log("This is from LogTest.jsp at " + new java.util.Date(),
➥e);
    }
%>
</body>
<% System.err.println("[error] Hi, I am in System.err!"); %>
```

For good or ill, there's no standard or convention for where a JSP container's logs will go, other than into a directory called log or logs, or what they should be called. Here are the names and locations of the logging directories for a few popular JSP containers:

JRun 3.0	JRUN_HOME/logs
Orion 0.9.6	ORION_HOME/log
Resin 1.1	RESIN_HOME/log
ServletExec 3.0	SERVLETEXEC_HOME/ se-hostname/ServletLogs
Tomcat 3.1	TOMCAT_HOME/bin/logs

Listing 15.2 shows what Resin 1.1 does with our logging JSP. I won't show the HTML browser output, which only shows the word Hello. Listing 15.2 is the entry from the RESIN_HOME/log/error.log:

LISTING 15.2   resin1.1/log/error.log—Testing Logging Capabilities Using a JSP

```
[2000/04/20 08:50:44] This is from LogTest.jsp at Thu Apr 20 04:50:44 EDT 2000
[2000/04/20 08:50:44] This is from LogTest.jsp at Thu Apr 20 04:50:44 EDT 2000
java.lang.ArithmeticException: / by zero
    at _jsp._LogTest__jsp._jspService(_LogTest__jsp.java:34)
    at com.caucho.jsp.JavaPage.subservice(JavaPage.java:83)
    at com.caucho.jsp.Page.service(Page.java:280)
    at com.caucho.jsp.QServlet.service(QServlet.java:161)
    at com.caucho.server.http.AbstractRequest.service(AbstractRequest.java:448)
    at com.caucho.server.http.AbstractRequest.service(AbstractRequest.java:391)
    at com.caucho.server.http.PageCache$Entry.service(PageCache.java:244)
    at com.caucho.server.http.PageCache.service(PageCache.java:103)
    at com.caucho.server.http.VirtualHost.service(VirtualHost.java:382)
    at com.caucho.server.http.Request.dispatch(Request.java:205)
    at com.caucho.server.http.HttpRequest.handleRequest(HttpRequest.java:189)
    at com.caucho.server.http.HttpRequest.handleConnection(HttpRequest.java:132)
    at com.caucho.server.TcpConnection.run(TcpConnection.java:145)
    at java.lang.Thread.run(Thread.java:484)
```

As you can see, the first `log()` method logs the string we put in, preceded by the name of the servlet, as the Servlet 2.2 API specification demands. The second `log()` method logs the string and servlet name, followed by the type and stack trace from the exception we caught. The `System.out` and `System.err` lines just go to their default locations (Resin doesn't redirect them anywhere), which when running in the foreground is the window from which Resin was started. So all we see there is

```
[info] Hi, I am in System.out!
[error] Hi, I am in System.err!
```

Orion does pretty much the same thing as Resin, except the file it uses for logging from the `log()` method is called `global-application.log`. Here's one place JRun 3.0 makes better sense; for each server instance you have running, JRun creates three log files in which the server name is prepended to the log name. Servlet `log()` calls are logged to an event log, while standard output and standard errors are redirected to separate log files. The directory structure looks like this (for the JRun server instance `default`):

```
JRUN_HOME/logs:
    default-err.log
    default-event.log
    default-out.log
```

Here's what JRun logs to `default-event.log` for `LogTest.jsp` (most of the stack trace is omitted to save space here):

```
04/20 05:42:47 info This is from LogTest.jsp at Thu Apr 20 05:42:47 EDT 2000
04/20 05:42:47 error This is from LogTest.jsp at Thu Apr 20 05:42:47 EDT 2000
➥[java.lang.ArithmeticException: / by zero]
java.lang.ArithmeticException: / by zero
    at jrun__LogTest2ejspc._jspService(jrun__LogTest2ejspc.java:42)
    at allaire.jrun.jsp.HttpJSPServlet.service(HttpJSPServlet.java:40)
    at allaire.jrun.servlet.JRunSE.service(JRunSE.java:896)
    at allaire.jrun.debug.StackManager.service(StackManager.java:61)
    at allaire.jrun.servlet.JRunSE.runServlet(JRunSE.java:808)
```

Of course, the `System.out` and `System.err` calls from `LogTest.jsp` go into `default-out.log` and `default-err.log`, respectively.

> **NOTE**
>
> Most if not all JSP containers allow you to specify which Java compiler you want to use with your JSPs. In working out this example, I realized that IBM's Jikes compiler treated the division by zero in `LogTest.jsp` as a compile-time exception rather than a runtime exception. Sun's javac ignored the obvious coding error at compile time and let the JVM catch it at runtime. That's pretty smart on Jikes part, but it just goes to show how you can sometimes get unexpected results from different vendors' software that does essentially the same thing (in this case, compile Java code to bytecode).

One last point on using logs. Always print out a stack trace of an exception when you get one, unless the JSP container does it for you. Particularly when working with JDBC, where every exception is an `SQLException` of some sort, it will behoove you to use the `printStackTrace()` method. The `printStackTrace()` method of the `Throwable` class writes out a stack trace from a caught exception. You can do this in your JSPs using `errorPages`. Just make sure you call `printStackTrace()` on the implicit `exception` object. By default, the `printStackTrace()` method prints to standard output using `System.out`. Wherever your JSP container writes standard output is where the output from `printStackTrace()` will go. Use the stack traces to determine exactly where your code (or your vendor's) went wrong.

15

Java Virtual Machine Problems

Hangs, deadlocks, JVM bugs, core dumps, and runtime exceptions due to configuration errors can ruin your day. This section covers common problems and things that are just good to know in dealing with problems related to the Java Virtual Machine.

There are a few exceptions you are more likely to encounter than others as you traverse the byways and backwaters of Java programming. For example, when doing Java database programming using JDBC, most `java.sql` API methods throw `SQLExceptions`. When programming servlets, the basic `javax.servlet` and `javax.servlet.http` API methods throw `ServletExceptions`. Aside from exceptions thrown explicitly by API methods, there are some general-purpose exceptions you are likely to see pop up no matter what type of Java programming you do. Some of those exceptions and other problems are covered in this section. An attempt is made to relate some of these generic Java exceptions to causes specific to JSP programming and development.

Getting an `OutOfMemoryError`

This error is caused by running out of memory for your JVM. Each instance of the Java Virtual Machine allocates objects from its heap. Java 1.2 and 1.3 JVMs from Sun have a default maximum heap size of 64MB. This is just not enough memory for an enterprise-level server application. IBM's JVMs use half of your machine's physical memory by default. Another possibility is that there is something extremely inefficient in your code that is causing the JVM to use more memory than it should, such as an infinite loop that creates objects until the JVM runs out of memory. In that case, increasing the maximum heap size will fix the problem only temporarily.

Sun Java Virtual Machines of Java 1.1 allow a maximum of only 16MB by default. Again, this is tunable. It's just good to know that the limitation is there by default. IBM JVMs set the maximum heap size at half of your machine's physical memory by default.

The syntax for increasing your JVM's heap size is vendor dependent, but most vendors adhere to the standards used by Sun. To increase the maximum heap size, configure your JSP container's properties wherever it allows you to pass arguments to the JVM on startup. The argument syntax for changing the maximum heap size for a 1.1 JVM is

```
-mx64m
```

For a 1.2 or 1.3 JVM it is

```
-Xmx128m
```

The default unit for memory settings is bytes. You must add a k or an m to specify that the number is to be interpreted as kilobytes or megabytes.

Here are a couple of URLs that are germane to the heap size for server-side Java applications:

The Java Virtual Machine Specification, Second Edition (see section 3.5) is at `http://java.sun.com/docs/books/vmspec/`.

"'Heap of Trouble' with the Wrong Heap Size" article from IBM at `http://www-4.ibm.com/software/developer/library/tip-heap-size.html`.

Getting a `NullPointerException`

A `NullPointerException` is caused by trying to use the value null as an object. The JVM automatically checks whether references being used in your code are null before letting them be used in an operation. If the JVM finds that a reference about to be used in an operation at runtime is null, it automatically throws a `NullPointerException`. No one intentionally tries to use null as an object. The source of these exceptions can often be traced to a method call that returned null instead of the expected value, which you then tried to use somewhere without realizing that the method returned null.

For example, you may have tried to get a reference to a file on the file system or get a hostname string from a DNS lookup. If the file did not exist or the network lookup failed because of a network problem, your method probably returned null. If you try to use that reference without providing an alternative action to take if it is null, then you will certainly get a `NullPointerException`. Other possibilities are basic coding errors, such as an uninitialized array or variable.

Getting a `NoClassDefFoundError`

This exception occurs when a class you referenced in your code cannot be found by the Java Virtual Machine. It is always due to a misconfiguration of your CLASSPATH or your JSP container's CLASSPATH or a misnamed JAR file or class file.

When you get a `NoClassDefFoundError`, the JVM should tell you the name of the class whose definition cannot be found. First make sure you spelled the class name correctly in your code. If it's not a typo, then just find the file that contains that class and make sure it is in the path of the JVM that you're using to run your JSP container. Usually this means making sure you've deployed all your classes and JAR files into the appropriate directories. If your Java classes are defined in packages, make sure the directory structure they are in reflects the package structure.

Unresponsive JSP Containers

If your JSP container becomes unresponsive yet is still shown to be running when you check its status with ps or TaskManager, it may have become frozen or hung. Often a hung JVM is due to a thread deadlock, when two threads are each simultaneously waiting to acquire a resource that the other is holding onto. But a JVM can also appear to be hung because of network or database connectivity problems.

The immediate solution is to restart the Java process, so that everything in the JVM is destroyed and restarted. That's drastic if you have potentially valuable information in live sessions, but often it's the only solution. There are steps you could take to try to alleviate the hangup in the future, such as making sure you have the latest version of the JVM from your vendor, not using the Sun JDBC-ODBC bridge driver to connect to a database, and making sure that the apparent hangup is not caused by some external factor, such as a broken network connection or DNS errors.

The last step in debugging a hung JVM situation (if it recurs) is to get a couple of stack traces from the JVM next time it hangs. A stack trace is a readout of all the threads currently running inside the JVM. The stack trace will show a list of every thread's execution stack up to a certain depth, along with some other information such as each thread's current state, a monitor dump for all the threads, and the name of each thread. The capability to generate stack traces on command is a built-in feature of most Java Virtual Machine implementations.

Stack traces are nearly impossible to read for beginners, but for seasoned programmers (and your JVM or application vendor) they can be extremely useful. For more information on how to obtain and interpret stack traces, see the following articles:

"An Introduction to Java Stack Traces" You'll find this article by Calvin Austin at `http://developer.java.sun.com/developer/technicalArticles/Programming/Stacktrace/index.html`.

"JRun: How to Generate and Capture Java Stack Traces" You'll find this at `http://www.allaire.com/Handlers/index.cfm?ID=12406&Method=Full`.

Getting Dr. Watsons or Core Dumps

Core dumps on UNIX and Dr. Watson exceptions on Win32 systems are essentially the same thing. You may or may not get a USER.DMP file created when Dr. Watson appears, but usually when the Dr. Watson error dialog pops on your screen, it's there to tell you that a fatal exception occurred in one of your programs.

Similarly, on UNIX systems a core file produced when the JVM dies unexpectedly indicates a serious problem. Here are some frequently asked questions about Dr. Watson and core dumps:

Q What causes them?

A There are three main causes of these kinds of fatal errors:

1. JNI (Java Native Interface) code you are using that has hit a fatal bug in the native code.

2. Bugs in your JVM implementation. Every thread, socket, or file you deal with in platform-neutral Java has to be translated into platform-specific operations by the JVM implementation (with the exception of green threads, which are seldom used anymore and which I won't go into here). At this native code level, there are sometimes bugs in the JVM. When one of these performs an illegal operation, the operating system will instantly kill the process and (usually) write out a core file.

3. Your OS is missing a patch or service pack necessary for the version of the JVM you are using.

Q Can I catch the problem in my code and log some data when it happens?

A No. These problems occur at the native layer, below the level of your JSP code and your JSP container's application code. You could log some information leading up to the crash (if it's predictable and that's practical), but once the JVM crashes, the JVM and your application are instantly dumped out of memory.

Q I send a core file to my Java application vendor and ask them to take a look at it? Can I get some useful data from the core file?

A No and no. For one thing, since it's either a bug in the JVM or in your own JNI code, there's nothing your JSP container's vendor can tell you about what is wrong. Secondly, unless you were running your JVM in debug mode in order to gather debug data for the next core dump that happens, there's nothing useful in the core dump file anyway. To run the JVM in debug mode for debugging core dumps, you should contact your JVM vendor. Most of the time, though, if you are not using the latest version and build of your vendor's JVM, the first thing they will do is tell you to upgrade.

Database Problems

One important thing to keep in mind when coding and debugging Java that connects to a database is that 99% of your problems are going to be reported in the form of SQLExceptions. Remember that the printStackTrace() method of class java.lang.Throwable is your ally. Use it when catching SQLExceptions so that you can look in the logs and get the maximum amount of information about what's going wrong.

Choosing the Best JDBC Driver

An important thing to know about JDBC programming is the type of driver you should be using. You would be surprised at the number of people who do JDBC coding without having learned the four main JDBC driver types. Knowing them is crucial for picking the best driver.

> **NOTE**
>
> To learn more about JDBC drivers and search for JDBC driver vendors in one convenient location, check out Sun's JDBC Drivers site at
> http://industry.java.sun.com/products/jdbc/drivers.

Type 1 Drivers

Type 1 drivers are JDBC-ODBC bridge solutions. They use native code to interact with the native ODBC drivers for the database vendor. The JDBC-ODBC bridge (sun.jdbc.odbc.JdbcOdbcDriver) that's part of the Sun SDK for Java is the most popular type 1 driver out there. Type 1 drivers, especially the Sun JDBC-ODBC bridge driver, should be used only for development or as a last resort. They are inherently slow because they rely on ODBC, which is typically slower than accessing a database's proprietary protocol, and they can crash the JVM running your JSP container if they hit a bug in their native code. Many, many people use the Sun JDBC-ODBC bridge driver to connect to Microsoft Access. That's fine for development and maybe even for production in a small site with just a few users. But in a production situation with any level of concurrent access to the database, it won't take long for you to crash your application using this type of driver.

Type 2 Drivers

Type 2 drivers are also part Java and part native code. They are generally faster than type 1 drivers because they use native code and communicate with your database using the database vendor's (usually) proprietary protocol (rather than the slower, older ODBC protocol). Because they rely on native code, they pose the same risk of crashing a JVM if a bug is present in the native code. Note that type 1 and 2 drivers connect directly to your database over the network, as do type 4 drivers. The type 3 driver is the only one that relies on middleware to connect to the database.

Type 3 Drivers

Type 3 drivers are pure Java, which means they won't crash your JVM even if there are bugs. They may cause a thread deadlock in the JVM if there's a threading bug, but they can't absolutely kill your JVM like a bug in a type 1 or type 2 driver can. Type 3 drivers talk to the database via an intermediate protocol (usually implemented as a special server) that translates between JDBC and the native API of the database you're using. The only thing better, because it's faster and doesn't rely on an intermediate layer, is a type 4 driver.

Type 4 Drivers

Type 4 drivers are also pure Java. The main advantage they have over type 1 and type 3 drivers is that they communicate with your database using the native protocol API of your database. Usually these drivers are provided by your database vendor, but type 4 drivers have also been written for Microsoft SQL Server and many other databases that may or may not have vendor-provided JDBC drivers. Since these drivers are pure Java and talk the native API of your vendor's database, they are usually the fastest and most stable type of driver you can get for JDBC programming.

Performance and Profiling Tools

There are lots of free and commercial tools available for profiling the performance of your application and your JSP container. Here are some links to get you started. The first five are free tools, and the final two are commercial ones. Remember, in this area you usually get what you pay for. If you want an easy-to-use tool that is full of features, you should look into buying one of the commercial ones. Fortunately, most commercial profilers have free evaluation versions.

The Java Heap Analysis Tool (HAT) `http://java.sun.com/people/billf/heap/`

Hpjmeter `http://www.unixsolutions.hp.com/products/java/`
`2_61_HPjmeter_content.html`

Jinsight `http://www.alphaworks.ibm.com/formula/jinsight`

Perfanal and Profiler `http://www.javalinux.net/JavaLinux/CDROM/`

15

ProfileViewer `http://www.capital.net/~dittmer/profileviewer.html`

Jprobe `http://www.klgroup.com/jprobe/index.html`

OptimizeIt `http://www.optimizeit.com/`

Using IDEs to Code and Debug JSPs

This is a huge topic, with lots of specific steps and requirements for each major IDE. Below are some links to get you started with coding and debugging JSPs in IDEs.

Unfortunately, the JSP debug and development support in many of the major IDEs is something of an afterthought. Allaire's JRun Studio (`http://www.allaire.com`) is designed with JSP coding and debugging in mind from the beginning. JRun Studio also incorporates all the functionality of Allaire's HomeSite, which is a very intuitive and easy-to-use IDE for Web site development. Of course, there are always the good old standbys, such as emacs (`http://www.gnu.org`), vim (`http://www.vim.org`), and TextPad (`http://www.textpad.com`), all of which have syntax highlighting and font-locking for JSP now.

Apache Tomcat Servlet and JavaServer Pages Development with VisualAge for Java
This can be found at `http://www7.software.ibm.com/vad.nsf/data/document2389`.

Borland/Inprise Jbuilder This has an optional JSP module, and it can be found at `http://www.inprise.com/jbuilder/`.

Forte for Java, Internet Edition This also has an available JSP module, and it can be found at `http://www.sun.com/forte/ffj/ie/index.html`.

JRun Developer Center This is a gateway to information on JRun Studio, JRun Forums, and so on. It can be found at `http://www.allaire.com/developer/jrunreferencedesk/`.

Kawa: Running and Debugging JSP classes Under Kawa This can be found at `http://www.tek-tools.com/kawa/docs/tutorial8.htm`.

Macromedia's Drumbeat 2000 This can be found at `http://www.macromedia.com/software/drumbeat/`.

VisualCafé Support Page This can be found at `http://www.visualcafe.com/Support/index.htm`.

JSP Syntax

IN THIS APPENDIX

The JSP is made up of a set of elements, all specified as tags. This appendix lists the elements that make up JSP 1.2. Please note the following:

- JSP elements are case sensitive.
- All attribute values should be enclosed within quotes.
- All JSP directives are enclosed between <% and %> and take no matching end tags.
- All JSP tags have a jsp: prefix and require a matching end tag (or a trailing /).
- Spaces are not allowed before or after the equals symbol (=) in attribute value pairs.

JSP Directives

JSP directives are used to specify page options or settings and to delimit blocks of code or expressions. Unlike tags, there is no mechanism for creating your own directives in JSP.

<% %>

Executes a code fragment (referred to as a *scriptlet*).

Syntax:

```
<% scriptlet %>
```

Example: The following scriptlet initializes a set of variables. This element takes no attributes.

```
<%
   String login_name = null;
   String login_password = null;
%>
```

<%-- --%>

Embeds a hidden comment in the page. Unlike standard HTML comments, hidden comments are not sent to the client (and can therefore not be read by viewing the client source). This element takes no attributes.

Syntax:

```
<%-- comment --%>
```

Example: The following example embeds a hidden comment in a page:

```
<%-- This is a hidden comment --%>
```

<%! %>

Declares one or more variables or methods. This element takes no attributes.

Syntax:

```
<%! declaration %>
```

Example: The following example declares two variables and initializes them with values:

```
<%! int n=0; i=1; %>
```

<%= %>

Evaluates an expression. This element takes no attributes.

Syntax:

```
<%= expression %>
```

Example: The following example uses an inline expression to retrieve a string to be displayed:

```
The correct answer is <B><%= quiz.getAnswer() %></B>.
```

<%@ include %>

Includes a file, parsing and processing its content. This element takes a single attribute, `file`, which is required. It specifies the relative URL of the file to be included.

Syntax:

```
<%@ include file="file" %>
```

Example: The following example includes (and processes) a file named `header.jsp` in the current directory:

```
<%@ include file="header.jsp" %>
```

<%@ page %>

Defines attributes that affect the behavior of a JSP page. Element attributes are listed in Table A.1.

Syntax:

```
<%@ page autoFlush="true|false" buffer="none|size" contentType="MIME type"
➥ errorPage="url" extends="package" import="package" info="information
➥ text" isErrorPage="true|false" isThreadSafe="true|false"
➥language="java" session="true|false" %>
```

TABLE A.1   <%@ page %> Attributes

Attribute	Required	Description
autoFlush	No	Flag specifying whether or not the buffer should automatically be flushed when full. Valid values are true or false; default is true.
buffer	No	Size of buffer used by the out object; default is 8KB.
contentType	No	The MIME type of the content generated by the page; default is text/html.
errorPage	No	Fully qualified name of a page to which exceptions are sent.
extends	No	Fully qualified name of a class that names the superclass to which a JSP page is transformed.
import	No	Comma-delimited list of types available to the scripting environment.
info	No	A block of text information that is written into the compiled JSP page. This value can be retrieved at runtime using the Servlet.getServletInfo() method.
isErrorPage	No	Flag specifying whether error pages are displayed. Valid values are true or false; default is false.
isThreadSafe	No	Flag specifying whether page is coded to be thread safe. If true, multiple requests will be processed simultaneously. Valid values are true or false; default is true.
language	No	Scripting language used; default is java.
session	No	Flag specifying whether page participates in session state management. Valid values are true or false; default is true.

Example: The following example creates a WAP page and specifies the MIME type accordingly:

```
<%@ page contentType="text/vnd.wap.wml" %>
```

`<%@ taglib %>`

Defines a custom tag library for use within the page. Element attributes are listed in Table A.2.

Syntax:

```
<%@ taglib prefix="prefix" url="url" %>
```

TABLE A.2   `<%@ taglib %>` Attributes

Attribute	Required	Description
prefix	Yes	Prefix to precede the custom tag name.
url	Yes	Absolute URL or url relative to tags.

Example: The following example specifies a tag library to be used in this page:

```
<%@ taglib prefix="game" url="/game/tags" %>
```

JSP Tags

JSP tags all begin with a jsp prefix. Additional tag libraries (specified using the `<%@ taglib %>` directive) will have their own prefixes.

`<jsp:fallback>`

Specifies fallback text to be displayed if a client cannot display and execute a bean or applet. This element takes no attributes and must be used in conjunction with `<jsp:plugin>`.

Syntax:

```
<jsp:fallback> text </jsp:fallback>
```

Example: The following example displays a Java applet, specifying two parameters and fallback text:

```
<jsp:plugin type="applet" code="game.class" codebase="/game/bin">
   <jsp:params>
      <jsp:param name="score" value="0" />
      <jsp:param name="round" value="1" />
   </jsp:params>
   <jsp:fallback>Your browser cannot execute this applet!</jsp:fallback>
</jsp:plugin>
```

`<jsp:forward>`

Forwards a request to another file for processing. Requests may be forwarded to any valid URL, and optional attributes may be specified using `<jsp:param>`. This element takes a single required attribute, page, which specifies the absolute or relative URL to which the request should be forwarded.

Syntax:

```
<jsp:forward page="page" />
```

or

```
<jsp:forward page="page"> ... </jsp:forward>
```

Example: The following example forwards a request to a login page:

```
<jsp:forward page="/login" />
```

`<jsp:getProperty>`

Obtains a property from a bean. This tag takes the name of an instance of a bean already created or located using `<jsp:useBean>`. Element attributes are listed in Table A.3.

Syntax:

```
<jsp:getProperty name="bean instance name" property="property name" />
```

TABLE A.3 `<jsp:getProperty>` Attributes

Attribute	Required	Description
name	Yes	Name of the instance of the bean from which to get the property.
property	Yes	Name of the property to retrieve.

Example: The following example retrieves text from a bean property and displays it:

```
<B>Question:</B> <jsp:getProperty name="quiz" property="question" />
```

`<jsp:include>`

Includes a static or dynamic page. Optional attributes may be specified using `<jsp:param>`. Element attributes are listed in Table A.4.

Syntax:

```
<jsp:include flush="true" page="url" />
```

or

```
<jsp:include flush="true" page="url"> ... </jsp:include>
```

TABLE A.4 `<jsp:include>` Attributes

Attribute	Required	Description
flush	Yes	Must always be `true` (no default value).
page	Yes	Relative URL of file to include.

Example: The following example includes (and processes) a file named `header.jsp` in the current directory:

```
<jsp:include page="header.jsp" flush="true" />
```

`<jsp:param>`

Defines a parameter to be passed to another page. This element is used in conjunction with `<jsp:forward>`, `<jsp:include>`, or `<jsp:plugin>`. Element attributes are listed in Table A.5.

Syntax:

```
<jsp:include name="name" value="value" />
```

TABLE A.5 `<jsp:param>` Attributes

Attribute	Required	Description
name	Yes	Parameter name
value	Yes	Parameter value

Example: The following example forwards a request to another page for processing, sending two parameters to it:

```
<jsp:forward page="/login">
   <jsp:param name="login_name" value="" />
   <jsp:param name="login_password" value="" />
</jsp:forward>
```

`<jsp:params>`

Designates a block of parameters to be passed to a Java applet or bean. This element is used in conjunction with `<jsp:plugin>` and contains one or more `<jsp:param>` elements. This element takes no attributes.

Syntax:

```
<jsp:params> ... </jsp:params>
```

Example: The following example displays a Java applet, specifying two parameters and fall-back text:

```
<jsp:plugin type="applet" code="game.class" codebase="/game/bin">
   <jsp:params>
      <jsp:param name="score" value="0" />
      <jsp:param name="round" value="1" />
   </jsp:params>
   <jsp:fallback>Your browser cannot execute this applet!</jsp:fallback>
</jsp:plugin>
```

`<jsp:plugin>`

Displays and executes an applet or bean on the client. It might include optional parameters specified using `<jsp:param>` and fallback text specified using `<jsp:fallback>`. Element attributes are listed in Table A.6.

Syntax:

```
<jsp:plugin align="bottom|left|middle|right|top" archive="url"
➥code="class file" codebase="path" height="pixels" hspace="pixels"
➥iepluginurl="url" jreversion="version" name="instance name"
➥nspluginurl="url" type="ben|applet" vspace="pixels" width="pixels" />
```

or

```
<jsp:plugin align="bottom|left|middle|right|top" archive="url"
➥code="class file" codebase="path" height="pixels" hspace="pixels"
➥iepluginurl="url" jreversion="version" name="instance name"
➥nspluginurl="url" type="ben|applet" vspace="pixels" width="pixels">
➥... </jsp:plugin>
```

TABLE A.6 `<jsp:plugin>` Attributes

Attribute	Required	Description
align	No	Object alignment. Valid values are bottom, left, middle, right, and top; default is bottom.
archive	No	Comma-delimited list of path names to be preloaded with a class loader to improve performance.
code	Yes	Java class file; class extension must be specified.
codebase	No	Directory containing code; defaults to current directory.
height	No	Object height in pixels.
hspace	No	Amount of space to the left and right of object, in pixels.
iepluginurl	No	URL of plug-in for Microsoft Internet Explorer client.
jreversion	No	Version of the Java Runtime Environment (JRE) that is required. Default is 1.1.
name	No	Instance name used for communication with other applets or beans.
nspluginurl	No	URL of plug-in for Netscape Navigator client.
type	Yes	Plug-in type; must be applet or bean.
vspace	No	Amount of space above and below the object, in pixels.
width	No	Object width, in pixels.

Example: The following example displays a Java applet, specifying two parameters and fallback text:

```
<jsp:plugin type="applet" code="game.class" codebase="/game/bin">
   <jsp:params>
      <jsp:param name="score" value="0" />
      <jsp:param name="round" value="1" />
   </jsp:params>
   <jsp:fallback>Your browser cannot execute this applet!</jsp:fallback>
</jsp:plugin>
```

`<jsp:setProperty>`

Sets a property within a bean. This tag takes the name of an instance of a bean already created or located using `<jsp:useBean>`. Element attributes are listed in Table A.7.

Syntax:

```
<jsp:setProperty name="bean instance name" property="*|property name"
➥value="value" />
```

TABLE A.7   `<jsp:setProperty>` Attributes

Attribute	Required	Description
name	Yes	Name of the instance of the bean in which to set the property.
property	Yes	Name of the property to set, or * for all parameters.
value	No	Value to be set for a specific property (not used if property is *).

Example: The following example passes all request parameters to a bean for processing:

```
<jsp:setProperty name="formMail" property="*" />
```

`<jsp:useBean>`

Locates or instantiates a bean for use. Beans must be instantiated with this element before `<jsp:getProperty>` or `<jsp:setProperty>` can be used. Element attributes are listed in Table A.8.

Syntax:

```
<jsp:useBean beanName="bean name" class="class name" id="id"
➥scope="application|page|request|session" type="type" />
```

or

```
<jsp:useBean beanName="bean name" class="class name" id="id"
➥scope="application|page|request|session" type="type"> ... </jsp:useBean>
```

TABLE A.8 `<jsp:useBean>` Attributes

Attribute	Required	Description
beanName	No	Bean name.
class	Yes	Bean class name.
id	Yes	Unique instance name, used by `<jsp:getProperty>` and `<jsp:setProperty>`.
scope	No	Scope in which bean exists. Valid values are `application`, `page`, `request`, and `session`. Default is `page`.
type	No	Bean type, if different from class from which it was instantiated.

Example: The following example instantiates a bean and then passes all request parameters to it for processing:

```
<jsp:useBean id="formMail" class="util.formMail">
   <jsp:setProperty name="formMail" property="*" />
</jsp:useBean
```

Using Popular JSP Servers

IN THIS APPENDIX

There are hundreds of commercial products available today falling under the very general category of "Internet application servers," and many of them claim support for the latest JSP and Servlet specifications. Unfortunately, due to brutal software marketing campaigns, there are different interpretations of what it means to *support* a particular technology. It might mean that the software product can work with a Servlet/JSP server, which may or may not be included. In general, this should be considered somewhat misleading. Other products achieve support for Servlet/JSP by embedding a third-party Servlet/JSP engine, such as the reference implementation or another commercial Servlet/JSP server. Finally, many vendors truly support Servlet/JSP by writing and providing their own concrete implementations of the Servlet and JSP specifications.

This appendix contains a listing of some of the commercial and open source Servlet/JSP engine (server) implementations that are currently available at the time of publishing. With the number of vendors that currently provide Servlet engines and the number of new products being added daily, this listing is not exhaustive. Visit the product Web sites for the most current information.

Different server products have considerable differences in features, such as support for other Java 2 Enterprise Edition technologies. However, the focus of this book is JSP, so we are highlighting the server's support for Servlet and JSP specifications and related features. We also will cover briefly a few of the most popular Servlet engines in use today and mention some of their Servlet/JSP–related features.

Organization (URL)	Server Name	Supports
Allaire (www.allaire.com)	JRun Server 3.0	2.2/1.1
Apache Group (www.apache.org)	Tomcat 3.1	2.2/1.1
BEA Systems (www.bea.com)	BEA Weblogic Server 5.1 BEA Weblogic Enterprise 5.1	2.2/1.1
Caucho (www.caucho.com)	Resin 1.1	2.2/1.1
IBM (www.ibm.com)	WebSphere Application Server 3.5	2.1/1.0
Orion (www.orionserver.com)	Orion Server 1.0	2.2/1.1
Unify (www.unifyewave.com)	Unify eWave ServletExec 3.0	2.2/1.1

JRun

JRun Server was the first commercially available Servlet/JSP engine. The most recent release implements the Servlet 2.2 and JSP 1.1 specifications, as well as EJB 1.0, JTA 1.0, and JMS 1.0. JRun can function as a standalone with its own HTTP server or as a plug-in with an external Web server, including Apache, Microsoft IIS, Netscape Enterprise/FastTrack/iPlanet, Zeus, and Website Pro. JRun features load balancing, a JSP Tag library, support for JavaScript as the JSP scripting language, a performance monitor, XML/XSLT processing, support for WAR files, automatic JDBC connection pooling, and a browser-based administration console. JRun is currently supported on Windows, Solaris, Linux, HP-UX, IBM AIX, SGI IRIX, and Compaq Tru64. Information and product downloads can be obtained at `http://www.allaire.com/jrun`.

Orion Server

Orion Server is a relatively new product offering; the 1.0 version was released in June 2000. It is a clean-room implementation of the full Java 2 Enterprise Edition platform, which includes full support for Servlet 2.2 and JSP 1.1, as well as EJB 1.1, JTA 1.0.1, JNDI 1.2, JDBC 2.0, and JMS 1.0. There are numerous additional Servlet/JSP–related features, including XML/XSLT processing, JSP Tag libraries, support for WAR files, application assembly tools, and HTTP session and context clustering/failover. The Orion team has performed various competitive benchmarking tests showing their server outperforming the Tomcat reference implementation by a factor ranging from 5 to 7. Information and product downloads for any Java 2 platform can be obtained at `http://www.orionserver.com`.

Resin

Resin is a commercial product released under an open-source license, touted as being one of the fastest Servlets and JSP engines available. Resin founder Scott Ferguson has performed benchmarking tests showing Resin outperforming native Apache modules such as `mod_perl` and `mod_php` and even defeating Jakarta Tomcat by a factor of 3. Other interesting features include support for JavaScript as the JSP scripting language, load balancing, and support for XSL, XSLT, and XPath. Finally, automatic bean compilation reduces JSP development time. Resin is supported with a standalone HTTP/1.1 server on UNIX and Win32; Apache on both UNIX and Win32, Microsoft IIS/PWS (ISAPI), and Netscape Enterprise/FastTrack/iPlanet (NSAPI). For Apache and IIS, you should use the Caucho Servlet engine packaged with Resin. Information and product downloads can be obtained at `http://www.caucho.com`.

ServletExec 3.0

Unify eWave ServletExec (formerly New Atlanta ServletExec) is one of the first Servlet engines to implement the Java Servlet and JavaServer Pages components from Sun Microsystems. ServletExec is a component of the Unify eWave platform, which supports EJB 1.1 and other advanced functions. ServletExec 3.0 allows for Web applications to be deployed on Microsoft IIS, Netscape Enterprise Server/iPlanet Web Server, and Apache Web Server. It can be run in-process as a Web server plug-in with Microsoft IIS, Netscape Enterprise Server, and iPlanet, or out-of-process for Microsoft IIS, Netscape Enterprise Server/iPlanet Web Server, and Apache Web Server. ServletExec has a Web-based administration console. You may plug in your own

JVM, including Sun, IBM, and Microsoft, and you can support multiple JVMs per Web server. It is currently supported on Windows 98/NT/2000, SPARC Solaris, AIX, HP-UX, and Linux. Information and trial software can be obtained at `http://www.UnifyeWave.com`.

Tomcat

Tomcat is the reference implementation for Servlets and JSP. The Jakarta Project is composed of members of the Apache Jserv Project, engineers from major corporations such as Sun, IBM, and Intalio, and also many other individual developers. It is an open-source project, and all interested developers are welcome to join and participate. Tomcat can run standalone or be integrated into the Apache Web Server, a popular HTTP server, originally designed for UNIX systems but now available in native builds for nearly every platform imaginable. Information and product downloads can be obtained at `http://jakarta.apache.org/index.html`.

Using Java Methods to Retrieve CGI Environment Variables

Some developers familiar with CGI or ASP might be wondering if there are CGI environment variable equivalents or HTTP server variable equivalents in Java. The answer is yes, but the method of access is slightly different. A CGI developer will reference the variables via `$ENV{'SOME_VARIABLE'}`, and the ASP developer will perform the same task using `Request.ServerVariables("SOME_VARIABLE")`. However, Java's generic environment variable method `request.getHeader("SOME_VARIABLE")` will not be able to address the most common of the CGI environment variables (National Center for Supercomputing Applications: `http://hoohoo.ncsa.uiuc.edu/cgi/env.html`) and ASP's HTTP server variables (Microsoft: `http://msdn.microsoft.com/servars.asp`). Instead, individual methods found in the `Request` object (`HttpServletRequest` interface) are generally used. Table C.1 shows a list of commonly referenced CGI environment variables on the left and the corresponding Java `Request` methods on the right.

TABLE C.1 Environment Variables: CGI Versus Java

CGI Variable	Java Request Method
AUTH_TYPE	getAuthType()
CONTENT_LENGTH	getContentLength()
CONTENT_TYPE	getContentType()
GATEWAY_INTERFACE	not implemented
HTTP_ACCEPT	getHeader("ACCEPT")
HTTP_ACCEPT_ENCODING	getCharacterEncoding()
HTTP_CONNECTION	getHeader("CONNECTION")
HTTP_COOKIE	getHeader("COOKIE")
HTTP_REFERER	getHeader("REFERER")
HTTP_USER_AGENT	getHeader("USER-AGENT")
PATH_TRANSLATED	getPathTranslated()
PATH_INFO	getPathInfo()
QUERY_STRING	getQueryString()
REMOTE_ADDR	getRemoteAddr()
REMOTE_HOST	getRemoteHost()
REMOTE_IDENT	not implemented
REMOTE_USER	getRemoteUser()
REQUEST_METHOD	getMethod()
SCRIPT_NAME	getRequestURI()
SERVER_NAME	getServerName()

TABLE C.1 Continued

CGI Variable	Java Request Method
SERVER_PORT	getServerPort()
SERVER_PROTOCOL	getProtocol()
SERVER_SOFTWARE	not implemented

The return types and descriptions for the methods listed above can be found in the ServletRequest and HttpServletRequest interfaces of the Servlet API. Please note that String methods containing empty values will return "null" in Java as opposed to empty strings returned by both CGI and ASP.

Looping Through Headers

If you are curious as to what headers are actually sent by the browser as part of the request, you can access those headers via the getHeader() method of the Request object. The getHeader() method will return an Enumeration of String objects, allowing you to loop through all the values as shown below.

```
<%@ page import="java.util.Enumeration" %>
<HTML>
<HEAD><TITLE>request.getHeaderNames()</TITLE></HEAD>
<BODY>
<%// Loop through the list of Header Names in the request
Enumeration e = request.getHeaderNames();
while( e.hasMoreElements() ) {
    String headerName = (String) e.nextElement(); %>
    <B><%=headerName %></B> = <%=request.getHeader(headerName) %><BR>
<% } %>
</BODY>
</HTML>
```

All the code seen above has been included on the accompanying CD-ROM as /AppendixC/serverVars.jsp.

INDEX

SYMBOLS

A

X-Y-Z